'This book is as fine an example of the first-class essay as you could hope to read. It is ingenious. It is witty. It compares and contrasts. Above all, it never bores' Niall Ferguson, *BBC History Magazine*

'His book is timely and a triumph…[Tony Blair] could do worse than read Andrew Roberts's book to remind himself of what it takes to achieve historical greatness' Michael Burleigh, *Evening Standard*

'This book…contains a rich selection of anecdotes about both [men] that will inform and entertain. It succeeds, above all, in pulling together strands of these two titanic figures in a way that ought to enlighten yet further even the most battle-hardened reader of books on the bloodiest war in history' Simon Heffer, *Country Life*

'Roberts has accepted the challenge on the back of his forthcoming television series exploring the qualities of leadership that brought the two men face to face across the English Channel in 1940. The result is lively, thought-provoking, and hugely entertaining…No one reading Roberts could fail to understand why Churchill topped the recent poll as our greatest Briton' Richard Overy, *Literary Review*

'As a straightforward "compare and contrast" essay, it is full of telling detail, often very wittily related' Craig Brown, *Mail on Sunday*

'This stimulating and highly readable book is more than a point-by-point comparison. It meditates on leadership itself, on history, history-makers and history writers, on ironies past and present'
Alan Judd, *Daily Telegraph*

'Fascinating and thought-provoking…Thoroughly well-worth reading'
Antony Beevor, *Sunday Telegraph*

'The best recommendation of this very entertaining and convincing book is that it is full, not just of funny and engaging stories very well told, but of some very startling illustrations' Philip Hensher, *Spectator*

'The study of history remains a constant joy, as well as a challenge and a path to enlightenment for Andrew Roberts. That is why indubitably, *Hitler and Churchill: Secrets of Leadership* is the most accomplished – and sexiest – historical work published so far this year. It is also one of the most pertinent' Michael Beaumont, *Yorkshire Post*

'A rattingly enjoyable book' *Economist*

'Roberts's strength is his unashamed selectiveness. The essential often lies in the detail. One may quibble or even disagree with some of the things he says, but the point of the book is to stimulate thinking and in that he most certainly succeeds' *Irish Independent*

'Andrew Roberts's stylish, analytical and often unexpectedly amusing study of these two adversaries is a brilliant and highly readable demonstration of how Hitler and Churchill's seemingly very different forms of greatness exhibited shared elements. Often, glorious humour leaps from the fascinating illustrations that so enliven and illuminate the author's text. With Roberts's light and elegant touch, and gimlet-sharp perceptions, this book is not to be missed' Colin McKelvie, *The Field*

'Andrew Roberts does a first rate job unmasking the man behind the medals' *Daily Express*

'It's testament to Roberts's elegant yet plain speaking prose that he manages to squeeze such an epic chunk of history into 350 pages'
Richard Warburton, *Birmingham Post*

'This fascinating book examines the very different leadership styles of Winston Churchill and his great adversary. In the process, Roberts dissects their personalities and lifestyles, right down to tastes in food, clothes and friends' *Western Daily Press*

'Andrew Roberts, in his own inimitable style, offers a contrasting study of leadership in *Hitler and Churchill*' John Yates, *Writers News*

'One of the merits of Roberts's Churchill is that, though his version is broadly orthodox, it is written with enough weight...to prompt us to think about Churchill historiography as a whole' Frank Johnson, *TLS*

'It is enthralling, informative, compelling and brilliantly written... History, unlike literary criticism, is lucky in that it has first-rank scholars who can write in a direct and simple way. Andrew Roberts is one of the very best' Eric Hester, *Catholic Times*

Andrew Roberts took a first in Modern History at Gonville and Caius College, Cambridge. His biography of Lord Halifax, *'The Holy Fox'* (1991), followed by *Eminent Churchillians* (1994), were published to critical acclaim. His publication of *Salisbury: Victorian Titan* (1999) won him the Wolfson History Prize and the James Stern Silver Pen Award for Non-Fiction. His next book, *Napoleon and Wellington,* has been reprinted several times in both hardback and paperback. He writes regularly for the *Sunday Telegraph* and reviews widely, and is a Fellow of the Royal Society of Literature. His website can be visited at www.andrew-roberts.net.

HITLER
AND
CHURCHILL

Secrets of Leadership

Andrew Roberts

PHOENIX

A PHOENIX PAPERBACK

First published in Great Britain in 2003
by Weidenfeld & Nicolson
This paperback edition published in 2004
by Phoenix,
an imprint of Orion Books Ltd,
Orion House, 5 Upper St Martin's Lane,
London WC2H 9EA

A CIP catalogue record for this book
is available from the British Library.

ISBN 0 75381 778 0

Typeset by Selwood Systems, Midsomer Norton

Printed and bound by Clays Ltd, St Ives plc

To Peter Wyllie

Contents

Illustrations

The Munich comedian Weiss-Ferdl in his dressing room in 1930; Hitler studied his timing, delivery and techniques.[1]

Hitler hamming it up for his favourite photographer Heinrich Hoffmann.[5]

Churchill broadcasts from the White House in 1943.[2]

Section Two

Hitler with Blondi.[6]

Hitler with Eva.[1]

Hitler posing with children.[6]

A very rare shot of the short-sighted Hitler wearing glasses.[6]

Benito Mussolini in his bathing trunks.[1]

Churchill didn't much care what he looked like.[7]

Hitler deliberately dressed down to emphasise his simplicity *vis-à-vis* his generals.[8]

Goebbels sharing a joke with the Führer.[6]

The architect Albert Speer and Hitler admire their handiwork at the opening of the new Reich chancellery in 1938.[6]

You had to walk through nine hundred feet of increasingly splendid halls before you reached the Führer's study.[6]

Churchill walking the streets of London on 26th May 1940.[2]

Hitler's secretaries smoked when his back was turned.[6]

Hitler at a party in 1937 with two Father Christmases.[4]

Churchill with his daughter Mary.[2]

Finance minister Hjalmar Schacht salutes the Führer's bust in 1935.[4]

Kingsley Wood and Anthony Eden advise Churchill after a Cabinet meeting, only hours before he became prime minister on 10th May 1940.[2]

Chamberlain's wartime cabinet in October 1939.[8]

Section Three

Lieutenant-General Erich von Manstein.[8]

General Walther von Brauschitsch, Hitler and General Franz Halder operating Mission Command.[9]

Air Chief Marshal Sir Hugh Dowding of Fighter Command.[2]

Bob Boothby, Churchill's close friend and confidant until he got involved in the sleaze story known as the Czech gold affair in 1941.[2]

Field Marshal Sir Alan Brooke and General Sir Bernard Montgomery with Churchill in France in 1944.[4]

Churchill, wearing military uniform, at the Teheran conference.[3]

Hitler inspects the damage after the Bomb Plot of 20th July 1944.[6]

Bruno Gesche, the commander of Hitler's SS Bodyguard.[10]

Some books have claimed that the Führer was gay.

A photo forged and then distributed as a postcard by the British Political Warfare Executive.[11]

Hitler wearing the Iron Cross 1st class, swastika armband and peaked hat.[2]

Churchill with a few favoured props: homburg hat, striped waistcoat, polka-dotted bow-tie and flamboyantly arranged handkerchief.[2]

The author and the publishers offer their thanks to the following for their kind permission to reproduce images:

1 The Bildarchiv Preussischer Kulturbesitz
2 Hulton Getty
3 Popperfoto
4 Ullstein Bild
5 Voller Ernst
6 The Walter Frentz Archive
7 The Imperial War Museum
8 AKG London
9 Heidemarie Schall-Riacour
10 Bayerische Staatsbibliothek
11 Richard Garnett

Acknowledgements

Since this book has been written in large part to accompany a BBC2 television series, I should like to thank Laurence Rees, director of *Timewatch*, for conceiving the idea and the Controller, Jane Root, for commissioning the series. Laurence is living proof that eccentric individuality can survive even in the largest organisations. I have hugely enjoyed making *Secrets of Leadership*, and especially working with the programme's producers, Jonathan Hacker, Detlef Siebert, Dominic Sutherland and Andrew Williams. Dani Barry, Lucy Heathcoat-Amory, Suzanne Hughes, Helen Nixon, Kate Rea, Lorraine Selwyn, Nancy Strang and Mark Walden-Mills were also a delight to work with for their professionalism and charm. Detlef Siebert and Dominic Sutherland very kindly read the manuscript of this book for me; of course the responsibility for any errors that still infest it is entirely theirs.

I would also like to thank the following people for their help, either through conversations or correspondence I have had with them: Joan Bright Astley, Paul Courtenay and Nigel Knocker of the International Churchill Society, Mr James Drummond, Professor Sir Michael Howard, Sir Anthony Montague Browne, Philip Reed, Director of the Cabinet War Rooms, the Hon. Celia Sandys and Lady Soames. I would further like to thank Mr Richard Garnett for his hospitality at Hilton Hall and his permission to research in, and quote from, his father's papers relating to the Political Warfare Executive; M. Robert Varoqui who kindly showed me around the Maginot Line; Major Ian Park-Weir who explained Churchill's time at the Royal Military College, Sandhurst; Herr Hoffmann who was very generous with his time showing me the German High Command's wartime headquarters at Zossen; Oberregierungsrat Hans Meissner for making Göring's Air Ministry (today the German Finance Ministry) and Herr Dr Palt for making Goebbels's Propaganda and Public Enlightenment Ministry (today the Federal Ministry for Labour and Social Welfare) open to me; Carole Kenwright and Judith Seaward were helpful during my visits to Chartwell.

I should also like to thank Chris Wren of the 11 Group Battle of Britain Operation Room at RAF Uxbridge; Wally Bennett, Andy Mahon and Stig Thornshon of the Warship Preservation Trust, Birkenhead, for allowing me the run of U-Boat 534; Fred and Harold Panton for allowing me on to their magnificent Lancaster Bomber 'Just Jane' stationed at East Kirkby, Lincolnshire; Harald Prokosch, head of the Siemens press department and Detlef Haumann, the maintenance manager of the Siemens Dynamo Works in Berlin; Squadron-Leader Ed Bulpett for a fascinating day at RAF Coltishall, Norfolk; Lieutenant Lucas Chevalier of L'École Militaire at Les Invalides, Paris; the FCO for allowing me access to Churchill's office in the Old Admiralty Building in Whitehall; the staff of the Maison Blairon in Charleville-Mézières for permitting access to General Gerd von Rundstedt's Army Group A headquarters; Lieutenant-Commander Rupert Nichol for my visit to the minehunter HMS *Ledbury*, and Dr Wilhelm Lenz, Head of the Deutsches Reich department of the Bundesarchiv Lichterfelde. Allen Packwood of the Churchill Archive Centre at Churchill College, Cambridge, was also very helpful to Detlef and Dominic in their researches for this series, for which many thanks.

As always I am profoundly indebted to my publishing team: the extremely talented and professional editor Ion Trewin, agent Georgina Capel and indexer Douglas Matthews, all of whom I am proud to say are friends as much as colleagues. Many thanks also to Jane Birkett who did the copy-editing and to Joanne King for her excellent picture research. I should finally like to thank Leonie Frieda for typing the manuscript, and for everything good that is happening in my life.

ACKNOWLEDGEMENTS

This book is dedicated to Peter Wyllie, my friend of twenty years, for giving me the best piece of advice I've ever received. His career shows that he already understands the secrets of leadership.

Andrew Roberts
www.andrew-roberts.net
February 2003

Introduction

'I keep my eyes open and their evidence makes me thought-
ful. The future is inscrutable but appalling; you must stand
by me. When I can no longer restrain and control, I will no
longer lead.'

Savrola by Winston Churchill

'How can one hundred people be led by a single person?' That
was one of the essay questions in my Cambridge University
entrance exam and, although it has long fascinated me, it has
taken me twenty years to get round to trying to answer it. Yet
this question lies at the heart of history and civilisation. If one
person could not command one hundred others there would be
no wars, but neither could there have been any cathedrals, space
exploration or philharmonic orchestras. The ability of one
person to make a hundred others do his bidding is the basic
building block upon which all collective human endeavour is
based, for better and for worse. So how does it happen?

One might reasonably expect that because politics and society
have changed so fundamentally over the centuries, so too would
the nature of leadership. Since agrarian societies based on feudal
obligation have been overtaken in the West by democracies based
on representative institutions, we ought to be swayed by different
imperatives and led by appeals to very different motives for
action. Yet the astonishing thing is that even in an age that

considers itself sophisticated and correspondingly cynical, in times of peril inspired leadership still relies to a large extent on the suspension of belief.

This unchanging vernacular is evident from the minimal alterations that have taken place in the language of leadership. To read Pericles' Funeral Speech of 431 BC ('Athens crowns her sons'), or Cicero's 'Amongst us you can no longer dwell' speech against the usurper Catiline in 63 BC, or John Pym's 'The cry of all England' speech of 1642, is to appreciate that the stock of human emotions to which leaders appeal is limited and remarkably constant. Were we listening to those three orators today we would probably be equally as moved now as their audiences were then. This stock of emotions can be plundered, plagiarised, but above all learned. The purpose of this book is to examine how two absolutely opposite personalities both pillaged that short lexicon in their different ways in order to win the prize both knew only one of them could attain: victory in the Second World War.

When in 1944 the film director Sir Alexander Korda wanted to exemplify Britain's spirit of resistance to Nazism, he hired Laurence Olivier to play the eponymous role in Shakespeare's *Henry V*. The King's speech before the breach at Harfleur was directly analogous to the speeches that Churchill was making that year, even though more than three centuries separated them. True leadership stirs us in a way that is deeply embedded in our genes and psyche. If the underlying factors of leadership have remained the same for centuries, cannot these lessons be learned and applied in situations fortunately far removed from the life-and-death ones of 1939–45?

Leadership – like courage and even sincerity – can be completely divorced from the concepts of good and evil. Adolf Hitler was both brave and sincere in his promotion of his beliefs, despite the fact that they were loathsome. Only to study the leadership qualities of people of whose actions one approves would be to deny oneself the examples of some of the world's most influential leaders. Undoubtedly the greatest criminal of our own times, Osama bin Laden, is a leader none the less and deserving of our investigation into how he could persuade so many people to wreak so much destruction. Just as Field Marshal Montgomery kept a framed photograph of Erwin Rommel in his caravan throughout the Desert campaign, we should try to study our enemy's leadership techniques in order to be able ultimately to defeat him.

Our world is still recognisably that which the post-Hitler settlement of 1945 bequeathed us. The Great Powers, allowing for Russia's and Eastern Europe's shrugging off of Communism in 1989–91, are much the same as they were when the United Nations was set up in San Francisco at the end of the war. Other than at the time of the implosion of Yugoslavia – which did not lead to any out-of-area conflicts – no European borders have altered. If one counts Korea as a United Nations police action, no wars have been fought directly between any Great Powers other than China's war with India in 1962. The past six decades have thus altered Europe less than in any similar period of time since the early Middle Ages. Decolonisation was already under way before Winston Churchill left office in 1955, and were he to return to earth today it would not take the Chiefs of Staff long to debrief him about the present state of the planet. Hitler – the Satan we cannot wholly put behind us – would need Hiroshima and Nagasaki to be explained to him, but the rest would be comprehensible enough. After all, he predicted in his bunker that the ultimate victors from his demise would be America and Russia, and although Germany's reunification might briefly excite him, the fact that it has turned out so peacefully and democratically would infuriate him satisfactorily. The events of 1939–45 still shape our world both with their lessons and their legacies. Hitler's and Churchill's continuing relevance to our lives is incontestable; Saddam apart, the West is presently enjoying those 'broad sunlit uplands' that Churchill promised us and Hitler tried so hard to raze.

That Churchill is still recognised as the personification of courageous leadership was indelibly underlined in the aftermath of the al-Qa'ida attacks on the United States of 11 September 2001. In their hour of pain and trial, Americans time and again turned to his example to express their deepest feelings about their sense of loss, their defiance and determination. Churchill once more emerged as a major figure in what can be called – after the title of one of his own books – 'the world crisis'. In his 2001 State of the Union address, President George W. Bush spoke of how, in their response to the attacks on America: 'We will not waver, we will not tire, we will not falter, and we will not fail.' It was a conscious echo of Churchill's broadcast to America of February 1941, in which he said: 'We shall not fail or falter; we shall not weaken or tire.' In his speech to the stricken survivors of the Pentagon on 12 September, the very morning after so many of their comrades had perished, US Defense Secretary Donald Rumsfeld said: 'At the height of peril to his own nation, Winston Churchill spoke of their finest hour. Yesterday, America and the cause of human freedom came under attack.' Rumsfeld returned to the subject of Churchill several times afterwards and the following August he told three thousand members of the US Marine Corps in California that there were direct parallels between America's relative diplomatic isolation over the projected war against Iraq and Churchill's lonely stand against the appeasement of Germany in the 1930s. Everything that I have read about Churchill's 'wilderness years' leads me to conclude that there are indeed just such parallels.

When President Bush was shown around the Cabinet War Rooms during his visit to London in 2001 he described Churchill as 'one of the really fascinating leaders', and he asked the British Embassy in Washington to furnish the Oval Office with an Epstein bronze bust of him.[1] (Ronald Reagan had already hung a portrait of Churchill in the White House's Situation Room.) Today it is Churchill who, thirty-seven years after his death, is helping to provide the vocabulary and the vernacular for the spirit of defiant resistance that America wishes to project to the rest of the world. 'Winston Churchill and his words are endlessly quoted and approved,' reported the *Boston Daily Record*, and when the President visited the devastated area of Manhattan's Ground Zero, comparisons were drawn with the Prime Minister's morale-boosting tours of the East End during the Blitz. As he prepared for war against Iraq, the President let it be known that he was reading a book entitled *Supreme Command: Soldiers, Statesmen and Leadership in Wartime* by the American academic Eliot A. Cohen, one of whose chapters is devoted to Churchill's relationship with his Chiefs of Staff.[2] (On a more mundane level, the comedian Jim Carrey quoted Churchill when he presented his far-from-mundane one-million-dollar cheque to the charity fund set up for the families of the victims of 11 September.)

At the highly charged ceremony to promote scores of New York firemen to fill the ranks of their fallen colleagues, Mayor Rudolf Giuliani quoted Churchill and earned the *Washington Post*'s accolade of 'Churchill in a Yankee's cap'. (Not such an inconceivable image, in fact, since Churchill loved wearing eccentric and sometimes outlandish caps and hats.) When he visited Britain in February 2002, Mayor Giuliani told Alice Thomson of the *Daily Telegraph*: 'I used Churchill to teach me how to reinvigorate the spirit of a dying nation. After the attack I'd talk to him. During the worst days of the Battle of Britain, Churchill never stepped out of Downing Street and said, "I don't know what to do", or "I'm lost". He walked out with a direction and a purpose, even if he had to fake it.'[3]

'*Even if he had to fake it.*' One of the contentions of this book is that for much of the time between the completion of the evacuation from Dunkirk on 3 June 1940, and Hitler's invasion of Russia fifty-five weeks later on 22 June 1941, Churchill did indeed regularly have to fake it. For all his superb oratory during that period, Churchill did not really know how Germany was going to be defeated. Faking it is sometimes a crucial part of leadership, but as St Paul wrote in his first epistle to the

Corinthians: 'If the trumpet shall give an uncertain sound, who shall prepare himself to the battle?' Churchill's certainty transmitted itself to the British people, even though in 1940 it was difficult to understand how on any possible rational analysis the war could be won.

Although both before and especially after the war, Churchill occasionally performed disappointingly in some of the high offices of state that he held, in those vital months of 1940–41 and for the rest of the conflict until 1945 he performed astonishing feats of leadership. At the heart of it all was a confidence trick of such staggering audacity that if he had not been proved right by events, he would probably have risked impeachment. (Of course if he had been proved wrong by events, and Britain had been successfully invaded, parliamentary retribution would have been the least of his worries.) This book will examine that benevolent confidence trick, as well as the malevolent ones employed by his antagonist.

The classical leadership paradigm

It has proved relatively easy throughout history for leaders to find people willing to kill for them; what has been far more difficult is to find people willing to die for them. People brought up in modern, rationalist-Christian Western countries have usually demanded at least the outside possibility of survival, but they have none the less volunteered in wartime for operations and units that have involved appallingly low survival-rates. The alternative that Shakespeare's Henry V offered to breaching the defences of Harfleur was, after all, to 'close the wall up with our English dead', and both twentieth-century world wars saw people willing to accept stupendously high attrition rates, especially in the infantry officer corps of the First World War and in Bomber Command in the Second. That was one kind of noble sacrifice; what the world saw on 11 September 2001 was its exact obverse image.

When Osama bin Laden was encouraging his followers to commit suicide, the methods he used seem to have been in essence indistinguishable from those employed by the Assassins in medieval times or the Mahdi and Khalifa in the Sudan in the 1880s and 1890s. They also seem to have borne a close resemblance to the Japanese *kamikaze* pilotry of 1944-5. Churchill, who fought against the Khalifa and was present at his army's final destruction at Omdurman in 1898, would immediately have recognised what he described (in a very different context) as 'a fakir of a type well known in the East'. The nature of this kind of charismatic pseudo-religious leadership – also exhibited by the cult leader Jim Jones when he persuaded over nine hundred of his followers to commit suicide in Guyana in 1978 – seems to be outside modern Western comprehension. Grigory Rasputin and some of the leaders of the earliest Crusades seem to have had something of the same appeal – Hitler certainly did – and it needs to be understood if the present threat to the West is to be overcome.

If bin Laden's leadership style is essentially Hitlerian in its vernacular and antecedents, and George W. Bush and his senior advisers look to Churchill for their inspiration, might not the War against Terror be legitimately seen as a re-fighting of the Second World War by proxy? I believe it can be, and the dichotomy between the charismatic Hitlerian versus the genuinely inspirational Churchillian techniques of leadership will be one of the central themes of this book. For the secrets of both types of leadership can be learned almost by rote, and harnessed to the benefit of anyone with an eye to history and the telling phrase.

Alan Bullock, in his joint biography of Adolf Hitler and Joseph Stalin subtitled *Parallel Lives*, demonstrated how many of the Nazis' totalitarian techniques were copied from the Bolsheviks. Of course the combined satanic but undeniable talents of Albert Speer, Joseph Goebbels and the film-maker Leni Riefenstahl made the Nazis' rallies far more visually impressive than the Red Square march-pasts so beloved of the

Soviet Politburo, but the amplified showmanship of both regimes amounted to little more than a showbiz spectacle done by microphones, lighting effects, smoke and mirrors.

In that beautiful and subtle critique of the dictatorial technique, the 1939 Hollywood movie *The Wizard of Oz*, the hitherto-terrifying wizard turns out to be a dwarfish mountebank who is kept busy behind an imposing façade pulling levers that produce flames and furious noises. Hitler, Stalin, Mussolini and Franco, the film suggests, actually amounted to no more than this, if only the Western democracies had the courage, decency and intellect to stand up to them. Yet for all that we have discovered about these men's personal inadequacies, they were responsible for the massacre of so many innocents as to leave the twentieth century forever besmirched as, in one distinguished historian's phrase, 'The Age of Infamy'.[4] In real life, instead of flying off in his balloon back to Kansas, the wizard would have shot the Scarecrow, the Tin Man, Cowardly Lion and Dorothy (and doubtless Toto into the bargain).

'No sadder proof can be given by a man of his own littleness than disbelief in great men,' wrote Thomas Carlyle in *On Heroes, Hero-Worship and the Heroic in History*, yet is not the reverse more true? Is there not pathos in our constantly casting about for leaders, when we have not yet perfected the art of being mature followers, sceptical of attributing superhuman qualities to people who we know perfectly well are no more than flesh and blood like us? A mature democracy should cringe at these periodic bouts of hero-worship, like the embarrassment a mature woman feels about her early-teenage crush on the captain of the school lacrosse team. 'One of the most universal cravings of our time,' wrote the American political thinker James MacGregor Burns, 'is a hunger for compelling and creative leadership.' It is a hunger that time and again has led to disaster, as when France cried out for leadership from Napoleon in 1799, Russia turned to Lenin in 1917 and compounded her error with Stalin less than a decade later, and no fewer than thirteen million Germans voted for Hitler in 1932. 'We won't get fooled again,' sang The Who in their eponymous political song. Yet we have been, time and again.

As Hitler's latest and finest biographer Sir Ian Kershaw pointed out in his 1987 book, *The 'Hitler Myth'*: 'The readiness to place all hope in "leadership", in the authority of a "strong man", has in itself of course not been peculiar to Germany. Promotion by threatened élites and acceptance by anxious masses of strong authoritarian leadership, often personified in one "charismatic" figure, has been (and still is) experienced by many societies in which a weak pluralist system is incapable of resolving deep political and ideological rifts and is perceived to be in terminal crisis.' Far from being, as Carlyle believed, a sign of bigness – or the absence of littleness – the glorification of leadership by 'great men' might merely be one sign of a country's Third World status.

Anarchist philosophers, and some modern libertarian thinkers, have argued with conviction that the underlying problem is the very existence of the concept of leadership itself, at least on a national scale. This also seems to be one of the complaints of the anti-globalisation protesters who descend on any town that is brave (or foolhardy) enough to host a summit of 'world leaders'. Were mankind to be able to organise itself in such a way that one man could not wield absolute power over a hundred, they argue, we would all be better off. Just as pure Marxists believe that the State would 'wither away' after the implosion of capitalism through self-contradiction, so anarchists such as Pierre Proudhon and Mikhail Bakunin contended that one day the very need for political leaders would eventually be dispensed with altogether. Yet although this argument has gained some ground since the war, especially in America during the 1960s and early 1970s, it is still as utopian as ever.

The briefest glance at the modern world shows how the ubiquity and visibility of 'world leaders' are, if anything, more in evidence today than at any time since 1945. Leaders have come to personify their countries in the public imagination and, even in an age of European integration, they have maintained a far higher public profile than might have been predicted even only thirty years ago. The influence that has led to this increase in the importance of world leaders – if not necessarily in their actual deployable power – does not look set to wane in the near future. This is largely due to the exponential increase in the speed and penetration of information technology, whereby more people in more places can be made aware far faster of more things that are happening. As the primary spokesmen for their countries, world leaders have taken full advantage of this development to raise their corporate profiles.

Far from meaning that we look more carefully at each issue the more conscientiously to be able to debate what is happening, the communications and information revolution has meant that we have bemusedly delegated more and more decision-making duties to our leaders. The 2002 Indo-Pakistan dispute over Kashmir was boiled down in the world's media to a stand-off between Prime Minister Vajpayee and President Musharref, and the issue of whether Osama bin Laden was dead or alive was considered more newsworthy than the liberation of Afghanistan itself from the Taliban. In 1780 the Whig MP John Dunning proposed the Commons motion that 'the influence of the Crown has increased, is increasing and ought to be diminished'. The same is today true of the influence of world leaders.

Leaders are likely to become more rather than less of a part of our daily lives because politics is being made ever simpler by the media, and nothing simplifies an issue better than to concentrate on the character of a single leader, or better still the personalities of two antagonistic ones. The need under universal suffrage to appeal to what is effectively the lowest intellectual common denominator in the electorate – at least among those likely to cast a vote – has inevitably led to the wholesale lowering of standards when it comes to persuasion, a process that politicians themselves nowadays wholeheartedly aid and abet.

Here is a single sentence from the peroration of William Gladstone's speech that destroyed Benjamin Disraeli's deficit-financing Budget of 1852 (and along with it the whole Tory ministry):

> I look back with regret upon the days when I sat nearer to many of my honourable friends opposite than I am now, and I feel it my duty to use that freedom of speech which I am sure, as Englishmen, you will tolerate, when I tell you that if you give your assent and your high authority to this most unsound and destructive principle on which the financial scheme of the Government is based – you may refuse my appeal now – you may accompany the right honourable gentleman the chancellor of the exchequer into the lobby; but my belief is that the day will come when you will look back upon this vote – as its consequences sooner or later unfold themselves – you will look back upon this vote with bitter, but with late and ineffectual regrets.[5]

It might have been one of the longer sentences of the Grand Old Man's œuvre, but can you imagine anyone in modern politics uttering anything like it? Three-word verbless sentences, intellectually patronising sound bites, references to footballing or soap opera catch-phrases – these are the stuff of modern political oratory.

The vocabulary of classical politics, involving speeches replete with literary and classical allusions, is simply not appropriate today because the decline in educational standards has made it impossible for much of the electorate to understand it, even if the politician himself has the intellectual wherewithal to deliver speeches of the necessary calibre. The great Whig lawyer and politician Lord Brougham said: 'Education makes a people easy to lead, but difficult to drive; easy to govern, but impossible to enslave.' It is a fearful thought that the opposite might also be true about the lack of education that is being imposed on the electorates of tomorrow.

This is not simply reactionary snobbishness – I have no desire to emulate the Princesse de Petitpoix in Disraeli's *Coningsby*, who felt it her duty in life 'to avenge the cause of fallen dynasties and a cashiered nobility' – but the fact remains that Gladstone, Disraeli, Rosebery, Balfour and Lord Salisbury believed in politics as an uplifting process, and they consciously sought in their speeches to educate almost as much as to persuade. Few political leaders today feel the same moral purpose in their speeches, and those who do seem to find it impossible not to sound like prigs.

With democracy has come demagoguery and, as Aristotle predicted, there is no more shameless type of government in the world than a perfect democracy, because it cannot admit of the possibility that its sovereign, the people, might ever be wrong. Social ills are blamed on political leaders today in a way that they rarely were under the old oligarchies. With blame comes the subconscious belief that leaders can change everything, even human nature. This absurd assumption is most evident at prime ministerial meet-the-people exercises, when Tony Blair is regularly asked to pass measures into law that would in earlier times rightfully be left to the bishops to implore through prayer, or in some cases the saints through divine intervention. Parliament could easily legislate that everyone should be kind and good, wrote Lord Salisbury in one of his *Saturday Review* essays in the 1860s, or that gravity should not cause window-cleaners occasionally to fall off window-sills, but there are limits to its true power.

The moment at which modern political leadership is most evident in peacetime comes during general election campaigns. These have always been toe-curling periods, hateful to anyone with even so much as a residual slither of human pride or dignity. The British election of 1992 saw a particularly low point in this regard, when the arguments were boiled down to accusations of 'double whammy' tax increases and the Government accused the Opposition of telling 'porkies' (which is cockney rhyming slang for lies).

What would Sir Max Beerbohm have made of it all? Consider his 1943 Rede Lecture on Lytton Strachey: 'This, they say, is to be the century of the common man. I like to think that on the morning of January 1st, in the year 2000, mankind will be free to unclasp its hands and rise from its knees and look about it for some other, and perhaps more rational, form of faith.' We have now passed that date, and there is no visible sign of anything but the same genuflection. If Francis Fukuyama's *The End of History and the Last Man* is correct in predicting the permanent global predominance of social democracy, there never will be.

'The wars of peoples will be more terrible than the wars of kings,' warned Churchill in his Commons speech on the Army Estimates in 1901. For, as he wrote in his novel *Savrola*, 'Chivalrous gallantry is not among the peculiar characteristics of excited democracy.'[6] Churchill, the paladin of democracy, underlined this problem when, one foggy afternoon in November 1947, he had a long day-dream about his father when painting in his studio at his country home, Chartwell. It was perhaps more of a vision, since according to his own handwritten account of the incident: 'I suddenly felt an odd sensation. I turned round with my palette in my hand, and there, sitting in a red leather upright armchair, was my father,' who had in reality died fifty-two years earlier. In the course of their 'conversation', the son told his father, who had been the founder of what was then called Tory Democracy: 'We have had nothing else but wars since democracy took charge.'[7]

Not only has democracy presided over the bloodiest wars in history, but some of them – such as Vietnam and the Gulf War – have been fought specifically in its name. When one fights for an idea rather than a particular geographical objective, such as Silesia or Alsace-Lorraine, it is almost impossible to compromise. Wars of democracy have tended to become wars to the knife; as a modern secular religion, democracy requires unconditional surrender. It despises compromise rather like the combatants of the eight wars of religion that France underwent between

1562 and 1595. The insistence on Germany's unconditional surrender in the Second World War elongated it, whereas earlier, eighteenth-century wars were limited dynastic affairs that generally ended when a province had been taken and a peace treaty could be signed. Churchill recognised this problem, and only managed to avert war against Franco's Spain in May 1944 by pointing out to the House of Commons: 'There is all the difference in the world between a man who knocks you down and a man who leaves you alone.' Had the Cold War of 1946–89 ever broken out into direct inter-superpower warfare it is likely that it would have ended only after massive destruction, because democracy, as Lord Salisbury said of militant Christianity, knows no middle way when faced with determined opposition.

The modern leadership paradigm

The thirteenth-century Sienese priest St Peregrino Laziosi is the patron saint of malignant growths, so it is presumably he who watches over the increase of the number of unelected public relations appointees who infest the British body politic to ensure that leaders are kept as far away as possible from the people they lead. Mr Wharton, in Trollope's *The Prime Minister*, 'was a Tory of the old school, who hated compromises, and abhorred in his heart the class of politician to whom politics were a profession rather than a creed'. Today's leaders in Britain and America – from all parties – are more and more drawn to politics as a profession, rather than out of a genuine sense of public duty, and have less and less 'hinterland', the current buzzword for non-political outside interests.

This process has been bad for the quality of leadership, since modern politicians find it almost impossible to resign on points of principle or for misdemeanours, having nowhere else to go in life. When in July 1954 Sir Thomas Dugdale, the Minister of Agriculture in Churchill's peacetime government, resigned over the compulsory purchase of land at Crichel Down before anyone had really suggested that he should, he returned to his traditional county pursuits with scarcely a backward glance at his severed career. Today ministers tend to hang on until they are threatened with dismissal. It is one of the least edifying spectacles in politics, and it further undermines the public's respect for their leaders.

This is not to argue that the leaders of the past were less ambitious than present-day ones, since they patently were not. As the British Prime Minister Lord Rosebery wrote in his biography of his friend and political opponent, Lord Randolph Churchill: 'The ambitious man who can watch without soreness the rise or success of a contemporary is much rarer than the black swan.'[8] It is merely to argue that the leaders of yesteryear tended to recognise when their time was clearly up, and go, in a way that is quite foreign to politicians such as David Mellor and Stephen Byers, whose grasps had to be slowly and painfully prised from the seals of office. In the fifth century BC Confucius said: 'There is no spectacle more enjoyable than to observe an old friend fall from a high roof', but the barely concealed *schadenfreude* which those two painfully prolonged resignations evinced in many other politicians – especially of their own parties – tended to disgust the public.

Politicians have long been drawn to the enjoyment of office for its own sake, regardless of where it might lead. When, in July 1834, Lord Melbourne was considering whether to accept King William IV's offer of the premiership, his notoriously outspoken private secretary Tom Young cried: 'Why, damn it all, such a position was never held by any Greek or Roman: and if it only last three months, it will be worth while to have been prime minister of England.' 'By God, that's true,' answered Melbourne. 'I'll go!' He did, and was prime minister for a total of six years and 255 days. Ambition *per se* is no bad thing in a leader, so long as it is allied to genuine talent, as it was in Melbourne's case. But as the former Tory Party Treasurer Alistair McAlpine found in John Major's Conservative Party: 'There is no room for either sentiment or principle in the lives of the overly ambitious.'

John Adair, the world's first professor of leadership studies, puts the importance of time and place in leadership succinctly when he says: 'It is difficult to be a great leader in Luxembourg in a time of peace.' Napoleon needed the Terror, Caesar needed the Gallic Wars and Churchill needed the Nazis to be raised to the pitch of greatness each achieved. (It must be said of Churchill, however, that had he died in April 1940 before becoming prime minister, he would none the less already have been a significant figure in twentieth-century politics.) One of the characters in A. N. Wilson's 'Lampitt Chronicles' emphasises the importance of historical opportunity succinctly when he observes of his own wasted life: 'I had never "done" anything: hard to see, after Suez, what one would "do", even if built with the same moral fibre of the old pioneers of Empire.'[9] Enoch Powell best enunciated this almost nihilistic feeling politically when he argued after Suez that the Empire no longer made sense and that the Commonwealth was no logical replacement.

In 1927 the American journalist Heywood Broun wrote of how, 'Just as every conviction begins as a whim so does every emancipator serve his apprenticeship as a crank. A fanatic is a great leader who is just entering a room.'[10] Leaders can appear before their time, and if it is not ready for them they can be forgotten, no matter how charismatic or inspirational they personally might be. Leaders need their John the Baptists more than they, their supporters, or history will readily admit. Oliver Cromwell required John Pym, General Franco needed General Mola, Gamal Abdel Nasser relied on General Neguib, and Ronald Reagan had to have his Barry Goldwater in order to pave their own ways to power. Tony Blair had the unaccustomed luxury of having two John the Baptists in Neil Kinnock and John Smith in order to make his ideas the more palatable and his path the smoother.

The process is often tough on the St John figure, as it was of course on the Baptist himself. They rarely get their rightful recognition and tend to be reminiscent of the Abbess del Pilar in Thornton Wilder's *The Bridge of San Luis Rey*, who 'was one of those persons who have allowed their lives to be gnawed away because they have fallen in love with an idea...before its appointed appearance in the history of civilisation'. Rather than being a fellow politician, 'the one who went before' is often an intellectual, someone whose thoughts make it possible for the leader to say and do things that would have been inconceivable even so much as half a generation earlier. Margaret Thatcher, for example, needed the economic views of Friedrich von Hayek, Milton Friedman, Sir Keith Joseph and Enoch Powell to be widely disseminated before she could undertake her wholesale free market reforms of the 1980s. She generously acknowledges these intellectual debts, but often leaders like to be seen as having constructed their ideology entirely on their own. Yet as Heine declared in *On the History of Religion and Philosophy in Germany*: 'Note this, you proud men of action. You are nothing more than the subconscious hodmen of the men of ideas...Maximilian Robespierre was nothing but the hand of Jean-Jacques Rousseau, the bloody hand that drew from the womb of Time the body whose soul Rousseau had created.' Neither Hitler nor Churchill was preceded by a John the Baptist character; they were no one's subconscious hodmen.

Hitler and Churchill: their continuing relevance

In order to try to estimate the continuing power that the Second World War exerts over us, I collected a number of press cuttings over two weeks in March 2000, a fortnight chosen entirely at random, snipping out anything that related to the Second World War, a six-year period that had, after all, ended fifty-five years before. In those fourteen days Israel released Adolf Eichmann's diaries; the David Irving *v* Deborah Lipstadt and Penguin Books libel trial about the Holocaust began to hear the concluding evidence from each side; the Austrian would-be Führer Jörg Haider finally and with evident reluctance denounced Hitler as the most evil man of the century, a place he had hitherto reserved for Churchill and Stalin; it was proposed that the empty fourth plinth in Trafalgar Square be filled by a composite statue of 'Women at War'; claims for compensation or restitution for art looted by the Nazis were estimated at between £800 million and £2.5 billion; the 97-year-old Leni Riefenstahl was reported to have survived a helicopter crash in the Sudan, and was about to be played by Jodie Foster in a film about her life; handwritten notes of a speech made by Hitler to the Reichstag in 1939 fetched £11,800 at auction; Neville Lawrence, the father of the murdered black teenager Stephen Lawrence, likened the experiences of young black people in Britain to those of Anne Frank; a man dressed as Hitler was arrested attempting to gatecrash the Vienna Opera Ball; fine obituaries appeared of Harold Hobday who breached the Eder Dam with a bouncing bomb, and Dominic Bruce, the RAF officer who made no fewer than seventeen attempted breakouts from German POW camps, including Colditz; the Queen Mother's wartime correspondence about the Duke and Duchess of Windsor aroused much media interest; and SS General Walter Schellenberg's 1940 Nazi invasion plan of Britain was published, complete with the list of 2,820 people who were going to be arrested. The Second World War was thus continuing to make headlines, almost on a daily basis, even over half a century on. For us Tommies, the war is far from over.

This is partly because the story of the 1939–45 period, and especially the year between June 1940 and June 1941, goes to the very heart of Britain's self-perception as a nation. It has aspects that appeal to both the Right and the Left. For the Right, those 386 days when we 'stood alone', albeit with the invaluable support of the Empire and Commonwealth, and also the alliance of Greece, represents the ultimate expression of sovereignty, proving the inestimable benefits of national independence. For the Left, it was the time when Fascism as a concept, rather than merely the nations of Germany and Italy, was faced down by the forces of democracy as represented by what Churchill dubbed 'the Grand Coalition' which included Clement Attlee's Labour Party. Michael Foot once said that 1940 was too powerful a symbol to be confiscated by the Right, and it is partly because both sides of the political spectrum take ideological succour from the events of that year that our pre-eminent *annus mirabilis* has survived as such a potent totem. As *The Times* wrote in a leader on 5 June 1990: 'Many countries celebrate the day that their independence was won or their *ancien régime* overthrown. Neither is applicable to Britain, a country without a national day of its own ... Britain remembers a national year ... The iconography of 1940 cannot be very far from those with Britain on their mind.'

There is a tribe in East Africa in which the witch-doctor's primary duty is to predict what a former great chief would have done in any given set of circumstances, and both sides of the debate over the extent of British integration into the European Union draw great inspiration from Winston Churchill. Euro-federationists such as Michael Heseltine like to cite Churchill as supporting the concept of European unity, although he tends to fail to add that the war leader did not actually wish Britain to be a participant in it. Sir Edward Heath also enjoys reflecting that it is to prevent future wars of the sort in which he fought that the Continent needs to federate. Similarly, those opposed to the Maastricht blueprint for Europe, such as Bill Cash MP and the historian Norman Stone – both of whose fathers died in the war – recall the disastrous results of trying to force Britain into a European superstate without her full-hearted consent.

It must always be back to 1940–41 that we return when we seek reasons for why Britons are proud to be so. There are plenty of things which Britain does very well indeed, but equally there always seem to be other countries that do exactly the same things better. It is hard to conceive of being proud of Britain simply because of pageantry, motor-racing, the pop music industry or the creation of the NHS, not least because Germany had her own national health insurance system far earlier. There has to be something more, and for many it is what Britain did over sixty years ago. Unlike any other Power, the British Empire stayed in the field from the start – except for the first two days from the German invasion of Poland – until VJ-Day signalled the end, and that is a cause for huge justifiable pride.

Such was the sense of catharsis generated by the war years that anything which took place afterwards was bound to be perceived as smaller, safer, more mundane, less magnificent. The post-war period in Britain has inevitably also been a post-heroic age. The Britain of Harold Wilson, Edward Heath and Jeremy Thorpe of the seventies simply could not hope to compare in terms of glamour and romance with that of Churchill, Eden and Montgomery of the early forties. Yet through all the various strains that were heaped on post-war Britain – the scuttle from Empire, periodic devaluations of sterling, mass New Commonwealth immigration, the Suez débâcle, appealing to the International Monetary Fund, British Leyland's industrial relations troubles, and the 1978–9 Winter of Discontent – the memory of 1940–41 was always a solace and a reminder that underneath all the humiliations there was a great nation.

Many another nation has had its golden age, its moment in history's limelight. The particular tragedy of my baby-boom generation is that ours should have been so recent. It is almost a recipe for nihilism, knowing that nothing can recapture that sublimely heroic period. Just as Greeks are still rightly proud of the achievement of fifth-century Athens, Frenchmen feel exalted when they contemplate the Arc de Triomphe (despite its presentation as victories of battles that France actually lost), Americans revere the Founding Fathers, and Mongolians still venerate (against strict government fiat) the memory of Genghis Khan, so we cannot wholly put behind ourselves the year in which, as T. S. Eliot wrote in his 1941 poem 'Little Gidding', 'History is now and England.'

There is little indication that interest in the war is lessening simply because its participants are leaving the stage, any more than interest in the Parthenon in Greece, Napoleon in France or the Constitution in America has waned with the death of their immediate protagonists and authors. The first quarter of the twenty-first century will see the Second World War veterans march off life's battlefield, but fascination with and admiration for their achievements will not die with them. Long after all the personal connections have been severed, the characters, events and lessons of what happened between 1939 and 1945 will be remembered by future generations. The re-introduction of the two minutes' silence on Armistice Day is an indication of the revived interest in, and veneration for, that time. Whenever I lecture on the war in schools I am repeatedly told by teachers that it is their pupils' favourite historical period by far.

Some people believe that Britain's obsession with the war is infantile, and even detrimental to the process of our maturing as a normal European state. They argue that the scars have largely healed, and are only picked open when hooligans sing xenophobic lyrics to the tune of 'The Dambusters' March' at international football matches. Yet the headlines of that fortnight in March 2000 ought to persuade them otherwise. As T. S. Eliot also put it in his poem: 'We are born with the dead: See, they return, and bring us with them.' Whether it is Swiss banks being sued by Jews demanding reparations, American schoolchildren venerating Hitler and then unleashing terror at Columbine High School, or audiences flocking to Spielberg movies such as *Schindler's List* or *Saving Private Ryan*, the echoes of Hitler's War will keep reverberating on and on, probably in ways that we cannot begin to guess at today.

Many factors would lead to final Allied victory and German defeat in World War II: not least the vast superiority in numbers and matériel. But Hitler's and Churchill's leadership also played a vital part in it. The lessons we can learn about how they behaved between 1939 and 1945 can help us in the way that we approach the far less momentous dilemmas of our own times. What were the leadership secrets that Hitler employed to mesmerise a nation? If we can see through him so easily today, why couldn't the German people then? Why were the warnings of his arch-opponent Winston Churchill not heeded when he was predicting precisely what Hitler was about to do next? He got it right in almost every respect, and such Themistoclean foresight is the essence of leadership. Unlike Hitler, Churchill had been educated and trained to exercise leadership since birth, yet he was not trusted with it until it was almost too late. Why not?

I believe that we need to understand how leadership works, how it is used and so often misused. We need to know what makes someone a good leader, but also how to spot all those tricks that would-be leaders use to try to gain our trust and support. We need to know how to identify the Führers of the future, because one thing can be taken for granted: next time they certainly won't be wearing the tell-tale jackboots and armbands.

Hitler and Churchill
to 1939

'You know I may seem to be very fierce, but I am fierce
with only one man – Hitler.'

Churchill to his new private secretary, John Martin

We are all familiar with the film footage of vast fawning crowds
lining the streets to greet Hitler on his various journeys through
the Third Reich in the 1930s. They were staged, of course, but
the adoration on the faces of the ordinary Germans generally
was not. How could such an unprepossessing specimen – with
his absurd little moustache, rasping voice and staring eyes –
have come to command such fanatical devotion?

To an extent rarely seen before outside a religious context,
the phenomenon of Adolf Hitler allowed intelligent people to
suspend the activity of that part of their brains which induces
rationality. The German Minister of Defence, Field Marshal
Werner von Blomberg, claimed that a cordial handshake from
the Führer could cure him of the common cold. Field Marshal
Hermann Göring said: 'If Hitler told you you were a woman, you
would leave the building believing that you were.' There are
endless further examples of intelligent people – men and women
alike – who were spellbound by Hitler. One of his senior staff
officers, General Walter Warlimont, recalled how: 'Hardly one of
the great theatre commanders, when summoned to make a presentation or report at the headquarters, was proof against the
overpowering presence of Hitler.'[1]

Churchill by contrast never seemed to exert this kind of personal, almost mystical power over others. While Hitler had charisma, Churchill did not. How was it possible that Hitler instilled so much more awe and adulation than Churchill? And why, despite that, did Churchill ultimately prove the more successful leader? What made Hitler and Churchill leaders anyhow, and what special skills and techniques did they employ to induce millions to follow them?

Various attempts have been made to liken Hitler and Churchill to one another. As one historian of the Churchill family, John Pearson, has put it:

> In a number of respects Churchill and Adolf Hitler were uncomfortably alike. Both were ruthless men, obsessed with military power and a driving sense of private destiny. Both were self-educated, intensely nationalistic, and powerfully aggressive in the face of opposition. Both, too, were strongly egocentric characters, overwhelming orators, natural actors and mesmeric talkers, more than capable of dominating those who fell beneath their spell. Both ... [found] their relaxation in painting, speculative monologue and nocturnal screenings of their favourite films. There was even an uncanny similarity in the way both sketched out strongly autobiographical fantasies of their intended paths to power, Churchill in [his novel] *Savrola* and Hitler in *Mein Kampf*.[2]

Unfortunately, any useful insights this passage might contain were wrecked when the author went on to claim that Churchill 'might well' have acted in the same way that Hitler did in his rise to power, whereas in fact the idea of Churchill wading up to his spotted bow-tie in the blood of his political enemies is utterly ludicrous. Most powerful leaders – certainly not just Hitler and Churchill – are 'egocentric characters' who are 'powerfully aggressive in the face of opposition', but where Churchill argued down his opposition and defeated it by votes in

Parliament, Hitler gunned down his opponents on the Night of the Long Knives and used Dachau and other concentration camps to dispose of the rest. Churchill would never have considered resorting to such tactics, even were Germany's internal stresses of the 1920s replicated in his own country. He did indeed intern Britons without trial under Regulation 18B in 1940, but he always considered it, in his own words, 'in the highest degree odious', and he released them as soon as he safely could. He reserved the use of gas for when – and if – the Germans invaded the British Isles, not as an instrument of genocide against civilians.

Churchill's nationalism was undeniably deeply felt and well-articulated, but it was never of the resentful, paranoiac and vicious kind that Hitler espoused. Rather than 'speculative monologue', Churchill actually excelled at dialogue and repartee; he would soon have tired of the unquestioning, mute, adoring audiences favoured by the Führer. Churchill was only 'obsessed with military power' in times of war; it just so happened that two of his periods of office coincided with the two most terrible wars of human history. In times of peace he concentrated on bringing in the legislation that forbade the employment of boys under fourteen in mines, introduced National Insurance, and gave one afternoon a week off for all workers. Furthermore Churchill's painting was done for relaxation and pleasure; Hitler painted houses for a living and ceased to do so when his need for cash eased.

The attempt to liken Hitler's *Mein Kampf* to Churchill's novel *Savrola* was perhaps the most absurd of Pearson's contrivances. Whereas the former book is a blueprint for Nazi Germany's quest for *Lebensraum* (living space) in the East and a treatise about the Aryan's racial superiority over the Slav, *Savrola* is a light romantic melodrama about the love affair between the wife of a president of a small European Latin republic and its leader of the opposition, the eponymous hero. Written in 1897 and published in 1900, *Savrola* does contain a few

3

references to politics, including some neo-Darwinist references to the survival of the fittest among nations that reflected the standard eugenicist thinking of the day, to which Churchill subscribed, but that is where any similarity to *Mein Kampf* ends. It certainly did not sketch an autobiographical fantasy about Churchill's rise to power, not least because Savrola advocates the appeasement of the dictator Molara, leaves the country when the Revolution starts and does not attain power in Laurania until the epilogue of the book in which everyone is living happily ever after.

Unlike *Mein Kampf*, *Savrola* was not a commercial success, and as Churchill admitted: 'I have consistently urged my friends to abstain from reading it.' It is easy to see why, with its absurd plot, one-dimensional characterisation and relentless clichés. Rats leave sinking ships, people stoop to conquer, petards are hoisted, the heroine loves the soil the hero walks upon, hours come, and 'All is fair in love and war'. It is also full of the politically incorrect remarks that one would expect from a work of its time: the King of Ethiopia has a 'black but vivacious' face, the lot of a woman is abdication and compliance, and of virtually the only working-class character in the book, we 'will read no more, for history does not concern itself with such'. The hero, Savrola, is a 32-year-old philosopher, amateur astrologist and statesman, who is drawn to politics more through ambition than his desire to contribute to the public good.

In almost every facet of their personalities, no two men could have been more different than Hitler and Churchill. The latter was a magnificent hedonist whose appetites were massive. On his way to the Quebec Conference on the *Queen Mary* liner in 1943, for example, Churchill ate a meal comprising 'oysters, consommé, turbot, roast turkey, ice with canteloupe melon, Stilton cheese and a great variety of fruits, *petit fours* etc, the whole lot washed down by champagne (Mumm 1929) and a very remarkable Liebfraumilch, followed by some 1870 brandy'.

The question of Churchill's drinking is an important one. He used to say that he had taken more out of alcohol than it had taken out of him, but then all drinkers believe that. In his case, however, with an ox-like constitution that served him well until his ninth decade, it was no more than the truth. Although Hitler believed that Churchill was a hopeless alcoholic, the evidence suggests otherwise. Churchill was clearly joking when he refused a cup of tea on medical grounds, claiming that: 'My doctor has ordered me to take nothing non-alcoholic between breakfast and dinner.' In fact, as he wrote in his autobiography *My Early Life*, 'I have been brought up and trained to have the utmost contempt for people who get drunk.' His friend Professor Frederick Lindemann once calculated that Churchill had drunk enough champagne in his lifetime to fill half a railway carriage, but that he took over half a century to do so.[3] ('The Prof' was the master of what would today be termed political incorrectness, once asking a civil servant: 'What is this foolish proposal to abolish hunger?')

Accusations of alcoholism made by the former historian David Irving in his multi-volume biography of Churchill, which is the kind of hymn of hate that would have been written if the wrong side had won the Second World War, parrot the standard Nazi propaganda line. Fortunately, though, Mr Irving gives us enough evidence in his books to refute his own allegations. Thus, when he states that on one weekend at Chequers in August 1941 the (non-claret) alcohol consumption consisted of two bottles of champagne, one of port, a half-bottle of brandy, one of white wine, one of sherry and two of whisky, he also lets us know how many people were consuming them. Sunday lunch alone found Lady Horatia Seymour, Lord and Lady Cranborne, Lord and Lady Bessborough, 'a Rothschild and his wife', an RAF officer and the (admittedly teetotal) Canadian Prime Minister, William Lyon Mackenzie King, around the Churchills' table. Once one divides the amount of drink consumed by the number of meals served and then again by the number of family members and guests present (in this case at least nine) it no longer seems excessive, especially in view of the generous standards of entertainment in grand country houses of the day.[4] On Irving's own statistics, therefore, Churchill cannot be accused of alcoholism, unless it is argued that he drank the whole of Chequers' entertainment budget himself. As we know from the testimony of several of his private secretaries, who did the mixing, Churchill liked his brandies and whiskies heavily diluted with water and soda.

(The author Clive Ponting has also complained that Churchill and Eden drank expensive 1865 cognac together in November 1940, but one might legitimately ask: if they did not deserve the luxury of drinking vintage brandy as they fought to save civilisation, who did? Mr Ponting's biography of Churchill and his book *1940: Myth and Reality*, which consistently denies the heroism of Britain in her finest hour, makes him reminiscent of no one so much as the balding clerks in John Betjeman's poem 'Slough', who 'daren't look up to see the stars / But belch instead'.)

Hitler, meanwhile, can be accused – and indeed convicted – of being an anti-smoking teetotal vegetarian. He was not a complete teetotaller because he would, he said, occasionally 'swallow water or beer because of the dryness of my throat', as he testified in his 1924 trial after the so-called 'Beer-hall Putsch'. A special dark beer with an alcohol by volume content as hopelessly low as two per cent was later brewed for him by the Holzkirchen brewery of Bavaria. During the Second World War, Hitler once remarked that there was little that could be done to alter the eating and drinking habits of the people in the short term, but that after the war he would 'see to the problem'. The ghastly prospect of a low-alcohol cholesterol-free Reich beckoned the Aryan peoples after victory.

In private, Hitler was one of those holier-than-thou vegetarians who sometimes give that perversion a bad name. During the twenties, when a friend called Mimi Reiter ordered a Wiener Schnitzel, he pulled a face and said: 'No, go ahead and have it, but I don't understand why you want it. I didn't think you wanted to devour a corpse...the flesh of dead animals. Cadavers!' He called broth 'corpse tea', and would tell what he considered a humorous story about a deceased grandmother whose relatives threw her corpse into a brook in order to lure crayfish for their supper. To a guest who was eating smoked eel he once remarked that eels were best fattened with dead cats, and to ladies eating suckling pig he said: 'That looks exactly like a roast baby to me.' Quite apart from the rudeness to his guests and the sick imagery employed, the sheer irony of Adolf Hitler lecturing others on the immoral aesthetics of corpses and death is delectable.

Hitler was once presented with a lobster by Heligoland fishermen, but he wanted to ban the eating of such 'ugly and expensive' animals and did not like being seen eating luxury foods. During the first few months after coming to power he signed no fewer than three separate laws providing for the protection and proper treatment of animals, and in January 1936 his Government decreed that 'Crabs, lobsters and other crustaceans are to be killed by throwing them rapidly into boiling water. When feasible, this should be done individually,' since, after much debate at high government levels, officials decided that this was the most humane method of killing them.

Hitler also liked caviar, until he discovered how much was being spent on it and he then moved on to roe, since the idea of a caviar-eating leader was incompatible with his conception of himself. Churchill had a robust attitude to people of this sort, minuting to Lord Woolton at the Ministry of Food in July 1940: 'Almost all the food faddists I have ever known, nut-eaters and the like, have died young after a long period of senile decay...The way to lose the war is to try to force the British public into a diet of milk, oatmeal, potatoes etc, washed down on gala occasions with a little lime juice.'

Hitler was almost entirely devoid of any but the blackest humour, and until the last hours of his life was a bachelor unable to commit himself emotionally to another human being. Churchill, by contrast, was a family man, compassionate and rightly famed for his wit. Nor could their artistic tastes have been more different. Hitler knew much about classical music in general and was inspired by the works of Richard Wagner in particular. Churchill preferred military marches, Gilbert and Sullivan, the music-hall comedian Harry Lauder, and the school songs he had sung at Harrow and remembered with fondness for the rest of his life. As a child, Diana Mosley, a cousin via Churchill's wife Clementine, remembers him singing 'Soldiers of the Queen' 'and other ballads of his youth, beating time as he did so with his shapely white hand'.[5] When he was attending the Quebec Conference Churchill 'made several of his entourage, including the fastidious [Permanent Under-Secretary at the Foreign Office Sir Alexander] Cadogan take part in the collective singing of old music-hall songs'.[6] Churchill was an exemplar of Noël Coward's quip in *Private Lives* about the potency of cheap music; he could not bear to hear the sentimental song 'Keep Right on to the End of the Road' because it made him cry.

Pretty much anything could induce tears in Churchill. Whereas many modern leaders struggle hard to manufacture genuine emotions, Churchill – who was essentially a Regency figure in the way that he openly exhibited his feelings – was regularly overwhelmed by them. If George W. Bush or Tony Blair were to cry in public it might well unnerve a large number of people during the War against Terror, but Churchill was so naturally lachrymose that he seems to have spent much of the Second World War in tears. 'I blub an awful lot, you know,' he once told his post-war private secretary, Anthony Montague Browne. 'You'll have to get used to it.' He soon did, not least when tears rolled down the Prime Minister's face as he contemplated the list of war dead at Boodle's Club in St James's. Churchill's earlier private secretary Sir John ('Jock') Colville explained how it was 'part of his character and quality, he wasn't scared to be emotional'.

Churchill wept at the news that Londoners were queuing for birdseed to feed their canaries during the Blitz; after his 'Blood, toil, tears and sweat' speech; at the baptism of his grandson and namesake Winston; at the cheering of his announcement in the Commons of the attack on the French Navy at Oran; touring the East End during the Blitz in September 1940; at the end of the visit to Britain of the American envoy Harry Hopkins; hearing of the sufferings of occupied France in June 1941;[7] watching Alexander Korda's movie *That Hamilton Woman* on the way to Placentia Bay; at the religious service on HMS *Prince of Wales* once there;[8] during the march-past after the Battle of El Alamein; on receiving the 1945 general election results;[9] at John Freeman's Address in Reply to the Gracious Speech in August 1945; at the first Alamein reunion at the Royal Albert Hall, meeting those blinded in the battle;[10] at Sir Stafford Cripps's funeral, and on many other occasions. The Duke of Windsor wrote to the Duchess at the time of King George VI's funeral in 1952: 'I hope to see Cry Baby again before I sail,' annotating: 'Nobody cried in my presence. Only Winston as usual.' It was rather un-English for a nineteenth-century aristocrat to wear his huge heart on his sleeve in this manner, but it was common in earlier times and entirely Churchillian.

(Anthony Montague Browne stayed on faithfully serving Churchill until the latter's death in January 1965, to the detriment of his Foreign Office career. It was he who had to register the death at Kensington Town Hall, choosing 'Statesman' over 'Retired' as the occupation of the deceased. Before the coffin was closed, Jock the marmalade cat, of whom Churchill was very fond, came into the bedroom, jumped into the coffin, peered into the still face, and went away, never to re-enter that room again. Montague Browne was the only non-family member to walk behind the catafalque at the State funeral. He recalled how, at the end of the long day of great national obsequies, he returned from Bladon churchyard in Oxfordshire 'submerged in a wave of aching grief for Britain's precipitous decline, against which

[Churchill] had stood in vain'. When he got back to his flat in Eaton Place he discovered that it had been burgled. It is as good a metaphor for modern Britain as any.)

While it is impossible to imagine two men more different than Hitler and Churchill, as leaders they had much more in common than one might think. The key attribute shared by both men was an almost superhuman tenacity of purpose that they held on to throughout their long years of adversity and failure. Hitler's early career was anything but promising. Landsberg prison in Bavaria, where Hitler wound up in 1923, was a forbidding place, although he was treated very leniently there. He had just tried to seize power, but instead his 'Beer-hall Putsch' failed pathetically. Indeed, up to the age of forty, Adolf Hitler was a failure in almost every respect. For most of the 1920s his NSDAP (nicknamed Nazi) Party was headed nowhere. In the elections of 1928, for example, it polled a mere 2.6 per cent of the vote. Most people at the time regarded Hitler as the joke leader of a joke party, thankfully devoid of any political future.

Churchill fully appreciated what Hitler went through in these German wilderness years. In his 1937 book *Great Contemporaries*, he reprinted an article of 1935 in which he had said that the story of Hitler's 'struggle cannot be read without admiration for the courage, the perseverance, and the vital force which enabled him to challenge, defy, conciliate, or overcome all the authorities or resistances which barred his path' in what Churchill described as Hitler's 'long wearing battle for the German heart'. (With commendable éclat, Churchill even retained those – and other – generous words about Hitler in the 1941 reprint of that book.)

Unlike Hitler – who had every disadvantage necessary for success in life – Churchill had every privilege that so often presages mediocrity. He was born at Blenheim Palace straight into the apex of Britain's political establishment; his father, Lord Randolph Churchill, was Chancellor of the Exchequer when Winston was at prep school. He had been bequeathed a far easier start than Hitler, who was the son of a simple Austrian customs officer. The grandson of a duke, whose heir presumptive he was until the age of ten, Churchill had had a promising career as Home Secretary before disaster overtook him as First Lord of the Admiralty in the First World War. Through a combination of military misjudgement and appalling luck, his brainchild, the Gallipoli campaign, was a costly failure, and he was forced to resign from the Cabinet in ignominy. His wife Clementine always remembered it as the lowest point in her husband's life, when he reputedly even briefly considered committing suicide.

Yet he refused to be broken. Politics were so deeply in Churchill's blood that he discussed them with Lloyd George in the vestry when waiting to sign the register during his wedding, and he was not about to leave that world. By 1924 Churchill was himself Chancellor of the Exchequer and after serving for five years in that high post he once again chose the political wilderness when he resigned from the Shadow Cabinet to pursue a long, bitter and ultimately doomed campaign against Indian self-government. His calls for enthusiastic British prosecution of the Russian Civil War and his air of over-excitability during the General Strike did not add to his reputation; instead, along with his eccentric and seemingly self-interested support for King Edward VIII during the Abdication Crisis, these made him look like a hopelessly reactionary imperialist warmonger and maverick in the eyes of most Britons. It was only by a vote of three to two that he escaped being deselected by his own constituency. There was indeed a sense, after he had warned of disaster so many times over so many different issues over so long a period, that by the time he got round to warning about the size of the Luftwaffe, Churchill was no longer taken seriously. He had himself written of this phenomenon in *Savrola*, when he described Laurania's anti-Molara press and the way that: 'The worst result of an habitual use of strong language is that when a special occasion really does arise, there is no way of marking it.... They had compared the Head of the State so often and so vividly to Nero and Iscariot, very much to the advantage of those worthies, that it was difficult to know how they could deal with him now.'[11]

For all but a few months in the 1930s, Churchill was yesterday's man. The writer Christopher Sykes called him 'a disastrous relic of the past' and even his friend the Canadian press baron Max Beaverbrook described him as 'a busted flush'. In 1931 there was a book published entitled *The Tragedy of Winston Churchill*. For a decade he was forced to spend much of his time at his home at Chartwell in Kent, painting, bricklaying and writing the biography of his great ancestor John Churchill, the 1st Duke of Marlborough. When the Tory MP Lady Astor visited Joseph Stalin in 1937, the Russian leader asked her about his old enemy's political prospects. 'Oh, he's finished,' she replied, a view of Churchill that would have been echoed by most other political commentators of the day.

Yet, like Hitler, Churchill clung unflinchingly to his beliefs, the principal one being that he was chosen by Providence to save his country. Despite widespread hostility and ridicule, he continued to warn against the threat of Nazi aggression. This started early; in March 1933 he pointed to 'the tumultuous insurgency of ferocity and war spirit' that was then raging in Nazi Germany. With Hitler only Chancellor for two months, Churchill drew attention to 'The pitiless treatment of the minorities' in Germany, and the way that she had 'abandoned her liberties to augment her might'. In particular he emphasised the rapid expansion of the Luftwaffe and the contrasting weakness of the Royal Air Force. Picturing the 'incalculable conflagration' which might be unleashed by an incendiary-bomb attack on London, Churchill was accused by the British Prime Minister Stanley Baldwin of being alarmist.

Part of the problem was that Churchill was not suited to subordinate posts. His restlessness and frustration, borne out by his unsuitability for other roles, misled nearly everyone about his leadership capabilities, but some of his colleagues recognised this early on. The Foreign Secretary at the time of the outbreak of the First World War, Sir Edward Grey, once remarked that: 'Winston, very soon, will become incapable from sheer activity of mind of being anything in a Cabinet but prime minister.' Churchill's decisiveness emerged as the vital quality required for national leadership, but he was not well suited for any position but chief executive. His energy, drive and encyclopaedic mind, when exercised in the subordinate positions he held throughout his career, simply alienated colleagues and superiors. Many of his peers viewed his move to Number Ten in 1940 with dread and alarm. The War Cabinet official Sir Ian Jacob wrote years later of how: 'They had not yet the experience or imagination to realize the difference of a human dynamo when humming on the periphery and when driving at the centre.'

Although Churchill longed for office in the thirties, afterwards he was hugely relieved that he had not been offered it, since it kept his hands entirely clean of any responsibility for the National Government's policy of appeasement. 'Over me beat invisible wings,' he later wrote. Throughout his life, Churchill believed he had been especially chosen by Fate for greater things and this was a key factor in his drive. Once, in the Great War, when his dugout was blown up by a high-explosive shell moments after he had left it, he said that he had 'a strong sensation that a hand had been stretched out to move me in the nick of time from a fatal spot'. Not by any means a conventional Christian, Churchill believed in a kind of providence that reserved him for a special destiny, although he had denounced such an idea in *Savrola*, when the hero tells the heroine: 'I have always admired the audacity of man in thinking that a Supreme Power should placard the skies with the details of his squalid future, and that his marriage, his misfortunes, and his crimes should be written in letters of suns on the background of limitless space. We are inconsequential atoms....I realise my own insignificance, but I am a philosophic microbe, and it rather adds to my amusement than otherwise.' As Churchill put it elsewhere, we are all worms, but he liked to think of himself as a glow-worm.

After he was run over by the Italian-American driver of a car crossing Fifth Avenue in 1931 he said: 'There was a moment...of a world aglare, of a man aghast...I do not understand why I was not broken like an eggshell or squashed like a gooseberry.' He might not have understood at the time, but he had his suspicions that Fate had especially marked him out to save his country. Therefore he continued to warn against the threat of Nazi aggression at every opportunity. (In a retort to Willie Gallacher, the only Communist MP in the Commons, Churchill said in 1944: 'I was for eleven years a fairly solitary figure in this House and pursued my way with patience; and so there must be hope for the honourable member.')

In one of the no fewer than seven hundred newspaper articles that he wrote – covering everything from iced water and corn on the cob to Mussolini and the rise of the Luftwaffe, for publications as diverse as *Cosmopolitan* and the *Pall Mall Gazette* – Churchill produced an essay on Moses that must have left readers in no doubt who Churchill believed would lead his people to the Promised Land. 'Every prophet has to come from civilisation, but every prophet has to go into the wilderness,' he wrote. 'He must have a strong impression of a complex society and all that it has to give, and then must serve periods of isolation and meditation. This is the process by which psychic dynamite is made.' All this self-referential philosophising must have been faintly irritating and ridiculous to many people in 1932, but it would have seemed very different eight years later, once the dynamite – psychic and physical alike – had exploded. If he had a political role model at this time, it was Clemenceau, of whom he wrote (surely semi-autobiographically) in *Great Contemporaries*: 'He was defeated in his constituency of the Var, and quitted its bounds under the taunts and insults of the mob. Rarely was a public man in times of peace more cruelly hounded and hunted. Dark days, indeed, and the leering triumphs of once-trampled foes!' But, years later in 1917, 'It was at that moment...that the fierce old man was summoned to what was in fact the Dictatorship of France. He returned to power as Marius had returned to Rome; doubted by many, dreaded by all, but doomsent, inevitable.' Once in power, Churchill wrote of Clemenceau (while dreaming about himself): 'He looked like a wild animal pacing to and fro behind bars, growling and glaring; and all around him was an assembly which would have done anything to avoid having him there, but having put him there, felt they must obey.' A better description of the British Conservative Party in May 1940 could scarcely be imagined.

Although Churchill's daughter Mary Soames has correctly written that he 'had a strong underlying belief in a Providential God', she has also pointed out that he 'was not religious in a conventional sense – and certainly no regular church-goer'.[12] The primary duty of the Almighty Being in whom Churchill believed, but to whom he paid little overt obeisance, seems to have been to watch over the physical well-being of Winston Leonard Spencer-Churchill. On one occasion when a visiting cleric over-generously described him as 'a pillar of the Church', he answered: 'Well, I don't think that could be said of me. But I do like to think of myself as a flying buttress.' He enjoyed the hymns, conformed outwardly as an Anglican in the way that most Conservative politicians did at that time, approved of the Church's then role as a bulwark of social stability, and applauded the part it had played in the development of the nation state. Moreover, he used the Bolsheviks' atheism against them politically, and although, as his friend Sir Desmond Morton put it, he 'did not believe that Christ was God...he recognised him as the finest character who ever lived'. He particularly admired the courage that Jesus had shown in the manner of his death, an aspect in a man's character that always mattered greatly to Churchill.

He was not entirely joking when he wrote to his mother from

India in 1897: 'I am so conceited, I do not believe the Gods would create so potent a being as myself for so prosaic an ending' as death in a skirmish on the North-West Frontier. When one considers how often and how closely Churchill brushed against the Grim Reaper's cloak in his long life it is hard to doubt that he might well have had an (admittedly somewhat blasphemous) point when he assumed that 'invisible wings' beat above him. For what was the actuarial probability of a man who lived his kind of life finally dying a nonagenarian? Consider the might-have-beens. He was born two months prematurely, after his mother took a fall out walking with the guns of a shooting party on the Blenheim estate, and had then taken 'a rough pony ride' back to the palace. Neither the London obstetrician nor his Oxford auxiliary could get there in time for the birth. Aged eleven, Churchill very nearly died of pneumonia at his Brighton prep school, a disease that was to recur during and after the Second World War. His son Randolph wrote that this attack in 1886 brought Churchill 'closer to death than at any time during his long and adventurous life'. His next brush was more self-inflicted, when aged eighteen he leapt off a bridge in a game of chase with his brother and cousin on the estate of his aunt Lady Wimborne near Bournemouth. He fell twenty-nine feet on to hard ground and knocked himself out for three days, rupturing a kidney. 'For a year I looked at life round a corner,' he recalled. He then nearly drowned in Lake Geneva.

The stories of his exploits in Cuba, where he witnessed action with Spanish forces, on the North-West Frontier of India with the Malakand Field Force, at the charge of the 21st Lancers in the Battle of Omdurman, and also in escaping from a Pretorian prisoner-of-war camp during the Boer War are well documented; indeed, the 17th/21st Lancers' regimental motto of 'Death or Glory' seems neatly to encapsulate the options with which Churchill sought to present himself between 1895 and 1900. Yet this seeming daring of death did not end in his mid-twenties. He even survived a plane crash.

After his enforced resignation from the chancellorship of the

Duchy of Lancaster as a result of the failure of the Gallipoli campaign in the Great War, Churchill took command of the 6th battalion of the Royal Scots Fusiliers in France. Not for him the
château-generalship of so many senior Allied officers far behind
the lines of that conflict. On occasion, when he was inspecting a
trench or dugout, a German high-explosive shell would land on it
just before he arrived or soon after he left.

Although Churchill was never subjected to an assassination
attempt – a curious oversight in an otherwise eventful life – he
did of course frequently court danger during the Blitz when he
would climb up on to the roof of the Admiralty to watch the air
battle, despite the ever-present danger of bullets, high explo-
sives, shrapnel blasts and plane crashes. He was up there in
September 1940, the same month that Buckingham Palace took
a direct hit in the courtyard at only the other end of the Mall.
Churchill, who hunted and took flying lessons, led a life that
could have been cut off on more than a score of occasions before
victory was won in the Second World War. Faith in his own star,
in what he called his 'guardian' and 'guiding hand', was a necessary prerequisite for a leader who wanted to follow the kind of
active existence that Churchill had chosen for himself.

The historian Paul Addison has characterised Churchill's
spiritual beliefs as 'a concoction of ambition, historical myth,
and a residue of religious conviction'. If they were what sustained his sense of self-belief during the months of doubt and
despair after the Dardanelles catastrophe, who can hold them
against him? There is anyhow a tremendous ambiguity to his
true religious beliefs. When in a Shadow Cabinet meeting in
June 1950 he referred to 'the Old Man' coming to his aid, he
later had to explain that he had meant God, yet three years later,
after his stroke, he told his doctors that he did not believe in the
immortality of the soul and that death was 'black velvet –
eternal sleep'. That is what he had called it in *Savrola*, half a
century earlier, when the Lauranian president faced death 'and
beyond he saw nothing – annihilation – black, black night'.[13]

Yet there is also an assumption that Heaven does exist in several of Churchill's letters, particularly the moving one that was to be delivered to Clementine were he to die in the trenches, in which he wrote: 'Do not grieve for me too much. I am a spirit confident of my rights. Death is only an incident, and not the most important that happens to us in this state of being. ... If there is anywhere else, I shall be on the lookout for you.' In his book *Thoughts and Adventures* (1932) he also wrote: 'When I get to Heaven I mean to spend a considerable portion of my first million years in painting, and so get to the bottom of the subject.'

Because Churchill was, in his own words, 'lacking in the religious sense' – and lost any specifically Anglican faith he might have had by about the age of twenty-three – he developed an elemental, almost pagan belief in Fate and Destiny rather reminiscent of Napoleon's. But not Hitler's. For Hitler increasingly saw himself as the Supreme Being who could control Providence, something that was quite alien to Churchill's (admittedly also highly egotistical) belief system. If anything, Hitler had a yet more unshakeable faith in his own star, a certainty about his ability to guide Fate himself. He believed that it was down to Fate that he was born at Braunau am Inn, close to the German border, and that nothing less than 'Divine Providence' had sent him to Vienna to share the sufferings of the masses; and of course – just like Churchill – it had also been an unseen hand that had protected him in the trenches during the First World War when so many of his comrades had perished.

All of this, Hitler reasoned, must have been done for a purpose, which equally clearly must be a great one. By the summer of 1937 he believed himself to be utterly infallible, stating: 'When I look back upon the five years that lie behind, I can say, this was not the work of human hands alone.' Imagine the invincible self-regard it is necessary to have in order to tell the German people, as he did in one speech: 'That is the miracle of the age, that you have found me, that you have found me among so many millions. And I have found you, that is Germany's good fortune.' In this he was encouraged by the Nazi Party: comparisons of Adolf Hitler to Jesus were only disparaged by SS Gruppenführer Schulz from Pomerania, for example, because whereas Christ had had a mere twelve disciples, Hitler had seventy million.[14]

Hitler also called on his *Schicksal* (Destiny) and *Vorsehung* (Providence) when he simply wanted to avoid making a decision. He only really chose to make decisions when events or his opponents forced them upon him; otherwise, as the historian Karl Dietrich Bracher has said, his trust in Fate was part of the rationalisation of his instinctive dislike of having to take them. Hitler stated that he would not undertake an action, 'Not even if the whole party tries to drive me into action. I will not act; I will wait, no matter what happens. But if the voice speaks, then I will know that the time has come to act.' The belief that one is a recipient of voices in one's head is a well-known symptom of schizophrenia. If the sense of Hitler as a national Messiah became a new kind of faith for Nazi Germany, it was one in which he himself was an enthusiastic co-religionist.

The sense of all-or-nothing that Hitler and Churchill both espoused in their wilderness years was also a consequence of neither having independent means, at least until the success of their books – in Hitler's case *Mein Kampf* and in Churchill's *The Second World War* – made them financially secure. Although he was never as poor as Adolf Hitler was during his wilderness period, Churchill lived for many years teetering on the brink of bankruptcy. People tend to assume that because Churchill was the grandson of a duke and born in a palace, he was also rich, but the truth is very different. Almost throughout his life, and certainly before the publication of his wartime memoirs in 1948, Churchill's debts left him constantly bordering on negative net worth. The outgoings on his splendidly luxurious lifestyle nearly always amounted to as much as he earned from his journalism and ministerial salary. His financial situation was so precarious at the time of his wife Clementine's fourth pregnancy in the summer and autumn of 1918 that it is thought that she even offered to put up her baby for adoption by General Sir Ian Hamilton's wife after it was born.

In May 1915, when forced to resign over the Gallipoli débâcle, Churchill did not return to his ministerial salary of five thousand pounds per annum until Lloyd George appointed him Minister for Munitions in July 1917. In the meantime he had to survive on the pay of an army officer and a backbench MP, in the days when neither was large. Clementine was no heiress, and could contribute very little to the family's finances. So short of money were they in 1918 that when the lease ran out on their London home in Eccleston Square they had to move into Churchill's aunt Cornelia's house in Tenterden Street off Oxford Street. Worse was to come later that year when Churchill received a letter from the Ministry of Agriculture complaining that the land at his country home, Lullenden in Sussex, was not being fully cultivated, at a time when producing food was a duty incumbent on all British landowners. (The civil servant Sir Maurice Hankey recalled spending a tea-time with Churchill in 1917 'rambling around his wild and beautiful property'.) In his reply to the Ministry, Churchill had to admit that he simply had not got the capital to invest in the machinery necessary to cultivate his land.

Although his journalism was later to provide him with a large income, he wrote relatively little during the First World War, and it was to be several years before the income from his history of that war, *The World Crisis*, came on stream. With his reputation at its nadir after Gallipoli, he could also not call on the generous group of rich friends who were occasionally to bail him out during the wilderness years of 1931–9 and who at one point bought him a Daimler car for his birthday. For all his genius in other areas, Churchill was an inept financial speculator, who lost the 2002 equivalent of a quarter of a million pounds in a single day of the Wall Street Crash of 1929.

Both Hitler and Churchill, therefore, knew hard times,

although they were hardly comparable since Hitler did not have the kind of friends who could bail him out to the extent of buying him a Daimler. Yet both men shared a tenacity, an unshakeable belief in their mission no matter what others said of them, and it was largely this that gained them followers once the political circumstances had changed. Today we think of Hitler and Churchill as powerful leaders, but we tend to forget how unlikely their rise to power seemed to people at the time. Both had been failures, Hitler in the 1920s and Churchill in the 1930s. So how could they become leaders of their countries such a short time afterwards?

Creation of the national myth

Hitler used his time in Landsberg prison to write a book, or rather he dictated it to his acolytes Rudolf Hess and Emil Maurice, who were also serving prison sentences for their participation in the Beer-hall Putsch. It reads like a work that has been spoken by a man walking up and down a prison cell, letting out the frustrations of his captivity in his rambling fury. *Mein Kampf* is a dreadful work in every respect: a garbled, unfocused mixture of manic hyper-nationalism, twisted Darwinism and repulsive anti-Semitism. Rather like Karl Marx who reduced history to merely the story of class struggle, Hitler's history of mankind is no more than a racial struggle, and the ills of the world are put down to an international Jewish-Bolshevik conspiracy. The subjugation of allegedly inferior peoples such as the Slavs is offered as the recipe for Germany's salvation. Yet *Mein Kampf* also holds the secret of Hitler's startling rise to his position as the Führer of Germany.

The creation of an all-encompassing national legend is epicentral to the formation of a modern political movement. For Hitler, this was *die Dolchstosslegende* (the stab-in-the-back myth). According to this explanation of Germany's defeat in the

Great War, the surrender of November 1918 came not as a result of unsustainable losses on the battlefield, still less of bad generalship by men like Hindenburg or Ludendorff, or even the incompetence of the Kaiser, but because a sinister conspiracy of socialists and Jews had betrayed the honest brave German *Volk* (people) from within. This analysis, which historians agree has no evidential historical merit whatsoever, was drummed into Germans at every available opportunity by the Nazis.

On occasion, Hitler would retell German history from the time of Arminius, the German who defied the Roman Empire, via the Emperor Barbarossa and Frederick the Great, creating a mythical heroic past for the whole of Germany which he could contrast powerfully with the humiliations of the 1919 Treaty of Versailles and which he put down to this alleged stab-in-the-back. In fact, of course, the defeat had been the result of German troops being stabbed in the front by the British, French, American and Canadian armies, rather than in the back by the Jews.

Even non-Nazis came to believe implicitly in the *Dolchstosslegende*, providing as it did the perfect psychological balm so desperately needed by a proud nation raw in defeat. In a biography published in 2002 it has emerged that in the 1920s the Prince of Pless, one of Germany's greatest aristocrats, was told by his father that he had dined the night before in the Pariser Platz in Berlin with the rich Jewish hostess Frau von Friedländer, who had allegedly told him:

> You don't perhaps realise that you nearly won the war because we were assisting you the world over and it was only because of us Jews that things went very badly for you afterwards. If you remember, in 1917 Balfour made his famous declaration in which he promised us a Jewish homeland in Palestine. Up to then we were on your side, because the Kaiser had promised us a homeland, but after the Balfour declaration it was decided that we should throw in our lot with the Allies. This

we did and the whole power of our worldwide organisation worked in that direction. You don't realise, of course, the great mistake you made here in Germany and in Austria by allowing Jews to obtain commissions in your armies, because it gave us the possibility to collect information on every level, up to and including the General Staff and to get an insight into the workings of your military machinery, which we could never have achieved otherwise. This information we passed on to the Allies. So they always knew far in advance what your plans were and where and when the next military move was going to take place.

The Prince of Pless recalled that 'My father was quite upset. He could not get over the fact that his Jewish friends, whom he had known for years before the war and who had pretended to be loyal German subjects and staunch friends and supporters of the Kaiser, in reality were all the time prepared to work against him if ordered to do so by their political leaders.'[15] If cultured aristocrats could have fallen for such ludicrous lies and conspiracy theories, how much easier would it have been for the less well-educated German masses?

However repugnant his core beliefs are to us today, in *Mein Kampf* Adolf Hitler offered a clear vision: that of a German *Reich* (Empire) that would one day dominate Europe. For a people who considered themselves downtrodden by sinister influences – however absurd the theories behind them – it proved irresistible. In his book Hitler wrote:

If the German nation today, penned into an impossible area, faces a lamentable future, this is not a commandment of Fate. Neither is to revolt against this state of affairs an affront to Fate... Germany will either be a world power or there will be no Germany. And for world power she needs that magnitude which will give her the necessary position in today's world, and life to her citizens.[16]

Few people took this vision seriously at the time. Yet such was Hitler's invincible sense of self-belief that he let none of this deter him. He had a deep sense of mission. 'The Jews have not brought about the 9th November 1918 for nothing,' he told the Czech Foreign Minister, Franzisek Chvalkovsky, in January 1939. 'This day will be avenged.' This warped, paranoiac conspiracy theory displayed what most modern psychologists would diagnose as the primary symptoms of a psychopath. Yet he would have been a psychopath few people would have heard of had it not been for the crisis of capitalism known as the Wall Street Crash.

Everything changed dramatically for Hitler when the American stock market collapsed in New York in October 1929. Soon afterwards the Great Depression hit Europe, bringing unemployment to millions and widespread social unrest in its wake. In May 1928 the Nazis had won 2.6 per cent of the popular vote and only a dozen seats, but by September 1930 – when Germany had five million people unemployed – they won 18.3 per cent and more than a hundred seats in the Reichstag. The month after the Lausanne Conference of June 1932, which terminated Germany's reparations payments under the Versailles Treaty, the Nazis won 37.4 per cent. In that election, anti-democratic parties won a majority of the vote; for the first time in history a large modern state had deliberately voted against democracy. Now that Germany was riven by crises, Hitler suddenly gained what every successful leader needs: followers. Six months later he was Chancellor.

Churchill too had a strong, unshakeable vision: that of a powerful British empire based on civilised values. During the 1930s, in his study in his country house at Chartwell in Kent, he wrote many speeches warning of the dangers that Nazi Germany posed to Britain and the world. This is an excerpt from one he made to the City Carlton Club in September 1935, as Italian threats to Abyssinia (modern-day Ethiopia) became ever more menacing and Germany's Nuremberg Laws outlawed the Jews and made the swastika the official flag of Hitler's Reich:

Germany is rearming on a gigantic scale and at an unexampled speed. The whole force and power of Nazidom are being concentrated on warlike preparations by land, sea and air. The German nation, under Herr Hitler's dictatorship, is spending this year at least six times as much as we are on the Army, the Navy, and the Air Force put together. German finance is a perpetuated war budget. I admire the great German people, but the rearmament of Germany, organized and led as she is now, must appear to anyone with any sense of proportion as the greatest and most grim fact in the world today.[17]

Recognising that Hitler's expansionist foreign policy must eventually mean war, Churchill time and again called for Britain to undergo a comprehensive programme of heavy rearmament. Few listened. He was variously denigrated as a 'fire-eater and militarist', a 'rogue elephant', or – by the *Daily Express* in October 1938 – as 'a man whose mind is soaked in the conquests of [the 1st Duke of] Marlborough'.[18] It was the same month that the Chamberlain Government had decided not to go to war with Germany over Hitler's plan to dismember Czechoslovakia, a stance that was greeted deliriously by the great majority of Britons. Clearly, Churchill's vision was completely out of tune with the times.

It was only on 15 March 1939, after the Nazis had marched in and occupied the rump of Czechoslovakia, that it dawned on the British people that Churchill might have been right all along about Hitler's true intentions. They understood how, in exploiting Britain's and France's lack of resolve, Germany was set to dominate Europe. Finally, after the warnings of half a decade, more and more people were willing to share Churchill's vision of a powerful alliance ready to defend freedom.

So both Hitler and Churchill gained followers through a vision which they clung to unflinchingly. Such a vision is the key to true leadership, and it is particularly powerful if the leaders have stuck to it through adversity, as both Hitler and

Churchill did. Leaders give people a common goal with which they can wholeheartedly identify. Managers don't have that guiding vision. As Ronald Reagan put it: 'To grasp and hold a vision, that is the very essence of successful leadership – not only on the movie set where I learned it, but everywhere.'

Hitler's vision, of course, was a fantastically evil one, but this is not how the German people saw it at the time. While to us his ideas seem utterly foul, many Germans believed that he really did offer them a glittering vision for a better future. Of course, most of it was defined by what he was against, rather than what he stood for. He was opposed to socialism, Bolshevism, the Versailles Treaty, liberalism, the Jews, big business, democracy, and old-style Wilhelmine aristocratic conservatism. Saying what one is against is far easier (and often more effective) in politics than stating what one is for, and Hitler took this truth to new heights.

Oratory

'The power which has always started the greatest religious and political avalanches in history has been, from time immemorial, none but the magic power of the word,' wrote Hitler. For him, words were 'hammer blows' which had the power to 'open the gates to people's hearts'. He admired the impassioned oratory of the British Prime Minister David Lloyd George, saying: 'The speeches of this Englishman [sic] were the most wonderful performances, for they testified to a positively amazing knowledge of the soul of the broad masses of the people.' When it came to propaganda, the Nazis pioneered a vast range of innovative ideas. For example, they invented what are today called 'photo-opportunities', and Hitler's rallies were undeniably impressive spectacles involving tens of thousands of people marching in perfect step. Yet for all their visual extravagance, it was at the centrepiece of these rallies – his oratory – that Hitler knew he had to excel. To that end he trusted only himself to write his speeches, as did Churchill. Neither man resorted to the phalanxes of speech-writers so favoured by today's politicians.

In his public performances Hitler used the old show-business trick of making people wait for him in order to build up excitement and expectation, both prior to his appearance and even when he had already stepped up to the dais. He would survey his audience, grasping his military belt with its *Gott Mit Uns* (God With Us) motto on the buckle, for sometimes up to half a minute before starting to speak. Commencing relatively slowly and with a low, deep voice, it was not until the end that he ranted and screeched in the manner so often seen on newsreels. He would also speak through the applause just after it had begun to drop off, and would wind up with shorter and punchier sentences. Many of these techniques, very different from the ones in common use in the Western democracies of the thirties, have become standard practice in political speech-making today.

Tenacity and charisma alone would not have made Hitler Germany's Führer. He still needed to sell himself and his vision. In order to succeed, leaders have to be able to convey themselves and their message to the public, and the primary means has always been – and probably always will be – the set-piece political speech. For all the penetration of the written word, graphics, text messaging and video link-ups, nothing is so politically persuasive as the power of direct oratory. Even today, for all the modern public-relations gimmicks offered by television, radio, the Internet and multimedia, we still judge our leaders largely by their ability to move us through their oratory. Politicians who are poor public speakers rarely make great leaders.

Both Hitler and Churchill have rightly gone down in history as highly effective orators, but surprisingly enough public speaking did not come naturally to either of them. While both undoubtedly showed talent eventually, they had to work very hard to develop it. Hitler liked to have a warm-up act to heighten the audience's anticipation of his public appearances. In a speech to workers at the Siemens Dynamo Works in Berlin on 10 November 1933, it was performed by his Propaganda Minister Dr Joseph Goebbels. This speech, given only nine months after Hitler had become Chancellor, provides a perfect illustration of the sinister but masterful method by which the Führer managed to create a sense of community between himself and his audience. It is worth considering in some detail for the various methods he used to play upon the emotions of an audience who were not necessarily positively disposed towards him.

'German compatriots, my German workers,' Hitler began, 'if today I am speaking to you and to millions of other German workers, I have a greater right to be doing this than anybody else.' He was aware that many in that largely working-class audience were likely to have left-wing sympathies, yet within a minute he had won them over with a reference to his wartime service in the trenches, something that many of them had also undergone. 'Once I stood amongst you. For four and a half years of war, I was in your midst. And through diligence, learning – and, I have to say, hunger – I slowly worked my way up. Deep inside me, I always remained what I had been before.' His reference to the widespread food shortages undergone by Germany in 1918–19 was a master-stroke, one of several in that speech.

He continued: 'But I was not amongst those who worked against the interests of the nation. I was convinced that the destiny of the nation had to find representation if terrible damage to the whole people, sooner or later, was to be avoided. This separated me from the others.' Then came an attack on the Versailles Treaty. By restricting Germany to an army of one hundred thousand, without armour or aircraft and a navy with no larger vessels than ten thousand tons, the Allies had tried to protect themselves from a resurgent Germany after the Great War.[19] It was nothing like so harsh as the terms that Germany planned to impose on the rest of Europe if victorious, but it disbanded the German General Staff, provided for the occupation of the Rhineland until its terms were accepted, demanded financial reparations and contained a clause blaming Germany for deliberately starting the war. Though each was perfectly reasonable in itself, collectively the clauses of the Versailles Treaty amounted to Hitler's best (and indeed only) rational political argument. As he put it in his Siemens speech: 'The theory that victor and vanquished have to remain in their legal position for ever, this theory has led to a new hatred in the world, to perpetuate disorder, to uncertainty, to distrust on one side and fury on the other.' It was a hatred and fury that Hitler would spend the next decade doing everything in his power to stoke up and then unleash.

Hitler knew very little about economics, but he did know that his audiences probably knew even less. So it was to the financial aspects of Versailles that he turned next:

The world was not pacified, as was explained at the time, but on the contrary, the world was plunged into ever-new haggling and ever-new discord. And the second thesis was equally mad: that you have to destroy the vanquished economically as well, so that the victor has a better economy. A mad theory, but one which runs like a red thread through the whole Versailles Treaty and which finally leads to the fact that for ten years they have tried, on the one hand, to burden the economy of a great people with an unbearable load, and on the other, to destroy it as much as possible, to cut off all its opportunities. We experienced the consequences of this. The way in which, in order to fulfil its economic obligations, Germany was increasingly forced to throw itself on to the export markets under any kind of conditions, the way in which the international competitive struggle began here and the way in which political debt was gradually changed into economic debts.

Economically this was drivel, not least because the Allies had

early on begun to lessen Germany's debt burden, which was significantly reduced by the Great Depression too. Yet it worked
rhetorically, which is all that mattered to Hitler as he got on to
another favoured topic: the Jews. The chief aim of the speech
was to promote rearmament without regard for international
restrictions. It was obvious that this would damage Germany's
international position, but Hitler made it clear whom he
intended to take the blame:

> The struggle between the people and the hatred amongst them
> is being nurtured by very specific interested parties. It is a
> small, rootless, international clique that is turning the people
> against each other, that does not want them to have peace. It
> is the people who are at home both nowhere and everywhere,
> who do not have anywhere a soil on which they have grown
> up, but who live in Berlin today, in Brussels tomorrow, Paris
> the day after that, and then again in Prague or Vienna or
> London, and who feel at home everywhere.

At that point a man in the audience shouted out: 'The Jews!'
Without pausing to consider him, or this, Hitler continued:
'They are the only ones who can be addressed as international,
because they conduct their business everywhere, but the people
cannot follow them. ... I know one thing about those who today
are agitating against Germany, about this international clique
which libels the German people in such a way: not one of them
has ever heard a bullet whistle past.' In fact, of course, the Jews
had a distinguished record of fighting in the trenches during the
Great War, as even the SS had to accept when, at the Wannsee
Conference that planned the Final Solution in 1942, Reinhard
Heydrich ordered that 'severely wounded veterans and Jews
with war decorations (Iron Cross 1st class) will be accepted in
the old-age ghettos' rather than being 'evacuated east'.[20]
Hitler never once actually mentioned the Jews by name in his
Siemensstadt speech, but it was obvious to everyone to whom

he was referring. It did not need the moron in the audience to shout it out. Hitler once remarked that if the Jews had not existed: 'We should have to invent them. It is essential to have a tangible enemy, not merely an abstract one.'[21] In the Nazi State, all social classes were supposed to be united in the so-called *Volksgemeinschaft* (people's community). Nothing creates more unity than a common enemy; hatred of the Jews thus constituted the backbone of Hitler's power. By overtly not mentioning the Jews by name in his speech, Hitler created another bond between himself and the audience, tacitly drawing them into his conspiracy.

The oration at the Dynamo Works continued, and by now he was indeed yelling:

> They should see that what I am saying is not the speech of a Chancellor, but that the whole people stands behind it as one man, man for man, woman for woman. What is bound together today is the German people itself. For centuries it has sought its destiny in discord, with terrible results. I think that it is time to seek our fate in unity, to attempt to realise our fate as an indivisible united community. And in Germany I am the guarantee that this community will not favour one side alone. You can see me as the man who does not belong to any class, to any caste, who is above all that. I have nothing but a connection to the German people.

This proclamation of the leader's classlessness and commitment to community was greeted with cheering and acclaim, along with the singing of the Nazi Party anthem, the Horst Wessel Song.

The German people, Hitler was emphasising, were completely separate from the Jews. Getting over this sense of the 'otherness' of non-Germans was just as important as emphasising the identity of the Aryan race itself.[22] The British philosopher Bertrand

Russell believed that 'Few people can be happy unless they hate some other person, nation or creed', yet why did Hitler hate the Jews? It is a straightforward enough question, and central to the history of the twentieth century, but there is still no entirely satisfactory answer. Various different theories have been adduced, from his having caught syphilis from a Jewish prostitute, via his having been cheated by the Jewish Dr Eduard Bloch, who treated Hitler's mother for breast cancer, to the allegedly Jewish professors who turned him away from the Visual Arts Academy of Vienna. Yet could there be a far more sinister answer than these naïvely monocausal ones? Might it be that Hitler actually had nothing personally against the Jews, but just spotted that demonising them would be a rewarding political move?

In a recent ground-breaking book, entitled *Hitler's Vienna: A Dictator's Apprenticeship*, the historian Brigitte Hamann has gone so far as to argue that during his 1908–13 sojourn in Vienna, between the ages of nineteen and twenty-four, Hitler actually liked and got on well with several Jews. Her researches left no Viennese stones unturned, from Dr Bloch's account-books to the racial background of the Visual Arts Academy's examiners. As a result, she managed to delve deep into the psychopathology of the future Führer, with fascinating results.

Much of what Hitler wrote about his Viennese years in *Mein Kampf* turns out either to be exaggerated or untrue. What is incontrovertible, however, is that although Hitler knew and lived among Jews during his poverty-stricken period as a painter and opera fanatic, they treated him well and he displayed no overt signs of hostility towards them at the time. During all the tedious, endless later monologues about his dog days in Vienna, Hitler never mentioned having a bad experience with a Jew there. It is even possible to state that some of Hitler's best friends were Jews, such as Josef Neumann and Siegfried Läffner. Far from it being instilled in him by his brutal, drunkard father or his provincial Austrian background, Hitler only appears to have taken to anti-Semitism much later, probably an entirely cynical manoeuvre to enhance his political ambitions after the Great War. Poor, shy, untalented, utterly asexual, introverted, socially envious and monomaniacal, the young Hitler was, in Albert Speer's later words, 'an insecure stranger in a large metropolis' when he lived in Vienna. Instead of adapting his personality in order to fit in, as most normal people would have done, Hitler withdrew further into himself and blamed the Viennese for not appreciating him properly.

It was the petty resentments of this unhappy time in the Austrian capital that established many of the outlines of what turned into Nazism. All that was needed was a huge European war to create the necessary conditions in which the bacillus of his views could thrive. Right on cue, only a year after Hitler left Vienna, came the cataclysm of August 1914. The dictator had served out his apprenticeship, and once anti-Semitism was cynically slotted into his creed he was ready to wreak his havoc. Of course it makes little difference whether Hitler's anti-Semitism was born of personal distaste, perceived wrongs or political opportunism, but it seems that the last was the case.

The writer Frederic Raphael has an interesting new theory that is a psychological twist on the one about the Jewish doctor of Hitler's mother having cheated and/or misdiagnosed her. According to this thesis:

If Dr Bloch failed to cure Frau Hitler's cancer, it is unlikely – not to say impossible – that in those days anyone could have. Nor does Hitler say so. That 'Adi' loved his mother is undoubted; so did Proust, who nevertheless, in a notorious *Figaro* article, defended matricide on the grounds that, after all, everyone sometimes longs to kill his mother. Is it too tricksy to suggest that Hitler, seeing his mother's sufferings, wished (humanely enough) that they would end but that, when they did, in her death, he felt so guilty that he transferred his shameful wish onto the Jewish doctor, who could then be the scapegoat for it?[23]

33

It probably is indeed far too 'tricksy', not least because Hitler might well have been among the millions of us who have never once wanted to harm our mothers, but it is certainly no weirder than many of the monocausal theories that have been produced to explain the Holocaust.

Some people consider that it is not just irrelevant where Hitler contracted his anti-Semitism but also morally wrong to investigate the issue too closely. They argue that it plays into the hands of people who, like David Irving, take the opposite view. As has been perceptively pointed out by the writer and critic Jonathan Meades, there is

> a school of charlatanism whose bickering adherents attempt to explain Hitler by inventing, or giving credence to, folkloric stories of psycho-sexual traumas: Hitler's mother was alleged-ly mistreated or misdiagnosed by a Jewish doctor and died; Hitler may have contracted syphilis from a Jewish prosti-tute – these speculations are hateful because they seek to make individual Jews culpable for the enormities their race was to suffer. There are, inevitably, one-ball theories and satanic abuse theories. There is the ludicrous tale of the infant Hitler having his penis bitten by a goat into whose mouth he was attempting to urinate.[24]

This last theory, if true, might explain much about Hitler, but presumably not his anti-Semitism. And even if Hitler was monorchid, that does not explain why thirteen million Germans voted for the NSDAP in 1932, since they were not told that he was short of a testicle (which, anyhow, he was not). What is inter-esting is not what drove him, so much as what drove the German people to abandon democracy and support a leader whose revanchism was so loudly proclaimed at every opportunity.

In his speech at the Siemens Dynamo Works it was only in carefully selected places that Hitler worked himself into a com-pletely deliberate and well-rehearsed rage. For the most part, he did not rant and foam during his speeches, despite the fact that he is shown in that state in most of the footage one sees. Reinhard Spitzy, private secretary to the German Foreign Minister Joachim von Ribbentrop, recalled how once, after a good lunch with Hitler and his staff, a servant entered the room to announce that a British diplomat had arrived:

> Hitler started up in agitation. '*Gott im Himmel!* Don't let him in yet – I'm still in a good humour.' Before his staff's eyes, he then worked himself up, solo, into an artificial rage – his face darkened, he breathed heavily and his eyes glared. Then he went next door and acted out for the unfortunate Englishman a scene so loud that every word was audible from the lunch table. Ten minutes later he returned with sweat beading his brow. He carefully closed the door behind him and said with a chuckle, 'Gentlemen, I need tea. He thinks I'm furious!'[25]

Leaders have to be actors, and Adolf Hitler understood this very well, even if he was something of a ham one himself. In the early days of his career he studied the performances of a Bavarian comedian named Weiss-Ferdl in order to learn how to captivate an audience. Just like an actor, Hitler would endlessly practise his poses and gestures in front of the mirror in his shabby room in Munich's Thierschstrasse. Photographs exist of him also doing this much later in his career. It was in the streets and beer halls of Munich that Hitler plied his early trade as a political agitator, sometimes speaking to audiences as small as a dozen people. There he learned just how much his effect on the public owed to careful planning and preparation of material. Anyone who has tried to address an audience at Speakers' Corner in London's Hyde Park will know just how quickly the experience toughens one intellectually and emotionally, especially when it comes to dealing with chance hecklers and outright opponents.

Hitler would personally examine the acoustics of the beer

halls so that he could change his tone and pitch accordingly. Once he made the mistake of delivering a speech on a Sunday morning. The audience was, as he later described, 'cold as ice'. From then on, he preferred to schedule his speeches for the evenings when his audiences were more receptive to his message. As he wrote in *Mein Kampf*: 'It seems that in the morning and during the day the human mind revolts against any attempt to have somebody else's will or opinion imposed upon it. In the evening, however, it easily succumbs to the domination of a stronger will.' (Professional actors bear out this contention; for some reason, audiences are far more receptive at evening performances than at matinées. It took a particular mind like Hitler's to put this phenomenon to a political use.)

Theatrical effects like martial music, seas of flags, massed ranks of storm troopers, and especially dramatic lighting – sometimes using military searchlights, sometimes hand-held flaming torches – were employed at meetings and rallies to increase the audience's receptiveness still further, and the Nazis pioneered means of propaganda that are now a commonplace in the modern political arena. The comparison to Churchill could not be more stark. He held few rallies and employed no spin-doctors or special effects. His preferred venue was the House of Commons or the wireless, where the audience physically present was relatively small. He relied on the power of the spoken word and the persuasiveness of the better argument. It wasn't demagogic tricks that made him the greatest orator of the twentieth century, but his exceptional command of the English tongue. As he wrote in *My Early Life*: 'I would make boys all learn English; and then I would make the clever ones learn Latin as an honour and Greek as a treat. But the only thing I would whip them for is not knowing English. I would whip them hard for that.'

Churchill was not a natural-born speaker; few people are. After a disastrous experience trying to address the Commons entirely from memory at the age of thirty, he abandoned the practice. Instead he would sometimes spend ten to fourteen hours preparing a single speech, occasionally to the accompaniment of gramophone records playing martial music, working and reworking it until he finally thought it perfect. As his friend Lord Birkenhead joked: 'Winston has spent the best years of his life writing impromptu speeches.' Churchill said that the best advice he ever got on parliamentary speaking came from the Tory politician and former Cabinet minister Henry Chaplin, who told him: 'Don't be hurried. Unfold your case. If you have anything to say, the House will listen.' It was advice Churchill put to good, and occasionally devastating, effect.

In *Savrola*, Churchill described the genesis of the hero's great speech in the Lauranian City Hall. It seems so plainly autobiographical an explanation of the process of creating a political oration that it bears repetition in full:

His speech – he had made many and knew that nothing good can be obtained without effort. These impromptu feats of oratory existed only in the minds of the listeners; the flowers of rhetoric were hothouse plants. What was there to say? Successive cigarettes had been mechanically consumed. Amid the smoke he saw a peroration, which would cut deep into the hearts of a crowd; a high thought, a fine simile, expressed in that correct diction which is comprehensible even to the most illiterate, and appeals to the most simple; something to lift their minds from the material cares of life and to awake sentiment. His ideas began to take the form of words, to group themselves into sentences; he murmured to himself; instinctively he alliterated. Ideas succeeded one another, as a stream flows swiftly by and the light changes on its waters. He seized a piece of paper and began hurriedly to pencil notes. That was a point; could not tautology accentuate it? He scribbled down a rough sentence, scratched it out, polished it, and wrote it in again. The sound would please their ears, the sense improve and stimulate their minds. What a game it was! His brain contained the cards he had to play, the world the stakes he played for. As he worked, the hours passed away. The house-keeper entering with his luncheon found him silent and busy; she had seen him thus before and did not venture to interrupt him. The untasted food grew cold upon the table, as the hands of the clock moved slowly round marking the measured tread of time. Presently he rose, and, completely under the influence of his own thoughts and language, began to pace the room with short strides, speaking to himself in a low voice and with great emphasis. Suddenly he stopped, and with a strange violence his hand descended on the table. It was the end of the speech.[26]

'Rhetorical power,' wrote Churchill, 'is neither wholly bestowed, nor wholly acquired, but cultivated.' He was a perfectionist, rather than a born orator, and in 1940–41 the result was indeed perfection. The cadences of Churchill's speeches of that year owed much to the hours when, as a young hussar subaltern stationed in India nearly half a century earlier, he had studied the historical works of Gibbon and Macaulay. Churchill created his own synthesis of the grandiloquent rolling sentences of the former and the biting wit of the latter. His oratory was also influenced by the late-Victorian rhetoric of William Gladstone, the Irish-American politician Bourke Cockran and his own father Lord Randolph Churchill, who was the most magnetic political orator of his day.

Churchill's grand, old-style idiom did not impress everybody; some found it insincere, others pompous, yet others derided him as a cross between a ham actor and a music-hall turn. There was even one point during the locust years of the 1930s when the House of Commons shouted him down when he tried to put the case for King Edward VIII during the Abdication Crisis. It was not really until 1940 that, in that supreme test of the British people, Churchill's rhetoric at last truly matched the perils of the hour to create the sublime beauty of the best of his wartime speeches. The defeat on the Western Front, the evacuation from Dunkirk, the Fall of France, the Battle of Britain, the Blitz, the threat of invasion – all produced speeches and phrases that will live for as long as does the English tongue.

In the summer of 1940, Churchill's speeches were just about all the British people had to sustain them. With Hitler in control of Continental Europe from Brest to Warsaw, even the Chiefs of Staff had no logical plan for victory. With neither Russia nor America in the conflict, all Britain could do was to hold on, grimly praying that something might turn up. Churchill could not really appeal to the head in his protestations of the certainty of ultimate victory, so he had to appeal to the heart.

Without having very much in the way of sustenance or good news for the British people, Churchill took a political risk in deliberately choosing to emphasise the dangers instead. Only three days after becoming prime minister he told the House of Commons: 'I have nothing to offer but blood, toil, tears and sweat.' He attempted no evasions about the nature of the task ahead, as his words swept away a decade of appeasement, doubt and defeatism, which he had once called 'the long, drawling tides of drift and surrender'. He unhesitatingly placed the conflict in the stark context of a Manichean struggle between good and evil, truth and falsehood, right and wrong. It was what Britons longed to hear. As he left the Commons he observed to his friend Desmond Morton: 'That got the sods, didn't it?'[27]

The effect was indeed extraordinary. As the writer Vita Sackville-West told her husband, the Information Minister Harold Nicolson: 'One of the reasons why one is stirred by his Elizabethan phrases is that one feels the whole massive backing of power and resolve behind them, like a great fortress: they are never words for words' sake.' The mention of Elizabethan England is instructive, for Churchill enlisted the services of the past to boost British morale, summoning up the ghosts of Drake and Nelson to emphasise to the people that Britain had faced such dangers and emerged victorious before. The subliminal message was that they would do so again. He was never above adapting successful lines for use in his speeches, both of his own and other people's; for example, his famous phrase about the RAF in the Battle of Britain might have owed something to Sir John Moore's declaration about the capture of Corsica in 1793: 'Never was so much done by so few men.'

Isaiah Berlin, in his essay-length book *Mr Churchill in 1940*, was at pains to point out how Churchill drew on 'an historical imagination so strong, so comprehensive as to encase the whole of the present and the whole of the future in a framework of a rich and multi-coloured past'. Churchill expected at least a working knowledge of British history from his listeners; he never talked down to them or patronised them by adapting his style to the perceived requirements of a modern mass audience. As Berlin put it: 'The archaisms of style to which Mr Churchill's wartime speeches accustomed us are indispensable ingredients of the heightened tone, the formal chronicler's attire, for which the solemnity of the occasion called.'

On 11 September 1940 Churchill broadcast to the nation on the likelihood of a German invasion, saying:

> We cannot tell when they will try to come; we cannot be sure that in fact they will at all; but no one should blind himself to the fact that a heavy, full-scale invasion of this island is being prepared with all the usual German thoroughness and method, and that it may be launched now – upon England, upon Scotland, or upon Ireland, or upon all three.

That speech was broadcast from deep within the Cabinet War Rooms, a bombproof underground complex of offices and private quarters in Whitehall. They had been constructed just before the war to house the central core of the Government in the event of air raids. Churchill made this speech shortly after the first bombing raids on London, knowing that even if Hitler had decided not to invade, the Luftwaffe's bombers were likely to continue to terrorise British cities.

This was how he conveyed the conviction that Britain could take it, whatever might come:

Therefore, we must regard the next week or so as a very important period in our history. It ranks with the days when the Spanish Armada was approaching the Channel, and Drake was finishing the game of bowls; or when Nelson stood between us and Napoleon's Grand Army at Boulogne. We have read all about this in the history books; but what is happening now is on a far greater scale and of far more consequence to the life and future of the world and its civilisation than these brave old days of the past.

Churchill made people feel that they were not alone in this struggle; they were walking with history. As an historian himself, he was in a perfect position to put Britain's plight in 1940 squarely in its historical context. To a people who were taught at school of the exploits of Drake and Nelson, this had an electrifying effect. Churchill had already demanded heroism from the British people when he appealed to the future millennium, with the words: 'Let us brace ourselves to our duties, and so bear ourselves that, if the British Empire and Commonwealth last for a thousand years, men will still say, "This was their finest hour."' Now he appealed to the past millennium, equating the situation with that of 1588 when the Spanish Armada bore down on Elizabeth I's England, and 1804 when Napoleon threatened to invade Britain. As prime minister, he once minuted to R. A. Butler at the Ministry of Education: 'Can you make children more patriotic? Let them know Wolfe won Quebec.' It not only worked with children; by mobilising British history in his support he encouraged people to think of themselves as being part of a long continuum, something which the huge success of books about the Napoleonic Wars during the Second World War implies was very successful.

In the context of today's politics and society, much of

Churchill's argument and the vocabulary in which it was couched were of course deeply politically incorrect. Clive Ponting has complained of the way Churchill continually referred to 'our own British life, and the long continuity of our institutions and the Empire', instead of 'coming up with a view of the future designed to appeal to a modern democracy'. This was because Churchill realised that the British nation was primarily fighting for its very identity and continued existence, before any utopian ideas about decency and democracy, let alone equality and fraternity. He therefore appealed to the ancient, tribal belief that the British people then had in themselves, largely based on the deeds of their forefathers and pride in their imperial achievement. It is no longer really an idiom that politicians can turn to, but it helped save us then.

There are those, such as the late Lord Hailsham – he chose the singular forum of Radio 4's *Desert Island Discs* to adumbrate his theory – who consider the emergence of Winston Churchill as prime minister in May 1940, within hours of Hitler unleashing his Blitzkrieg upon the West, as a proof of the existence of God. No theologian, I prefer to subscribe to the opinion of the American broadcaster Ed Murrow on the phenomenon of Churchill in 1940: 'He mobilized the English language, and sent it into battle.' The printed page is not the correct medium for these speeches, of course. To feel the shiver down one's spine at Churchill's words only recordings will do. They alone can convey the growls, the sudden leonine roars, the lyrical sentences, the cigar-and-brandy-toned voice, the sheer defiance coming straight from the viscera insisting upon no surrender in a war to the death.

Churchill suffered from a slight stammer and a lisp, which affected his public speaking. Like his father, he had difficulty all his life pronouncing the letter 's'. As a young man he would try to remedy the problem by rehearsing such tricky phrases as: 'The Spanish ships I cannot see for they are not in sight.' Later, when he was on the American lecture circuit, he began to cure his lisp and the inhibitions that it had caused him. Although he worked hard at overcoming his speech impediment, he never mastered it entirely. 'Those who heard him talk in middle and old age may conclude that he mastered the inhibition better than he did the impediment,' his son Randolph later joked. Churchill's lisp is noticeable even in his most famous speeches that inspired the nation during the war, leading detractors to assume – wrongly – that he was slurring his lines due to drink.[28]

Hitler's Siemensstadt trick of not referring to his enemies directly was also occasionally used by Churchill, who made a radio broadcast in November 1934 on the probable causes of a future war, in which he warned of a 'nation of seventy millions a few air-hours away being taught that war is a glorious exercise', a clear, but indirect reference to Nazi Germany. Yet whenever he felt he was able to mention his enemies directly, he greatly relished it. His wartime estimations of Ribbentrop and Mussolini in particular were fine knockabout stuff, displaying part music-hall turn and part sincere disdain. Mussolini he variously described as 'this whipped jackal', 'a lackey and serf' and 'the merest utensil of his master's will'. His very pronunciation of the word 'Nazis', which he lengthened to sound like 'Narrzies', illustrated his contempt for them. 'Everybody has the right to pronounce foreign names as he chooses,' was his robust maxim.[29]

Jokes, often with himself as the butt, were an essential part of Churchill's speeches. I have only come across one occasion when Churchill failed to get a joke: when Jock Colville, his private secretary, interjected (in a discussion on Montgomery's extravagant self-promotion) that the general had banned the Eighth Army bands from playing 'The British Grenadiers'. When Churchill asked why, Colville replied that it was because of the first line: 'Some talk of Alexander...' (General Harold Alexander was Monty's rival in the desert.) There was a gratifying laugh from the other guests around the dining-room table, but the next morning, to Colville's horror, he found that Churchill had taken the story seriously and had dictated a minute to the Chief of the Imperial General Staff that Montgomery's order be immediately rescinded. As Colville recalled: 'When I explained with embarrassment that I had only said it as a joke, he was far from amused.' That single rule-proving exception apart, Churchill was a man for whom humour was a vital part of life. He also had a tremendous propensity for the arresting, amusing simile such as: 'Punishing China is like flogging a jellyfish.' Witticisms tend to accrete to the genuinely witty – like Oscar Wilde, George Bernard Shaw and Noël Coward – even if they did not actually utter them, and Churchill has undoubtedly benefited from this phenomenon.

Hitler, while supposedly being a good mimic in private, almost never made jokes in public. Mimicry is anyhow something of a harlot's trick, and otherwise his humour was of the cruel kind; nothing amused him more than other people's discomfiture. After the war, Albert Speer recalled the cruel practical joke that Hitler and Goebbels had played on the Nazis' official foreign press spokesman, Ernst 'Putzi' Hanfstaengl, whose close personal ties to the Führer were a source of uneasiness to the rather splendidly titled Minister for Propaganda and Public Enlightenment. Hitler owed Hanfstaengl much; they had been friends since 1923 when he lent Hitler the $1,000 with which the Nazis began printing the *Völkischer Beobachter* as a daily newspaper. As a Harvard graduate, Hanfstaengl had given Hitler an air of respectability in polite social circles in the early days of the movement. None of this could protect him from the spite of Goebbels, however, who

> began casting aspersions on Hanfstaengl's character, representing him as miserly, money grubbing, and of dubious honesty. He once brought in a phonograph record of an English song and attempted to prove that Hanfstaengl had stolen its melody for a popular march he had composed. The foreign press chief was already under a cloud when Goebbels, at the time of the Spanish

Civil War, told the table company that Hanfstaengl had made adverse remarks about the fighting spirit of the German soldiers in combat there. Hitler was furious. This cowardly fellow who had no right to judge the courage of others must be given a lesson, he declared. A few days later Hanfstaengl was informed that he must make a plane trip; he was given sealed orders from Hitler which were not to be opened until after the plane had taken off. Once in the air, Hanfstaengl read, horrified, that he was to be put down in Red Spanish territory where he was to work as an agent for Franco. At the table Goebbels told Hitler every detail: How Hanfstaengl pleaded with the pilot to turn back; it must all be a misunderstanding, he insisted. But the plane, Goebbels related, continued circling for hours over German territory. Finally the pilot announced that he had to make an emergency landing and set the plane down safely at Leipzig airport. Hanfstaengl...only then realized that he had been a victim of a bad joke...All the chapters of this story elicited great merriment at Hitler's table – all the more so since in this case Hitler had plotted the joke together with Goebbels.[30]

Hardly surprisingly, soon afterwards Hanfstaengl left Germany to live abroad in American exile, where he acted occasionally as an adviser to Roosevelt when the President wanted to delve into the mind of his chief antagonist.

Nor was that an isolated example: Goebbels understood how the Führer's sense of humour and fondness for these kinds of practical jokes could be used to promote himself and sideline potential opponents. True leadership involves noticing when one is being manipulated, but Hitler did not seem to do so with Goebbels, who was probably the most intelligent Nazi of the Third Reich. When a senior Party member Eugen Hadamowski set his sights upon promotion to control the Reichsrundfunk (the Reich broadcasting system), Goebbels decided to set up another elaborate joke. He had earmarked that job for one of his own cronies, but he suspected that Hitler might prefer

Hadamowski, who before the Nazis came to power had won his gratitude for having organised very efficiently the public address systems for their election campaigns.

Albert Speer described Goebbels's cruelly brilliant campaign to undermine his *bête noire*:

> He had Hanke, state secretary in the Propaganda Ministry, send for the man and officially informed him that Hitler had just appointed him Reichsintendant (General Director) for radio. At the table Hitler was given an account of how Hadamowski had gone wild with joy at this news. The description was, no doubt, highly coloured and exaggerated, so that Hitler took the whole affair as a joke. Next day Goebbels had a few copies of a newspaper printed reporting on the sham appointment and praising the new appointee in excessive terms. He outlined the article for Hitler, with all its ridiculous phrases, and acted out Hadamowski's rapture upon reading these things about himself. Once more Hitler and the whole table with him was convulsed. That same day Hanke asked the newly appointed Reichsintendant to make a speech into a dead microphone and once again there was endless merriment at Hitler's table when the story was told.

With Hadamowski's credibility ruined behind his back (and probably with absolutely no justification) Goebbels was able to appoint his own man to the still vacant job. As Speer appreciated: 'From one point of view, Hitler was the real dupe of these intrigues. As far as I could observe, Hitler was in fact no match for Goebbels in such matters.... But it certainly should have given one pause for thought that Hitler allowed this nasty game to go on and even encouraged it. One word of displeasure would certainly have stopped this kind of thing for a long while to come.'[31]

Such practical jokes are hardly a high form of humour, and the knowledge that Hitler would be party to the humiliation of an efficient and hard-working official simply because he was alleged to be overambitious tells us much about the contempt he felt for the human race in general. Compare this to the superb sallies and brilliantly funny jokes of Winston Churchill and the dichotomy is obvious. (The genesis of perhaps Churchill's most famous joke, the punch-line of which is 'And you madam are ugly, but in the morning I shall be sober', can perhaps be found in *Savrola*, in which he wrote of President Molara's wife, Lucile: 'It is hard, if not impossible, to snub a beautiful woman; they remain beautiful and the rebuke recoils.'[32])

So many of Churchill's jokes are too well known to bear repetition here, but there is one that for some reason has not been included in the standard 'Wit and Wisdom' anthologies of his humour (perhaps because it might be apocryphal). After he had been lecturing in the United States in the thirties on the multifarious positive aspects and benefits of the British Empire, an aggressively anti-imperialist American woman asked a long question about British policy towards Mahatma Gandhi's independence movement, culminating in the words: 'So, Mr Churchill, what do you intend to do with your Indians?' 'Leastways, madam,' the great man is said to have replied, 'not what you did with yours.'

Hitler avoids Churchill

It had been Putzi Hanfstaengl who had nearly organised an encounter between Hitler and Churchill in August 1932, when Churchill was in Germany on a tour of Marlborough's battlefields as part of the research for his biography of his great ancestor. Churchill's son Randolph had covered Hitler's election campaign of the previous month for the *Sunday Graphic*, even flying in the putative Führer's plane from meeting to meeting, and he was keen for his father to meet the man who he was even then convinced 'will not hesitate' to plunge Europe into war as soon as he had built an army capable of so doing.[33] Hanfstaengl knew Randolph through his foreign press contacts, and so he and Churchill dined together at Churchill's hotel in Munich.

At the dinner Hanfstaengl spoke of Hitler 'as one under a spell' – his 'mission' over 'Red Spain' still being several years in the future – and told Churchill that since Hitler came to that same hotel at tea-time every afternoon it should be easy for him to engineer a meeting between them. According to Hanfstaengl's memoirs – which were written after he left Germany and so therefore might well have been heavily biased – Hitler was unhappy about meeting someone 'whom he knew to be his equal in political ability', adding: 'In any case, they say that your Mr Churchill is a rabid Francophile.' This showed that Hitler at least knew of Churchill by that stage of his career, and from later remarks of his it is clear that he had also read at least some of Churchill's autobiographical writings.

Hanfstaengl held out the hope that on one of the afternoons or evenings of Churchill's stay, Hitler – who had recently turned down the office of vice-chancellor in the declared expectation of soon being offered the chancellorship itself – might be curious enough about the British wartime First Lord of the Admiralty to come to the hotel to join Churchill, his daughter Sarah, Randolph, the *Daily Telegraph* owner Lord Camrose and Professor Lindemann for coffee. At the dinner that evening, Churchill had told Hanfstaengl, in a discussion about the 'extensive representation' of Jews in Germany's professions, to 'Tell your boss from me that anti-Semitism may be a good starter, but it is a bad sticker'.

Churchill never had the chance to tell Hitler anything directly because he did not appear, but the next day Hanfstaengl made a final attempt to talk the Nazi leader into meeting the man who was – unbeknownst to any of them – eventually to prove his nemesis. Hitler made precisely the same mistake that was being made by so many in British politics at the time; he had written Churchill off, telling Hanfstaengl: 'In any case, what part does

Churchill play? He's in opposition and no one pays any attention to him.' Nor did Hanfstaengl's cheeky reply – 'People say the same thing about you' – serve to change his mind. Two days later Churchill and his party had left the city to return to England, with Hitler keeping away until they had gone.

One of the great interviews of history had thus been missed, possibly out of an inferiority complex on Hitler's part, but most likely owing to his acceptance of the received wisdom that Churchill was 'a busted flush' and not worth his time. If so, it should be added to the list of Hitler's fundamental miscalculations. Of course, it is impossible to surmise what might have taken place had the two men met, but if Churchill was tempted to relay his message about anti-Semitism it would hardly have lasted long or been much of a meeting of minds, particularly as neither spoke the other's language. More likely it would have resembled the weighing-in of two opponents before a boxing match. At its worst it could have been one of history's great disappointments, with a formal and mutually insincere exchange of pro-forma diplomatic *politesses* and some generalisations about their Great War experiences. Perhaps it is therefore better that it did not take place after all.

Charisma

Whereas Churchill never really projected charisma, Hitler radiated it. Churchill had a commanding personality that many people might mistake for charisma, but charisma is different. Charismatic leadership is based on the almost mystical qualities that followers attribute to their leaders. This form of power has no roots in tradition or basis in institutional authority; it acknowledges no constitution and is quite separate from the power of an elected statesman in a democracy. No one ever wanted to give Churchill dictatorial powers for life, as were accorded to Hitler. Churchill was the archetype of the inspirational leader but not regarded as superhuman, ethereal, or existing on a different plane from the rest of mankind. (Not everyone would agree with this estimation: the young scientist R. V. Jones, who was summoned to the Cabinet Room in June 1940 to explain the Luftwaffe's radio beam guidance system to Churchill, found that 'whenever we met in the war I had the feeling of being recharged by contact with a source of living power' which he naturally found exhilarating.[34])

There are endless examples of people who were spellbound by Hitler. How did he do it? Firstly, Hitler discovered early in his career that he could intimidate and dominate others simply by staring at them without blinking. It gave him an aura of determination and unshakeable conviction. As in the children's game of 'Who blinks first?' Hitler rarely blinked when he glanced at someone he wished to impress. It could be fantastically disconcerting to those who had no inkling of what he was up to. Albert Speer recalled that he once had a 'blinking duel' with Hitler over dinner. When Hitler stared at him, Speer decided to try to hold his gaze. Hitler kept staring at Speer, waiting for him to cave in. As Speer put it: 'Who knows what primitive instincts are involved in such staring duels...this time I had to muster almost inhuman strength, seemingly for ever, not to yield to the ever-mounting urge to look away.'[35] Fortunately, at that moment Hitler had to attend to the request of the woman seated next to him, and so he had to break off the duel.

It helped that Hitler had his mother's eyes, which were an unusual shade of light blue with a strange admixture of greenish-grey. There are hordes of people who bear witness to the weirdly compelling effect that Hitler's eyes had upon people. The French Ambassador Robert Coulondre seemed transfixed by them, and the playwright Gerhart Hauptmann described seeing them as the greatest moment of his life. Martha Dodd, the American Ambassador's daughter, testified that they were 'startling and unforgettable'. Nietzsche's sister Elisabeth said of them: 'They...searched me through and through.' Slightly protruding and almost lashless, the Führer's eyes had a curiously hypnotic effect, or at least they did once Nazi propaganda put it about that they did. A great deal in the creation of charisma is auto-suggestion, for if Coulondre, Hauptmann and Dodd had not been told of the power of Hitler's eyes beforehand, they might well not have noticed them.

Of course there was more to Hitler's charisma than just his glance. Most people believe that charisma is a natural personal quality that one either has or does not have. It is in fact an acquired trait, and indeed something of a confidence trick. It is our perception that provides a leader with charisma; after all, no one is born charismatic. Nobody who knew Hitler as a corporal in the trenches of the Great War or as a failed artist in Vienna remembered him as being charismatic, or even much of a leader. He only acquired charisma through his political success and his own unceasing efforts to create a cult of his own personality. Hitler deliberately nurtured this status of infallible superman until millions proved willing to accept him at his own outrageously inflated estimation. His biographer Sir Ian Kershaw describes his state of mind by 1936 as one of 'narcissistic self-glorification'.[36]

Once we attribute an unchallengeable authority to a leader, he (or occasionally she) simply acquires charisma, which derives from the Greek word for spirit. Religious leaders sometimes have – at least in the eyes of their followers – charisma, because their authority is founded on faith. As a secular religion, Nazism was no different. The historian Michael Burleigh has shown how much Nazi ideology had in common with a religious cult, above all in its deification of the Messiah figure.[37] The authority of the Führer was beyond question, and Hitler deliberately emphasised the charisma that was attributed to him by nurturing this status of superman. He avoided being connected to anything likely to be unpopular or that could have made him look fallible. He rarely displayed emotion and deliberately kept himself detached from situations requiring the exhibition of ordinary human feelings.

Nearly everyone who knew Hitler personally confirms that it was hard to relax in his presence. Although cine film taken by his girlfriend Eva Braun shows that he was generally friendly and polite on social occasions, nevertheless genuine warmth or affection were entirely lacking. Instead Hitler chose to surround himself with an aura of unapproachability. He never developed a genuine personal relationship with other human beings; indeed his Alsatian, Blondi, was the closest he came to having a friend.

Until a few hours before his suicide, Hitler remained unmarried. Eva Braun was kept out of the public eye and was known only to his inner circle. All witnesses agree that Hitler never showed any real interest in her; she was attractive enough to look at and pleasant to have around, but that was about it, until her undeniably brave and devoted decision to stay with him to the very end. She wanted to die an honest woman, a legally wed German bunker-frau, and at least he accorded her that honour as the price of her willingness to join him in his suicide. Afterwards they probably parted company, since she had not done anything to justify her joining him on his journey over the Styx.

Public relations

Hitler liked to be photographed with children and animals, never quite kissing babies but undergoing all the rest of the debasing crudity of modern political photo-opportunities. His cultivation of an image of simplicity was perhaps one of his most effective public relations devices, maybe even more effective than the bombastic Nazi rallies. Joseph Goebbels was intent on presenting Hitler as 'the People's Chancellor', emphasising his simple tastes and closeness to the ordinary German. While many Germans perceived the Party officials as bigwigs – whom they nicknamed 'golden pheasants' – the Führer remained, in their eyes, 'one of us'. It is a populist propaganda trick used by many modern leaders. (Few are the American politicians who keep their jackets on in town-hall meet-the-people exercises nowadays.)

Despite being short-sighted, Hitler never wore glasses in public. His secretaries used an especially large font when typing his speeches because he felt that to be seen with glasses might impair his superman image.[38] He also avoided being photographed taking any sort of strenuous physical exercise. Nor would he let even his valet see him anything less than fully dressed. Once, when to Hitler's deep disapproval Mussolini was photographed in bathing shorts, the Führer said he would never allow that to happen to him; indeed, he expressed the fear that 'some skilled forger would set my head on a body in bathing trunks'![39] He was embarrassed to disrobe before a doctor and would never permit an X-ray of his sensitive stomach. He also refused to have a masseur, as suggested to him by Heinrich Himmler, the head of the SS. He liked to have his body covered at all times, and even in the hottest weather he wore long white underwear, as became apparent in the aftermath of the Bomb Plot when his trousers were blown off on the warm summer day of 20 July 1944.

By contrast, Churchill could not have cared less about his physical appearance. He almost never stood on his personal dignity, although he was always conscious of the respect that he felt ought to be accorded to what he occasionally called 'the King's first minister'. When Churchill was ill in Morocco in 1944 two retainers dragged him up a hill to a picnic in the Atlas Mountains using the tablecloth as an ungainly makeshift hammock. The complete absence of dignity involved in this mode of transportation could not have troubled him less. He could often be found at work in his dressing gown and slippers. He would sometimes unselfconsciously undress or take a bath in the presence of his staff and colleagues. On one occasion he even received a startled President Roosevelt as he got out of the bath, with the joke: 'The prime minister of Great Britain has nothing to hide from the president of the United States.' Churchill also had an inherently uncharismatic penchant for funny hats and fancy uniforms. He was the only prime minister, even including the Duke of Wellington himself, who ever wore military uniform while in office. In photographs taken with Roosevelt, one shows Churchill in the uniform of an honorary air commodore, another in the uniform of a colonel of the 4th Hussars, and yet another as an honorary colonel of the 4th/5th (Cinque Ports) Battalion of the Royal Sussex Regiment. While most people will find such eccentric taste in clothes immensely attractive, it tends to make Roosevelt look Churchill's superior. In *Savrola*, Churchill had shown that he was aware of the advantages of dressing simply, even if he had not followed the advice himself. He described the eponymous hero entering the Lauranian State Ball: 'No decorations, no orders, no star relieved the plain evening dress he wore. Amid that blaze of colour, that multitude of gorgeous uniforms, he appeared a sombre figure; but, like the Iron Duke in Paris, he looked the leader of them all, calm, confident, and composed.'[40]

Certainly by the time Churchill became prime minister he seemed to care little about dress codes. In 1940 he invented what he called his 'siren-suit', a garment based on his bricklaying boiler suit only made in velvet, with a full-length zip up the front. While his office staff ridiculed it as his 'rompers', Churchill wore it even on some formal occasions, visiting troops or receiving foreign dignitaries. It was not appreciated at the Kremlin, where, he said: 'They thought I was pushing democracy too far.' It confirms what Hitler already knew: that by dressing down a leader can actually make himself more visible rather than less.

The Nazis, of course, loved dressing up. It is hard to imagine anything more grandiose than the full-dress uniform of Heinrich Himmler, until one comes to the uniform of Hermann Göring. He loved medals and even invented a few new ones, secure in the knowledge that he would be the prime candidate to receive them. Yet the uniform of Adolf Hitler himself had no gold braid, no epaulettes, no lapel badges, no sashes or orders, just the Iron Cross decoration of the simple but courageous soldier in the First World War, a Nazi Party badge and one other small badge. Hitler encouraged other Nazi leaders to dress flashily while he himself deliberately dressed down. This was part of his populist image as the 'People's Chancellor'. He was sending a message to the people that, unlike other leaders, he was so powerful that he didn't need special uniforms or insignia to emphasise it.

When in 1938 Hitler travelled to Rome for a meeting with Mussolini, he had special uniforms made for everybody accompanying him. The task fell to Benno von Arent, Reich Stage Designer and Reich Commissar for Fashion, whose talent for medal design earned him the nickname 'Tinsmith of the Reich' from Albert Speer. Arent was best known for his sets of operas and operettas, and the diplomats on the trip were dressed in frock coats heavily laden with gold braid. Only the Führer dressed, as usual, in a simple outfit. As he said: 'My surroundings must look magnificent. Then my simplicity makes a striking effect.'

A place of their own

Part of Hitler's entirely manufactured charisma was the result of the carefully co-ordinated photo-opportunities that portrayed him as a man in love with simplicity and Nature. To effect this, it was necessary to have both a good deal of privacy and a perfectly chosen base away from the city. Leaders need to be occasionally physically inaccessible in order to emphasise their power over events, and that was something Hitler well understood. The town of Berchtesgaden in the Bavarian Alps is inextricably linked with Adolf Hitler, whose country home, the Berghof, was built above the village of Obersalzberg, just up the mountain. Hitler was very proud of his long connection with the region that had begun when he went on an incognito visit to a fellow Fascist politician Dietrich Eckart before the Beer-hall Putsch. He stayed in several inns in the area over the years and later on bought a house that became the centre of a huge compound for the Nazi top brass. Martin Bormann, Hermann Göring and Albert Speer all had houses built on the hillside, largely in order to protect their all-important personal access to the Führer. Three thousand yards of concrete bunkers built for them underneath the hillside still exist, although much of the rest was blown up by the American Army in 1945 in order to prevent the site becoming a shrine to neo-Nazis. (It was a genuine concern; the hotel on top of the Gran Sasso mountain in the Abruzzi region of Italy from which Mussolini had been liberated in a daring paratroop coup incorporates a museum that nostalgically commemorates the SS commando unit's action.)

'Yes, there are many links between Obersalzberg and me,' Hitler reminisced to his cronies in January 1942. 'So many things were born there, and brought to fruition there. I've spent up there the finest hours of my life. It's there that all my great projects were conceived and ripened. I had hours of leisure, in those days, and how many charming friends!' If Hitler's ghost can be said to haunt anywhere, it is not in the anonymous, flattened area off the Wilhelmstrasse in Berlin where his bunker used to be, but up there on the Bavarian Alpine mountainside.

The Berghof itself was not the architectural masterpiece that Hitler believed it to be. For some reason the Führer loathed varnished furniture, preferring stripped pine. His biographer Norman Stone has described it as 'a building fit for an Ian Fleming villain. Huge slabs of red marble adorned it; looted pictures hung on the walls; there was a vast, thick carpet; a huge fire burning in the grate; oversized armchairs were placed an uncomfortable distance apart, in such a way that the guests would have to half shout their platitudes at each other as the sparks leapt from the fire in the gathering twilight.'[41] For his fiftieth birthday, the Nazi Party presented Hitler with the civil-

The eyes have it:
Hitler in 1930.

Churchill striding purposefully out of Downing Street on 4 July 1940, speech
in hand, to tell the Commons of the sinking of the French fleet at Oran.

The League of Maidens (some more like matrons) worship their idol as Heinrich Himmler looks on.

The Reich Party Rally for Honour and Freedom at Nuremberg, 1936.

Churchill tiling a roof in his Wilderness Years, the seam of his overcoat ripped.

Churchill wearing his siren suit, or 'rompers', at Chartwell in 1939.

A laurel halo
for the Führer
in gaol at
Landsberg.

Field Marshal Werner von Blomberg
believed that meeting Hitler could cure
him of the common cold.

Hermann Göring thought that Hitler could
make him believe he was a woman.

Chancellor of the Exchequer Winston Churchill, accompanied by his parliamentary private secretary Bob Boothby, his daughter Diana and his bodyguard Inspector W.H. Thompson, walks to the Commons to present his 1929 Budget.

Churchill, still convalescing ten months after his accident on Fifth Avenue, is carried into his London home in October 1932.

The newly elected Chancellor, in an uncharacteristically meek pose, meets his former commander-in-chief President Hindenburg at Potsdam on 21st March 1933.

The Führer inspects his troops outside the Hradschin Castle in Prague on the day of his unopposed invasion of the rump of Czechoslovakia, 15th March 1939.

The Munich comedian Weiss-Ferdl in his dressing room in 1930; Hitler studied his timing, delivery and techniques.

Hitler hamming it up for his favourite photographer Heinrich Hoffmann.

Churchill broadcasts from the White House in 1943.

engineering miracle of 'the Eagle's Nest', a stone building six thousand feet up, reached through the middle of the mountain, from which he could view the entire region, including his beloved Salzburg.

Yet the breathtaking panoramic scenery did not calm what passed for his soul. Paradoxically, those beautiful views seemed only to have helped Hitler to come to his most drastic decisions. It was while he was staying at Obersalzberg that he plotted to grab absolute power in Germany, that he hit upon the infamous Berchtesgaden plan to dismember Czechoslovakia, and where he planned the invasion of Russia. Joseph Goebbels, a regular visitor, regularly complained to his diary about the amount of time the Führer spent at Obersalzberg, but was gratified by the way that 'the solitude of the mountains' tended to spur his Führer on to ever more fanatical efforts. It was in late March 1933, while staying here, that Hitler decided upon a boycott of all Jewish businesses, services, lawyers and doctors across the whole Reich. Staggeringly beautiful scenery clearly had the opposite effect on Hitler that it tends to have on most other people; rather than softening and humanising him, it hardened his heart and filled him with dreams of racial domination. There was a legend that under one of the highest peaks of the Berchtesgadener mountain range, the Untersberg, the German Emperor Barbarossa lay sleeping, and it was thus no coincidence that the German invasion of Russia in June 1941 was codenamed 'Operation Barbarossa'.

In the summer of 1933 Obersalzberg became a place of pilgrimage for many Germans. As Sir Ian Kershaw has written: 'Such were the crowds of admirers trying to glimpse the Reich Chancellor that Himmler, as Commander of the Bavarian Political Police, had to lay down special traffic regulations for the Berchtesgaden area and to warn against the use of field-glasses by those trying to observe "every movement of the people's Chancellor".' In the end, such was the interest that the whole area had to be cordoned off during Hitler's afternoon walks in order to ward off the sightseers. So a tradition was begun of a daily march-past, when 'up to two thousand people of all ages and from all parts of Germany, whose devotion had persuaded them to follow the steep paths up to Obersalzberg and often wait hours, marched, at a signal from one of the adjutants, in a silent column past Hitler'. For one of his closest adjutants, Fritz Wiedemann, such unrestrained adulation had quasi-religious overtones, and it doubtless helped lead Hitler to believe himself to possess almost superhuman powers.

It was also in Bavaria that propaganda opportunities were given full rein. There are photographs of the Führer in traditional lederhosen leaning against a tree; the Führer with smiling, adoring, blond children; the Führer patting his Alsatian, Blondi; the Führer poring over architectural drawings of the cities he intended to build; a happy, relaxed Führer taking tea with Eva Braun; the Führer as Father of his Aryan people; a becloaked Führer welcoming distinguished guests such as David Lloyd George and the Duke of Windsor to the Berghof; the statesman at work, comforting the old, walking on a snowy hillside.

Having a place away from the city where he could think, write and entertain was important to Churchill too. Chartwell in Kent was bought in September 1922 for five thousand pounds, a knock-down price because it was dilapidated and had been put up at auction with a reserve of £6,500 but had received no bids. The only reason Churchill was able to afford it was because of a bequest from a first cousin once removed, Lord Herbert Vane-Tempest, who had been killed in a Welsh railway accident just at the time that Churchill had been appointed Colonial Secretary.

Churchill in addition had to spend almost twenty thousand pounds on renovating the house over the next eighteen months, and it was a constant drain on his resources for years afterwards, to the point when Clementine continually fretted that it would bankrupt them. It was none the less precisely the kind of retreat that a man who occasionally suffered from 'black dog' depression needed, commanding as it does superb views over the Kentish Weald that can only be uplifting to the spirits.

If Obersalzberg was the most Wagnerian and Teutonic place in Central Europe, there is no more quintessentially English county than Kent. Just as the Berghof's geographical situation and aspects encouraged Hitler in his dreams of conquest, so the Kentish Weald reinforced Churchill's determination to resist them.

Architecture

Hitler was obsessed with the power of architecture to emphasise his and Germany's new-found greatness. He would have whole-heartedly echoed Churchill's perceptive remark that: 'First we shape our buildings and then they shape us.' Hitler had megalo-maniacal building plans for Berlin. While Goebbels staged huge rallies celebrating the quasi-religious Führer-cult, Speer was ordered by Hitler to build a new Reich Chancellery that would simultaneously impress and intimidate visitors, just a few hundred yards from Potsdamer Platz in Berlin. Nothing of it is left today; the site is now a block of flats and – rather imagina-tively – a kindergarten. The blueprints show that Hitler's New Chancellery was some twenty times bigger than the old one that it augmented. The date of the New Chancellery's construction – 1938 – is highly significant since it was in that year that Hitler annexed Austria in March and the Sudetenland in October, thus winning two of his greatest foreign-policy objectives without recourse to war.

Setting out for huge territorial expansion in his quest for *Lebensraum* for the German people, Hitler was keen to make the greatest possible impression on foreign visitors. He explained to Speer, whom he had earmarked to be the architect of 'Germania', his new capital: 'I shall be holding extremely important conferences in the near future. For these, I need grand halls and salons that will make an impression on people, especially on the smaller dignitaries.' The New Reich Chancellery stretched a quarter of a mile. While its address was Voßstraße 2–6, this was not where the entrance was found. Speer purposely chose a seemingly illogical place for it on the side of the building, in the Wilhelmstrasse. This meant that an arriving dignitary had to walk along nine hundred feet of halls of ascending grandeur, with the imposing Marble Gallery at the centre, before reaching the Führer's study. Hitler was delighted with Speer's work, saying: 'On the long walk from the entrance to the reception hall they'll get a taste of the power and grandeur of the German Reich!'

Hitler's study was a vast room of twelve hundred square feet, adorned with ponderous chandeliers and an immense pastel-coloured carpet. The friezes of three great heads adorned the front panels of the Führer's huge desk: one of them was that of the Medusa with writhing snakes emerging from her head. In classical mythology, anyone who saw the Medusa fell instantly under her spell and was turned to stone. Hitler rarely did any work in this study; its sole purpose was to receive visitors and leave them in awe of his charisma and Germany's power.

Compare this to Number Ten Downing Street, a terraced house in Whitehall, which in size and style looks nothing special, at least from the outside. Roy Jenkins has described it as 'one of the most rickety large houses in London, built early in the eighteenth century, a well-known period for jerry-building'. Number Ten is a little like Dr Who's Tardis, with far more space than seems possible from the outside, since it sprawls into the area of neighbouring houses and connects with other parts of Whitehall through passageways that cannot be externally observed. It could therefore not be more different from the very showy but impractical Reich Chancellery. Even so, almost the entire working area of Number Ten would have fitted into Hitler's study alone.

Small wonder that it is nearly impossible for a British prime minister to develop the kind of charisma that Hitler projected. British political leaders before the war used to walk around the streets without the retinues of bodyguards, political advisers and aides that they have today, and this very approachability also made it hard for them to acquire charisma. Even during the war, Churchill would often walk from Downing Street to Parliament. Today, even in peacetime, prime ministers tend to be driven the three hundred or so yards, only wishing to walk the short distance when – as during the Queen Mother's funeral in 2002 – it is hoped that they might be able to make political capital out of it.

Props, logos and trademarks

Hitler and the Nazis mastered the use of props and trademarks through their uniforms, jackboots, swastika logo, armbands, flags, anthems, and the salute – which all bestowed a distinctive corporate identity on their party and followers. Even Hitler's most potent facial characteristic, his absurd little toothbrush moustache, went through various stages of development as he altered its width occasionally. Churchill also understood how politicians needed distinctive trademarks. In an essay on politicians' props – Gladstone's collars, Baldwin's pipe, and so on – he once wrote, disingenuously: 'I have never indulged in any of these.' Did he really think that normal people wore those homburgs, spotted bow-ties, high wing-collars, and smoked that size of Romeo y Julieta cigar? He adopted the V-for-victory sign in the summer of 1941, and he also owned literally dozens of hats: military and naval headgear, pith helmets, an Australian bush hat, Russian astrakhans, homburgs, panamas, top hats – one of which recently fetched £10,000 at auction – stetsons, even an American Indian chieftain's feathered war bonnet. He rarely inhaled cigars, but as he was about to walk into a public occasion he lit one up and advised the Tory MP beside him: 'Never forget your trademark!'[42]

Hitler, by contrast, was a fanatical non-smoker who considered tobacco to be 'the wrath of the Red man against the White man for having been given hard liquor'. It took the Führer to find a racial motive behind even smoking. The Nazis instituted the world's most powerful anti-smoking movement between 1933 and 1945, which instituted bans on smoking in public spaces, restrictions on tobacco rationing for women, and developed the world's most refined tobacco epidemiology, linking tobacco use to lung cancer for the first time. Fears that tobacco might prove hazardous to the physical well-being of the Aryran race meant that German doctors – half of whom were Nazi Party members by the outbreak of the war – led the campaign against smoking. Advertisements pointed out that while Hitler, Mussolini and Franco were all non-smokers, Stalin and Roosevelt puffed away on cigarettes and Churchill was rarely seen without his cigar.[43]

Yet for all these campaigns, German cigarette consumption actually increased during the early years of Nazi rule, from 570 cigarettes per capita per annum in 1932 to 900 in 1939. (In France during the same period it only rose from the same base figure to 630.) The German anti-tobacco activists complained to the Führer about the 'American-style' advertising with which they had to contend, but he was reluctant to act against the tobacco firms since they had declared themselves as early and enthusiastic supporters of his regime, to the point of bringing out a special brand of *Sturmzigaretten* (Brownshirts' cigarettes). They also provided an invaluable stream of revenue for Hitler's perennially hard-pressed Treasury, contributing no less than one billion Reichsmarks in the financial year 1937/38. By 1941 taxes on tobacco were providing around eight per cent of the Government's entire income and so were crucial for the war effort.

Despite the Luftwaffe and Post Office both banning smoking, as well as many factories, government and Nazi Party offices, rest homes and hospitals – and Himmler announcing a smoking ban on all uniformed SS officers on duty – consumption none the less continued to rise. Although some air-raid shelters provided special rooms, in general smoking was banned there, as it was on buses and trains in sixty of Germany's larger cities by 1941. The Nazis announced 'the beginning of the end' of smoking throughout the Reich when they increased tobacco taxes to their highest levels in November of that year. The result was that although more soldiers smoked than ever before (some 87.3 per cent), they were smoking 23.4 per cent fewer cigarettes. In 1940–41 Germans smoked an astonishing 75 billion cigarettes, enough to form a cylindrical block 436 feet high with a base of a thousand square feet.

People management

Who would you assume was better at people management – Hitler or Churchill? While Hitler kept himself detached and did not really care for anybody else but himself, he did look after his staff, who pretty uniformly adored him. When they fell ill, he visited them in hospital. He enjoyed giving presents on their birthdays and at Christmas, and even paid personal attention to selecting appropriate gifts. Some, like his valet, saw in him their second father.

Even up to her death in 2000 at the age of eighty-three, Hitler's favourite secretary, Gerda Christian, retained fond memories of the man she always – even after 1945 – called 'The Chief'. With him in the bunker until just before the end, she never afterwards had a bad word for her 'kind and fair' former boss. There is no leader so evil that he will not have his defenders. It was doubtless possible to find sixteenth-century Muscovites who would recall the reign of Ivan Vasilievich with nostalgia. He was a harsh Tsar, they would concede over their vodka, but he was fair and his torturing should be seen in its proper historical context. 'The Terrible' was really more a respectful term of endearment than any kind of criticism.

Genghis Khan probably had supporters who would aver years later that he had had a bad press, probably didn't know what was being done in his name, was misunderstood, and anyhow at least he had made the yaks run on time. You always knew where you were, sentimental Transylvanians would recall, with Vlad the Impaler.

Eric Hobsbawm, who is regularly described as our greatest living historian – though heaven knows why while his near-contemporaries such as Robert Blake, Asa Briggs, Alan Bullock, Antonia Fraser, Paul Johnson and Hugh Thomas are still breathing – has still not tired of pointing out how Joseph Stalin modernised the Soviet Union, and so could not have been all bad. Kim Il Sung, Fidel Castro, even Pol Pot have had their Western apologists. It is a well-known phenomenon that intellectuals and writers, who proclaim their objectivity and atheism at every opportunity, are often the first to worship naked power, and it seems that the more brutally that such power is exercised the more devout is the obeisance.

The remarkable hero-worship shown by intelligent and sensitive Englishmen to Napoleon, even while he had the Grande Armée stationed at Boulogne in 1804, is a fine example of this baleful phenomenon. In his book *Napoleon and English Romanticism*, the historian Simon Bainbridge chronicled what he calls the 'obsession' which Byron, Hazlitt, Wordsworth, Coleridge and Southey felt for the thrusting Corsican upstart. In politics, too, the Whigs sailed perilously close to treachery in their outspoken admiration for their country's enemy. While an undergraduate at Cambridge, William Lamb – later Lord Melbourne – wrote a Latin ode to Bonaparte, and his letters to his mother recorded joy at French victories and sorrow at Allied successes. He and Charles James Fox admired Napoleon's 'energy', in much the same way that British writers and aristocrats admired the 'energy' of Nazi Germany in the thirties. The historian Arthur Bryant went so far as to describe Hitler as 'the Unknown Soldier come to life' in June 1939, only three months before the outbreak of war, and he did not have Frau Gerda Christian's excuse of having known the Führer personally.

The way that intellectuals have been mesmerised by tyrants in the twentieth century, with genuinely brilliant men such as Jean-Paul Sartre and E. H. Carr falling in politically platonic love with Stalin, has had a terrible effect on the rest of their countrymen. Critical faculties were lulled, potential opposition stymied. What might perhaps be excusable in a young secretary who had seen little of life outside the Berlin bunker is entirely unforgivable in hardbitten hacks like Walter Duranty, the *New York Times* correspondent in Moscow in the thirties who actually witnessed Stalin's deliberate policy of famine-creation in the Ukraine and yet still wrote favourably about the Bolshevik regime. Another American journalist, Lincoln Steffens, famously went further and reported on his return from Russia: 'I have seen the future and it works.' Even now that Marxist-Leninism has been confined to the dustbin of history – except of course in China, Cuba, and the sociology departments of Western campuses – and shown conclusively not to have worked despite seventy years of experimentation, the Hobsbawms remain unrepentant.

Just as apologists for the Kray twins are quick to argue that they kept the East End streets safe, and Irish republicans claim that the IRA are effective in combating small-time drug dealers, there seems to be no one too vicious to rate hagiography, however specious the grounds. There is also a certain perversity in human nature that makes us wish to say the opposite to everyone else, to be the child who points out the emperor's nudity. Of course, properly harnessed that impulse can sometimes even be good for democracy. Even when the American House of Representatives voted to declare war on Japan after the surprise attack on Pearl Harbor, one person – Mrs Jeanette Rankin of Montana – voted against it. She was one against 388, she was foolhardy and wrong but she was not browbeaten for her brave pacifist stand. Only dictatorships require absolute unanimity, and election results such as that in North Korea in 1985, where the Great Leader claimed to have won 100.0 per cent of the popular vote, often hint at weakness rather than strength.

For Frau Christian there was a final irony. 'I cannot complain about my time with the Führer,' she told friends. 'We were even allowed to smoke at a time in Germany when it was not the done thing for women to smoke.' As it was only after a long and painful battle against lung cancer that she died, so it might be argued that her boss even did for her in the end too.

Churchill, by contrast with Hitler, was a tough boss for whom to work. Very often he failed to display what he described in *Savrola* as 'That charm of manner of which few great men are destitute'. When it came to people management, he could on occasion be rude and sarcastic. His secretaries had difficulty in interpreting what they described as his 'inarticulate grunts or single words thrown out without explanation', and he could often be wounding to those who failed to grasp his intentions. 'Where on earth were you educated?' he would growl. 'Why don't you read some books?' Had Churchill exhibited the same kind of behaviour in today's working environment he could have wound up in front of an industrial tribunal. He had a terrible temper, although his great charm usually allowed him to unruffle feathers afterwards. To his credit, he was just as bad with colleagues and superiors as with underlings.

When, as Chancellor of the Exchequer in the 1920s, Churchill had a disagreement with the then Minister of Health, Neville Chamberlain, he was reported to have remonstrated with the Prime Minister, Stanley Baldwin, by marching 'about the room shouting and shaking his fist' and launching into 'a tremendous tirade'. Chamberlain thought Churchill's temper 'childish and contemptible' and wrote to Baldwin: 'Not for all the joys of Paradise would I be a member of his staff! Mercurial! A much abused word, but it is the literal description of his temperament!'

Under the terrible strain of leading the country in the summer of 1940, Churchill received a letter from his wife that read: 'There is a real danger of your being generally disliked by your colleagues and subordinates because of your rough, sarcastic and overbearing manner', and adding, 'I must confess that I have noticed a deterioration in your manner...and you are not so kind as you used to be.' Churchill took notice and tried to reform, but as the Australian Prime Minister Paul Keating used to say: 'Leadership is not about being nice. It's about being right and being strong.'[44]

Churchill even publicly acknowledged his rudeness in a speech in the House of Commons in June 1941, when he said:

> I do not think any expression of scorn or severity which I have heard used by our critics has come anywhere near the language I have been myself accustomed to use, not only orally, but in a stream of written minutes. In fact, I wonder that a great many of my colleagues are on speaking terms with me.

Taking advice

The very fact that Clementine Churchill was able to write to her husband so honest a letter was indicative of their strong, open, enduringly loving marriage. On 16 April 1908 Churchill wrote, in a courting letter to Clementine Hozier, 'What a comfort and pleasure it was to me to meet a girl with so much intellectual quality and such strong reserves of noble sentiment.' On 18 April 1964, fifty-six years, two world wars and two premierships later, and after the exchange of several hundred letters and telegrams, Clementine Churchill was writing to her husband to say that the three party leaders would like to call on him to mark the close of his parliamentary career. Their genuine love was apparent from the first; 'the empty bunny [bed] is melancholy,' he wrote when she was away. It is quite wrong to suggest, as did the Hollywood actor Kevin Costner in May 2001 – while producing no evidence whatever – that Churchill was ever unfaithful to Clementine. That Clementine might have had, in Mary Soames's phrase, 'a classic holiday romance' with the art dealer Terence Philip is a matter of historical contention. Under the sundial in the Golden Rose Walk at Chartwell was buried Clementine's souvenir of the brief fling, the corpse of a dove Philip gave her with the W. P. Kerr quotation:

Here lies the Bali dove.
It does not do to wander
Too far from sober men,
There lies an island yonder,
I think of it again.[45]

(If Churchill was one of the 'sober men' to whom the rhyme was referring, it makes the verse yet more intriguing.)

This romantic streak notwithstanding, Clementine Churchill was something of a battleaxe. She did not have much time for many of her husband's most interesting friends, such as Lord Beaverbrook, Brendan Bracken and Lord Birkenhead, but she retained the valuable ability to silence men like Generals de Gaulle and Montgomery with her basilisk, Aunt Agatha-style glare. Anyone of lesser mettle would probably not have survived marriage to such a restless and demanding spirit as Winston Churchill. It was always in defence of him that her harshest words were said. At a lunch party given by the French Ambassador in 1953 she overheard the former Foreign Secretary Lord Halifax saying that her husband had become a handicap to the Tory Party, and viciously retorted: 'If the country had depended on you we might have lost the war.' By comparison with Clementine's open and equal relationship with Churchill, even several years into their relationship Eva Braun was still calling Hitler 'mein Führer' and it is inconceivable that she would have taken him aside to warn him of his effect on his subordinates, even if he had requested it.

It has been suggested that the reason why Hitler's relationship with Eva Braun did not result in marriage until he was fifty-six years old and hours away from death was because he was homosexual. According to a well-researched and well-argued, but ultimately unconvincing book entitled *The Hidden Hitler* by Dr Lothar Machtan of Bremen University, published in 2001, the Führer was about as gay as his depiction in Mel Brooks's *The Producers*. Machtan claimed that not only was Hitler a promiscuous homosexual before 1933 and a severely repressed one afterwards, but it is even argued that he instituted the Night of the Long Knives massacre of July 1934 to cover up this guilty secret.

Unfortunately, as is almost inevitable in theories of this kind, the evidence is at best doubtful and scrappy, and at worst mere insinuation. Although since the twenties there have been dozens of autobiographies published with titles such as *I Was Hitler's Pilot*, *I Was Hitler's Doctor* and *I Was Hitler's Valet*, no one has stepped forward with the sure-fire sensational bestseller *I Was Hitler's Lover*. Dr Machtan's explanation for this is that among the 150 people killed on the Night of the Long Knives were many Brownshirts and others who knew about Hitler's predilections and that this mass 'elimination of witnesses and evidences' was near total.

Dr Machtan's theory is open to any number of doubts, however. Joseph Goebbels is known to have loathed homosexuals: would he have been content to serve under and ultimately to kill himself, his wife and six children for a man he suspected of being one? Generals who were suspected of homosexuality found their careers ruined, and homosexuality was made a crime punishable by the concentration camp. Although Dr Machtan repeats much anti-Hitler propaganda from the twenties and early thirties in support of his case, this is inherently suspect by its very nature, coming as it did from Hitler's most committed political enemies.

After the posthumous 'outing' by historians and television documentary-makers of Lords Baden-Powell, Kitchener and Montgomery, it was perhaps inevitable that questions would be asked about a man who only enjoyed something in the nature of a shotgun wedding. Nor is it only the Führer's reputation that has been blackened. According to a former comrade of Hitler's from the trenches, his fellow soldiers used to put boot blacking on Hitler's penis when he was asleep in the trenches, an activity which Dr Machtan describes as 'evidently a common occurrence' in the German Army.

The person who made this and several other such claims about Hitler was a man called Hans Mend, nicknamed 'the Ghost Rider'. Although he did indeed serve in Hitler's unit during the war, Mend was a blackmailing paedophile who wound up in prison for sex offences and had a series of unrelated money grievances against Hitler. His eventual death in Dachau is taken as evidence that Hitler had him silenced, but it might just as easily have been as a result of his other activities. Anyhow, Hitler allowed Mend to live for years after the Brownshirt leadership had met their death at his hands, which would have been a curious oversight if he had been primarily concerned with silencing those who knew about his secret past.

Far from being new, the accusation of homosexuality was regularly levelled at Hitler by German Social Democrat and Communist newspapers before 1933. It is hardly a taboo subject, as Dr Machtan claimed, since many of the tens of thousands of publications on Hitler have gone into this possible side to his personality, and into the nature of his relationships with Rudolf Hess and Albert Speer in particular. If we are to believe Dr Machtan, Hitler was an insatiably promiscuous and predatory homosexual who acted out his crushes on chauffeurs, fellow soldiers, Viennese rent-boys and casual street pick-ups, but for some reason, he says, 'we must limit ourselves to conjecturing how and to what extent the Hitler–Speer relationship bore a homoerotic imprint'. Dr Machtan would even have us believe that he only married the 'tomboy' Eva Braun – who chose to die with him, despite presumably knowing that she was merely his 'beard' – in order to put future historians off the scent of his homosexual past.

Professor Norman Stone looked deeply into the whole subject of the Führer's sexuality back in 1980 for his biography *Hitler*, and he came up with a far more credible theory than that of an active homosexual who suddenly changes on becoming Chancellor of Germany. Stone argued that Hitler was 'semi-sexless', and that he had only half the normal levels of testosterone in his blood: 'No one knew what was going on in Hitler's head, and he never revealed anything.' Furthermore he might still have been a virgin at thirty-five.

Stone believed that Hitler's one true love was architecture, which involves its own paradox, considering how many beautiful buildings he was instrumental in destroying. He had little or no use for either men or women as sexual beings, for the sex act would merely bring him down to their base level. He was close to Hess, who was not homosexual, and to Röhm, who was, and addressed them in the familiar as 'du', but that certainly does not constitute evidence that he ever sodomised either of them, or wished to.

Ernst 'Putzi' Hanfstaengl, who knew Hitler as well as anyone in the early days of the Nazi Party, thought him 'the repressed, masturbatory type', at least before it was in his interests to exaggerate about the sexuality of his former boss for the American secret services. Since Hitler probably did have an affair with his own niece Geli Raubal, which possibly led to her suicide in September 1931, at best he must have been bisexual anyhow. 'He was a very lonely man, but he was prepared to settle for a long romance with power,' was Professor Stone's verdict, and it is a vastly more convincing one than that presented by Dr Machtan.

Even if Hitler had been homosexual, it would be of absolutely no use in explaining what he did politically, or how he did it. His carefully created charisma aside, Hitler was a rather ordinary person. As the professor of modern history at Cambridge University, Richard Evans, has observantly pointed out: 'The only really extraordinary thing about Hitler was his talent as a rabble-rousing orator, a talent he discovered after the First

World War almost by accident. For the rest, he seems to have been normal in his private life, unoriginal in his ideas, and fanatical but by no means exceptional among the ideologues on the far right in Weimar Germany in his visceral but ultimately politically motivated hatred of the Jews.'[46] Churchill, on the other hand, was an extraordinary individual according to virtually any criteria one cares to employ.

Delegation versus Meddling

Churchill was notorious for his tendency to micromanage and meddle in other people's business. On a professional level, he would today be termed a 'micromanager'. His private secretary during his time at the Treasury, Percy James Grigg, recalled: 'It might easily happen that the minutes of a single morning covered the whole region between the draft of an important state paper or ideas for the next Budget and some desired improvement in the make-up of files or the impropriety of the Office of Works supplying Czechoslovakian matches in a British Government establishment.'

Every morning, while still in bed, Churchill would churn out endless instructions and inquiries about anything that came to his most fertile and questing mind. Before lunch one day while Chancellor of the Exchequer in the 1920s, for example, he asked his financial secretary to look into the question of withholding any increase in teachers' salaries; he asked the Cabinet Secretary whether it was really necessary to increase the number of submarines based in Hong Kong; and inquired at the Foreign Office about the cost of their telegrams from Persia. This kind of micromanagement created tensions and made Churchill unpopular with some long-serving Treasury officials, who did not appreciate the Chancellor's attempts to interfere in matters that they thought could be perfectly adequately dealt with at the appropriate lower levels.

As Chancellor, Churchill also attempted to run the *British Gazette*, the Government's propaganda news-sheet during the General Strike of 1926, to the point that its editor tried desperately to have him kept out of the building where the newspapers were printed. During the first night's production he complained to the Prime Minister, Stanley Baldwin, that Churchill had tried 'to force a scratch staff beyond its capacity' and had 'rattled them badly'. Five days later he complained again: 'He butts in at the busiest hours and insists on changing commas and full stops until the staff is furious!' Even worse, Churchill seems to have insisted on showing the printing staff how to operate their own machines.

Hitler dealt with the business of government in a completely different way. He loathed holding meetings and reading reports and was very reluctant to put anything in writing. 'A single idea of genius,' he said, 'is worth more than a whole lifetime of conscientious office work.' Churchill, by contrast, was a hard worker, who, in his own words, 'found I could add nearly two hours to my working day by going to bed for an hour after luncheon'. This regime, to whose efficacy the author can attest, did allow Churchill to be something of a pest to his staff during the war since it enabled him to stay up until around 2 a.m., which those who had not had the luxury of snoozing in the afternoon found exhausting.

Hitler was by contrast rather indolent. Whereas Churchill immersed himself in complex economic questions, although not always successfully, Hitler rarely bothered at all. 'I have the gift of reducing all problems to their simplest foundations,' he said in 1932. He knew what he wanted: no unemployment and massive rearmament. So he appointed Germany's leading economic expert, Hjalmar Schacht, as Minister of Economics and Plenipotentiary of Rearmament and then let him get on with the business of managing the economy. 'Inflation is lack of discipline,' Hitler told Schacht, 'lack of discipline in the buyers and lack of discipline in the sellers. ... I will see to it that prices remain stable. That is what my Brownshirts are for.'[47] His economic views give the phrase 'command economy' an even more sinister meaning than the overtly statist one that it has already.

Schacht in fact generated a surprising economic upturn, but at a price. The deficit financing of Hitler's rearmament programme meant that after three years of a booming economy the food shops in Germany were running low of supplies by the mid-1930s. The Minister of Agriculture, Richard Darré, was worried about the situation. He bombarded Hitler's office with memoranda and tried for two whole years to gain an audience with the Führer, but in vain. Hitler wasn't interested in what he considered petty economic questions, which were better left to the experts.

Hitler only got personally involved when it became clear that his plans for military expansion were at risk. Schacht warned that Germany was heading for ruin unless the spending on rearmament was radically cut back but Göring understood better than Schacht what Hitler wanted to hear, he boasted: 'I know nothing about economics, but I have an unbridled will.' As Schacht was trying to restrict the rearmament programme, Göring sensed an opportunity both to please his boss and to extend his power base. He promised to provide a 'Four-Year Plan' that would supply both food and guns. So Hitler appointed him Reich Plenipotentiary of the Four-Year Plan and, within a few months, Göring had numerous experts for specific economic questions installed, who each competed with their counterparts in Schacht's Economics Ministry.

In May 1937 Schacht protested to Hitler about Göring's intrigues, but the Führer waved him away. He wanted nothing more to do with the matter and told Schacht to take it up with Göring directly himself. A few months later, Schacht saw no other course but to resign. This was a typical example of how Hitler ran the Nazi State. He wasn't interested in the details of policy or administration. Instead, he set the overall objectives and then let his subordinates fight it out among themselves.

The best way for a subordinate to deal with Hitler was to

adopt the tactics of Colonel-General Walter Model, who used to avoid making requests of the Führer, always came up with forceful proposals that exuded energy, occasionally ignored orders that he judged impossible to execute, and very often simply presented Hitler with a fait accompli, reporting what he had already done. This very often worked, especially if Model managed to get him to believe that a particular strategy had been originally thought up by the Führer himself, in which case his support was assured. Model had a rough manner, but was absolutely loyal. Nicknamed 'the Lion of Defence' and 'the Führer's fireman', because Hitler switched him constantly from front to front attempting to hold up the Red Army's advance in 1944–5, Model finally shot himself on 20 April 1945.

Hitler even used to encourage competition between different areas of the state apparatus, promoting a kind of neo-Darwinist contest between ministries and acolytes. In the very opposite of the 'team-playing' management technique, Hitler never minded if some parts of his Government were at the throats of others. Thus the Foreign Minister Joachim von Ribbentrop was despised by the Propaganda Minister Joseph Goebbels, who was in turn loathed by the Party boss Martin Bormann, who was hated by the SS chief Heinrich Himmler, who was feared by the Armaments and Architecture Minister Albert Speer, who was disliked by the Luftwaffe commander Hermann Göring, who was in turn hated by Ribbentrop. Stirring this cauldron of seething animosities was the Führer, to whom they all ultimately and individually answered. This situation was patently absurd, but it suited Hitler well since it fitted in with his Darwinist views and secured his personal power, putting him in the position of ultimate arbiter between all the rival factions.

As an illustration of Hitler's technique, Albert Speer recalled how he

took delight in having Ambassador [Walter] Hewel, Ribbentrop's liaison man, transmit the content of telephone conversations with the Foreign Minister. He would even coach Hewel in ways to disconcert or confuse his superior. Sometimes he stood right beside Hewel, who would hold his hand over the mouthpiece of the telephone and repeat what Ribbentrop was saying, while Hitler whispered what to answer. Usually these were sarcastic remarks intended to fan the Foreign Minister's suspicions that unauthorized persons might be influencing Hitler on questions of foreign policy, thus infringing his domain.

It was no way to run a government.

On the outbreak of war in 1939, Churchill was given the post of First Lord of the Admiralty, in charge of the whole naval theatre of operations. It immediately became evident that his exile in the political wilderness hadn't diminished Churchill's tendency to micromanage. From his office in the Old Admiralty Building – today called the Churchill Room – he bombarded both his subordinates and his Cabinet colleagues with memoranda that covered almost every aspect of the war. One naval officer confided to his diary: 'Winston Churchill is taking a great personal interest and tends to interfere with the sailors' business. He is an extraordinary man and has an astonishing grasp of the situation, but I wish he would keep to his own sphere.'[48] Churchill acknowledged this part of his nature, telling the House of Commons three years later: 'I am certainly not one of those who needs to be prodded. In fact, if anything, I am a prod.'

As he saw it, his 'sphere' as First Lord of the Admiralty extended far beyond responsibility for the Royal Navy. In a letter to the Foreign Secretary, Lord Halifax, on 10 September 1939, only a week after taking office, Churchill wrote to say that he thought that Halifax's friend, the British Ambassador to Italy Sir Percy Loraine, 'does not seem to understand our resolve', before going on to comment on telegrams from Egypt. He wound up with what read like a gentlemanly threat: 'I hope you will not mind my drawing your attention from time to time to points which strike me in the Foreign Office telegrams, as it is so much better than that I should raise them in Cabinet.' A few days later, Churchill sent Halifax a memorandum urging him to bring Bulgaria into the Balkan defence system. Meanwhile he was writing 'My dear Sam' letters to the Lord Privy Seal Sir Samuel Hoare, in which he questioned the need for petrol and meat rationing, entertainment restrictions, blackouts, and proposed the formation of 'a Home Guard of half a million men over forty'. This too had a final line that sounded dangerous: 'I hear continual complaints from every quarter of the lack of organisation on the Home Front. Can't we get at it?'

This propensity to interfere and micromanage is not unusual for energetic leaders, nor is it necessarily a bad thing. Hands-on management can be very effective, but it depends how it is done. The general problem with micromanagement is that the better people are at their jobs, the more they mind being told how to do them. Most of Churchill's staff and colleagues were content to put up with his meddling only because he generated the vitality and fighting spirit that was so desperately needed. He was, in the words of one of his secretaries, not just 'a tremendous nuisance' but also 'a tremendous tonic'.[49] Thankfully it was the latter that prevailed. Churchill's energy and spirit more than compensated for all his faults and failures, and even for the Norway operation in the spring of 1940.

The idea for the operation had originally been Churchill's own. As early as September 1939 he had proposed cutting Germany off from some of her iron-ore supplies by mining the waters of Norway, which was neutral territory. Legal and diplomatic concerns delayed the operation for several months. When finally, in April 1940, the Royal Navy was sent towards Norway, the Germans struck first. Fully aware of Allied intentions, they occupied the major Norwegian ports before the British fleet arrived. After several weeks of fighting, the British did capture the key port of Narvik, only to have to evacuate it the following day. Soon Norway was in Hitler's hands and the world's greatest naval power had suffered a humiliating defeat. It is one of the many paradoxes of this period that it was the Norway débâcle that forced Chamberlain to resign and made Churchill prime minister, despite the fact that the First Lord bore far more direct responsibility for the unhappy Allied blunders during the operation than the Prime Minister. But leaders are often judged more by their spirit than by their actions, and usually rightly so. And Churchill possessed one key skill that great leaders need above all: the ability to inspire others.

Both Hitler and Churchill were able to draw on a powerful sense of nationalism during the war. Like Charles de Gaulle, who had 'a certain idea of France', Churchill had his own certain idea of what Britain was and could be, and it was an heroic one born of his (often over-romanticised) conception of British history. Hitler had no such instinctive understanding of the true nature of the German people and their innate national characteristics. He could play up to their anger and resentment, but it was the only tune in his repertoire, whereas Churchill could adjust his message to the changing times.

For all Churchill's talk of Trafalgar, Napoleon and Nelson, Hitler was still far from his Waterloo, as Churchill had to admit in July 1940 when he said that he hoped that by 1942 'the War will, I trust, take a different form from the defensive, in which it has hitherto been bound'. He was correct in his prediction, of course – late 1942 was to see the first great Allied victories of the war at El Alamein and Stalingrad – but he was still unable to provide any logical cause for optimism. He called for blind faith, and due to his leadership, oratorical skills and the lack of any honourable alternative, he got it.

Hitler too encouraged the belief that Germany's present struggle was an extension of its glorious struggles of the past. He presented himself as the spiritual descendant of the great German heroes in direct line of apostolic succession from giants such as the Emperor Barbarossa, Otto von Bismarck, after whom one of the greatest German warships was named, and Frederick the Great, whose exploits he had read to him by Goebbels as the Red Army marched on his Chancellery in April 1945.

Both Hitler and Churchill demanded great acts of sacrifice from their countries, a superbly counterintuitive form of leadership. The leadership manuals and books published by management gurus instruct us that: 'The fundamental task of leaders is to prime good feeling in those they lead. That occurs when a leader creates *resonance* – a reservoir of positivity that frees the best in people.'[50] For all the ghastly management-speak of that last sentence, the fact remains that people can feel good when making sacrifices, which can bring out the best in them – at least in wartime. Politicians do not always have to be resolutely upbeat in order to be popular. At dinner on 15 December 1940, during the Blitz, one of Churchill's junior ministers Richard Law put his finger on this truth when he told Churchill's private secretary that 'The secret of Hitler's power was his demand for sacrifice. The P.M. understood this and his own speeches were brilliant in that respect, but [the Minister for Labour Ernest] Bevin thought that he could buoy people up by promising them higher wages and better times. He was wrong.'[51]

The one thing that Churchill never asked the British people to sacrifice was hope. Before the entry of Russia and America into the Second World War in 1941, it was impossible to predict how Hitler was going to be defeated – even Churchill himself could not have known for certain – but his broadcasts none the less left no one in any doubt that it would eventually happen one day:

> It is a message of good cheer to our fighting Forces on the seas, in the air and in our waiting Armies in all their posts and stations, that we send them from this capital city. They know that they have behind them a people who will not flinch or weary of the struggle – hard and protracted though it will be; but that we shall rather draw from the heart of suffering itself the means of inspiration and survival, and of victory won not

for ourselves but for all – a victory not only for our own time,
but for the long and better days that are to come.

The driving force behind Hitler's charismatic leadership was the
quest for power. Yet Churchill demonstrated that leaders don't
need charisma or dictatorial powers to inspire others. After
meeting Hitler people felt that he, the Führer, could achieve
anything. But when people met Churchill they felt that they
themselves could achieve anything. Genuine inspiration beats
artificially created charisma.

'Working towards the Führer'

One of Hitler's leadership techniques that proved very effective
was the encouragement of the concept of what was called
'working towards the Führer', or carrying out tasks that it was felt
would please him, even if he had not directly authorised them.
Nowhere was this more in evidence in Nazi Germany than in the
war against the Jews. Following Göring's take-over from Schacht,
increasingly radical steps were taken to eliminate the Jews from
the German economy. By April 1938 more than 60 per cent of
Jewish firms had been liquidated or 'Aryanised'. In the course of
1938, following the Anschluss of Austria, anti-Jewish violence
increased throughout the Reich. Hitler saw it as important for his
international standing that he should not be personally associated
with this anti-Jewish campaign as it gathered momentum. No
discussion of the 'Jewish Question' was, for example, permitted
by the press in connection with his visits to different parts of
Germany in 1938.

The day after the assassination of Ernst vom Rath, the third
secretary in the German Embassy in Paris, by the Polish Jew,
Herschel Grynszpan, on 7 November 1938, local Party leaders
instigated anti-Jewish demonstrations and pogroms all over
Germany. On the evening of 9 November, Nazi leaders met in the

Old Town Hall of Munich to celebrate the fifteenth anniversary of the Beer-hall Putsch. By the time the reception began, vom Rath had died from his wounds. Goebbels wrote in his diary: 'I explain the matter to the Führer. He decides: let the demonstrations continue. Pull back the police. The Jews should for once get to feel the anger of the people.'

Goebbels seized upon the opportunity to improve his standing with the Führer, which had suffered greatly from the marital difficulties stemming from his relationship with the Czech film actress Lida Baarova. Here was his chance, by 'working towards the Führer' in such a key area, to win back favour. After Hitler had left the Old Town Hall, Goebbels gave an inflammatory speech suggesting that the Party should organise and carry out 'demonstrations' against the Jews throughout the country. The Party leaders relayed this immediately to their local offices, and Party and SA activists were turned loose on synagogues, lives and property.

Hitler was adamant that the SS itself was kept away from the Kristallnacht pogroms. The 'demonstrations' were meant to be seen as the 'spontaneous outburst of public rage', as Goebbels put it, and the involvement of the SS would have made the violence look far too much like an organised operation. In the event, few were fooled. Only six weeks after the Munich agreement had been signed, the true nature of the Nazi regime was once again highlighted for the world. Hitler hastened to dissociate himself from the events, but it is clear that Goebbels really had his full support, despite what his apologists have since tried to make out. In a secret speech to one hundred leading press men on the day after the pogroms, Hitler praised Goebbels's propaganda triumphs. A few days later, on 15 November, Goebbels's diary records that the Führer 'is in fine fettle. Sharply against the Jews. Thoroughly endorses my, and our, policies.' Indeed, Hitler now encouraged Göring to find a co-ordinated solution to the 'Jewish Question'.

Göring seized upon the opportunity to get a cash injection for his floundering Four-Year Plan. Insurance companies were told that they would have to cover losses, if their foreign business was not to suffer. As for the Jews, they were grotesquely enough held liable for the damage done to them. The insurance payments were made to the Reich, not to the Jews, and Göring imposed an 'atonement fine' of one billion marks on them. As from 1 January 1939 all Jews were to be completely excluded from the economy.

The overwhelming need on behalf of underlings to impress Hitler led to a radicalisation of Nazi policy. Kristallnacht taught the world, as if it had not had warnings enough – not least from Churchill – that Nazism was an evil creed that would most likely envelop the world in war. Economically, Göring's Four-Year Plan was simply not sustainable and the money spent on rearmament had somehow to be recuperated. War was the solution, and it was what Hitler had wanted all along. Churchill had been right. On the day war was declared, Neville Chamberlain appointed Churchill to his old post of First Lord of the Admiralty. Winston was back.

Hitler and Churchill
from 1940

'War is a beastly thing now, all the glamour has gone out of
it. Just a question of clerks pushing buttons.'

Churchill to Robert Bernays MP in the House of
Commons tearoom in the 1930s

From the very first month of the war, during the period known
as the 'Phoney War' or 'Sitzkrieg', while others were advocating
caution, Churchill was agitating for action, not just at home, but
abroad too. Yet his confidence in Britain's anti-submarine measures proved to be ill-founded. The carrier HMS *Courageous* was
torpedoed in the Bristol Channel in September 1939. In the next
month, a German submarine penetrated the defences of Scapa
Flow and sank the battleship HMS *Royal Oak*. In the first nine
months of the war, Britain lost 800,000 tons of shipping to a relatively small number of cncmy submarines and magnetic
mines. Yet in the late spring of 1940, Churchill publicly maintained that the Royal Navy had reduced the front line of the U-
boat force to fewer than a dozen vessels. If this estimate had
been accurate, the Navy would have nearly accounted for the
better part of the whole front line of the German force.
Unfortunately it was not, and Churchill had to arrange for the
transferral to active duty of the Director of Anti-Submarine
Warfare who kept telling him the truth.

On 20 January 1940 Churchill broadcast to the neutral

nations, urging the Dutch, Belgians and Scandinavians to 'stand together with the British and French Empires against aggression and wrong'. This only encouraged Hitler to take a forestalling action. The captured records of Hitler's conferences reveal that in early 1940 he still considered 'the maintenance of Norway's neutrality to be the best course for Germany', but that in February he came to the conclusion that: 'The English intend to land there and I want to be there before them.' His definite decision to order an attack on Norway was taken a few days after Churchill had ordered the British destroyer HMS *Cossack* to sail into Norwegian waters and board the German ship *Altmark*, in order to liberate British prisoners. Churchill capitalised on this success and much was made of the event. The Norwegian Government protested against the violation of its territory, but their passive acceptance served to convince Hitler that Norway was actually Britain's accomplice, and it became the detonating spark of the pre-emptive action that he now ordered: the invasion of Norway.

On the evening of 9 April 1940, Churchill was enjoying a good dinner at the home of his Cabinet colleague, the Secretary of State for Air Sir Samuel Hoare. He was in a fine mood. A long-cherished project of his, the mining of Norwegian waters, was finally getting under way, and he hoped it would interrupt the vital German iron-ore imports from Scandinavia. Hoare recorded in his diary: 'Winston very optimistic, delighted with mine laying, and sure he had scored off the Germans. He went off completely confident and happy at 10.30.'[1] Yet when he returned to the Admiralty Churchill found that it was he and not the Germans who had been undermined. A large German naval force was reported to be steaming towards Norway. The next morning the Nazis captured the vital Norwegian port of Narvik and only a few weeks later all of Norway was in Hitler's hands.

Eduard Dietl, the German commander, had only two thousand mountain infantry and 2,600 sailors with whom to oppose

24,500 Allied troops, including the Norwegian 6th Division, so what had gone wrong?[2] The Germans had received excellent intelligence on British intentions; Churchill's designs had been let loose by none other than himself. He dropped a series of hints in a secret conference with neutral press attachés in London on 2 February that had soon become known to German Intelligence. By late March 1940 the world press had slowly filled with speculation about the Allied designs on Scandinavia and suspicions were raised further when it was discovered that Churchill's nephew, Giles Romilly, had been sent to Narvik.

By contrast, not a word of Hitler's own daring plan had leaked out. A top-secret unit had been established within the German High Command, the Oberkommando der Wehrmacht (OKW), under Hitler's personal supervision. He appointed General von Falkenhorst in charge of the preparations for 'Weser Exercise'. To retain maximum secrecy, this soldier was at first given no maps to help him with this task. Instead he bought himself a Baedeker pocket-map of Norway and retired to a hotel room, returning in the afternoon with the plans to show Hitler, who instantly approved them. The Führer did not even mention a word of the scheme to Ribbentrop. It went off very successfully, the result of secrecy, daring and enterprise. Hitler himself called it one of the 'cheekiest operations' in recent military history, with good reason.

By contrast, Britain had a cumbersome governmental structure that tended to hold up operations of this sort. The Cabinet, the Foreign Office, the French, the Dominions and other important bodies had to be consulted – and world opinion had to be considered – before Churchill could violate Scandinavian neutrality by the mining of harbours. There was no single authority from which Churchill could swiftly obtain permission for such an operation. With so many parties involved in the decision-making, it was small wonder that the Germans were fully aware of British intentions.

Hitler's dictatorial powers made it much easier for him to

keep his plans secret than for the British leadership. His Cabinet hadn't met since 1938 and it wouldn't do for the remainder of the war. And while the concerns of the British Foreign Secretary, Lord Halifax, did much to delay Allied action, his German counterpart Ribbentrop had been cut out of the decision-making process entirely. Such secrecy was in line with the Führer's Basic Order No. 1, which hung in every military office: 'Everybody must know only as much as is necessary to carry out his tasks, and then no earlier than need be.'

Yet during the Norwegian campaign, Hitler displayed a worrying loss of nerve. In a fit of funk over the situation at Narvik, the Führer had Field Marshal Wilhelm Keitel draft an order for the force there to withdraw to neutral Sweden and have itself interned. Only prompt action by a relatively junior officer, covering for his boss who was on sick leave, saved the situation. When Lieut.-Col. Bernhard von Lossberg received Hitler's message to the commander in Narvik at the OKW's Berlin office, he immediately sought out Keitel and Field Marshal Jodl and refused point-blank to send the Führer's order. It reflected, he said, the same loss of nerve that had lost Germany the Battle of the Marne in the First World War, which had led to four years of trench warfare and eventual defeat.

Jodl made it clear that he was in no position to countermand the order, but he found a way around the problem by sending another telegram to the commander in Narvik congratulating him on his recent promotion, while Hitler's orders were torn up. The following day Jodl explained to Hitler that the telegram had not been sent as it contradicted the congratulatory message that had just been telegraphed. Hitler's military staff were thus compensating for his own weaknesses. His second thoughts in the Norwegian campaign were no isolated incident either; the same thing was to happen in the French campaign during the summer of 1940. A close look at the famed Blitzkrieg success in the West reveals both the strengths and the weaknesses of Hitler's military leadership.

The Allied mentality before May 1940 can best be summed up in the two words: 'Maginot Line', the name given to the elaborate bulwark of French fortifications on the border with Germany. Constructed in the late 1920s and early 1930s, and named after the long-serving French Defence Minister André Maginot, it was considered the most advanced fortification system of its time and thought to be impenetrable to German attack. In reality, these fortifications contained the seeds of the most ignominious military defeat that France has ever suffered in her long history of subjugation and surrender. The French High Command expected a war with Germany to be a repeat of the trench warfare of the First World War. The Maginot Line was basically a Western Front in reinforced concrete. It was a model case of bad leadership; what the French High Command failed to appreciate was that history rarely repeats itself exactly and that leaders who cling to the recipes of the past are almost certain to fail. As Churchill joked in the House of Commons in 1944 on being warned to avoid the mistakes of 1914–18: 'I am sure that the mistakes of that time will not be repeated; we shall probably make another set of mistakes.'

When the Nazis prepared for their attack on France, they were clearly inferior in numbers and matériel. The Allies had more men, more guns, and more and better tanks. But the German Army had one inestimable advantage: it had better leaders. Their commanders recognised that the military circumstances had entirely changed since 1918. The Polish campaign had demonstrated the speed and destructiveness which a combined attack of panzers and Stuka dive-bombers could achieve. While the German High Command was preparing to unleash in the West this new form of warfare, dubbed 'Blitzkrieg' (lightning war), the British Parliament was engaged in a full-scale political crisis, as a significant proportion of the House of Commons revolted against the premiership of Neville Chamberlain.

Churchill takes charge

Between 7 and 10 May 1940 a sensational parliamentary coup replaced Neville Chamberlain, the incumbent wartime Prime Minister, with Winston Churchill, then First Lord of the Admiralty. Chamberlain, who had been one of the senior men responsible for the pre-war policy of appeasement, had presided over the mainly Tory National Government for three years and still enjoyed considerable support from the Conservative Party and in the country. A spontaneous outburst of anger at the British Expeditionary Force's poor performance in the recent Norwegian campaign, however, was about to be voiced in the House of Commons. With the Whitsun bank holiday approaching, it was agreed that the traditional debate on the adjournment of Parliament would be held on the issue of the military débâcle in Norway and the Government's general handling of the war so far. Unbeknownst to the Westminster MPs, Hitler was preparing to unleash his Blitzkrieg in the West, and as they met on the evening of Tuesday, 7 May 1940, an all-out German invasion of Holland, Belgium and France was only fifty-five hours away.

Few, if anyone, expected Neville Chamberlain's National Government to fall as a result of the debate, least of all the Prime Minister himself. Just before it began he told Lord Halifax that he doubted it would 'amount to much'. None the less, an extraordinary combination of factors – including inflammatory speeches from respected individuals, a lack of support from Tory backbenchers, a disastrous personal performance by the Prime Minister, incessant behind-the-scenes intrigues and deals, and an uncharacteristically lacklustre speech by Winston Churchill – meant that after two days of debate a new mood had settled on Westminster, one which forced Chamberlain from office.

One backbench Tory MP, John Moore-Brabazon, surreptitiously took some blurred photographs of what thereafter became known as the 'Norway Debate' with his tiny Minox camera from the Bar of the House, quite against Commons' rules. From these we can tell that when Chamberlain rose to defend the performance of his ministry the chamber and galleries were packed. The Prime Minister was at pains to explain away his complacent statement of 4 April that Hitler had 'missed the bus', which only four days later had been followed by Germany's attack on Norway, forcing British forces to evacuate the country from 2 May.

Facing regular interruptions from the Labour benches, Chamberlain soldiered through a long, self-exculpatory and uninspiring defence of his Government and himself. 'For my part I try to steer a middle course,' he said in a sentence typical of the whole speech, 'neither raising undue expectations which are unlikely to be fulfilled, nor making the people's flesh creep by painting pictures of unmitigated gloom.' It was hardly the leonine wartime leadership that Britain had enjoyed from the two Pitts, Lord Palmerston and David Lloyd George.

Answering him, Clement Attlee, the leader of the Opposition and of the Labour Party, struck some heavy blows against the planning, organisation and execution of the operations in Norway, arguing that the Government had entirely failed to learn from the lessons of Hitler's Blitzkrieg tactics as employed against Poland the previous autumn. 'The war is not being waged with sufficient energy, intensity, drive and resolution,' he said, quipping that Chamberlain had 'missed all the peace buses, but had caught the war bus'. In his peroration, Attlee proclaimed his confidence that Britain would win the war in the end, but in order to do so 'we want different people at the helm from those who had led us into it'.

Following him Sir Archibald Sinclair, the leader of the Liberal Party, drew attention to the way 'the complacent and, alas, ill-founded boastings of ministers contrast pitifully with the hard, swift blows of the German forces'. So far, so predictable. With a Tory majority from the 1935 general election of 249, the Government had little to fear if the debate went along strictly party lines. But after a pro-Chamberlain speech by the imperialist Tory backbencher Brigadier Sir Henry Page Croft and a crushing rejoinder from the Labour MP Colonel Josiah Wedgwood, who attacked Croft's 'facile optimism' and predicted a 'lightning strike' invasion of Britain, the fragile façade of party unity suffered its first crack.

Admiral of the Fleet Sir Roger Keyes, Conservative MP for Portsmouth, stood up in his full-dress naval uniform, complete with six rows of medal ribbons, and described the handling of the Norway campaign as 'a shocking story of ineptitude, which I assure the House should never have been allowed to happen'. Coming from the hero of the legendary Zeebrugge Raid of 1918, his views carried great weight. Of the many contemporaneous accounts of that day found in the diaries and correspondence of spectators, almost all refer to the power and authority of Keyes's speech. The admiral somehow managed to relieve his friend Churchill of any personal responsibility for the Norway débâcle, despite the fact that it had been almost entirely run from the Admiralty. 'The whole country is looking to him to help win the war,' he said of Churchill, before sitting down to much cheering.

Soon afterwards Leo Amery, a distinguished Conservative former Cabinet minister, rose to deliver another hammer blow against the Government front bench. Of diminutive height and not a naturally gifted speaker, Amery none the less carried extra weight because he sat for one of the seats in Chamberlain's home town of Birmingham and had himself been First Lord of the Admiralty. As his philippic progressed, Amery sensed that the mood of the House was with him, so he decided to take the risk of winding up his speech using the same words that Oliver Cromwell had employed in dismissing the Long Parliament in 1653: 'You have sat too long here for any good you have been doing. Depart, I say, and let us have done with you. In the name of God, go!' The effect was as dramatic as it was crushing for the Government, and is thought to have persuaded several MPs to vote against Chamberlain.

Oliver Stanley, the Secretary of State for War, tried his best to rescue the situation, and a couple of backbench National Government supporters also came to its defence, but by the end of the first day's debate it was clear, from one Labour MP's intervention, that it was not just the handling of the Norway campaign that was on trial, but the very existence of the Government itself.

By the time that Labour's Herbert Morrison opened the second day of the Norway Debate on Wednesday, 8 May 1940, the fate of Neville Chamberlain's National Government was indeed hanging in the balance. The first day had gone disastrously for ministers and it was obvious that a significant body of National Government supporters, mainly those who had opposed the appeasement policy in the thirties but also including the usual selection of disappointed office-seekers, sacked former ministers, rebels and 'awkward squad' types, were going to take this opportunity to try to oust Chamberlain by voting with Labour and the Liberals. The presence of several of the younger MPs in military uniform was felt to augur ill for the Government, considering the angry mood in the Armed Forces about what was seen as administrative incompetence. Even more worrying for the government whips was the number of usually loyal MPs who were considering either abstaining or absenting themselves altogether from the final division.

Morrison argued that 'the whole spirit, tempo and temperament of at least some ministers have been wrong, inadequate and unsuitable', citing by name Chamberlain himself, Sir John Simon the Chancellor of the Exchequer and Sir Samuel Hoare the Air Minister. He also announced that Labour had demanded a formal division at the end of the debate which would, he told MPs, 'broadly indicate whether they are content with the conduct of affairs or whether they are apprehensive about the conduct of affairs'.

At this point Chamberlain rose to accept the challenge, but in a very ill-advised manner. Mentioning 'my friends in the

House', the Prime Minister said: 'I accept the challenge. I welcome it indeed. At least we shall see who is with us and who is against us, and I call on my friends to support us in the lobby tonight.' This was understandably characterised as a blatant appeal to narrow party loyalty at a time of great national peril, and as such it backfired disastrously.

Sir Samuel Hoare, the arch-appeaser of the thirties, spoke next and was badly mauled by a series of interventions from Admiral Keyes, the Labour front-bencher Hugh Dalton, and no fewer than seven other MPs. As Secretary of State for Air, Hoare was reduced to admitting that the RAF was 'not nearly big enough', a damaging remark from a government that had been in office for almost the whole of the previous decade.

Next to speak was David Lloyd George, who had waited eighteen years for his chance to revenge himself upon the men who had turned him out of the premiership in 1922. With his famed Welsh eloquence and reputation as 'the man who won the [Great] War', he contended that Britain was in a far worse position than in 1914, and blamed Chamberlain personally for his inability to 'rouse' and 'mobilise' the British Empire. It was a scornful, bitterly personal but highly effective attack. When heckled by a Tory backbencher, he sarcastically retorted: 'You will have to listen to it, either now or later on. Hitler does not answer the whips of the Patronage Secretary [Chief Whip].' Of Chamberlain's guarantee to Poland and the neutrals he said: 'Our promissory notes are now rubbish on the market.'

With Churchill ready to accept full responsibility for all that had taken place in Norway, Lloyd George made one of the most telling remarks of the whole debate and employed a powerful metaphor: 'The right honourable gentleman must not allow himself to be converted into an air-raid shelter to keep the splinters from hitting his colleagues.' His devastating peroration mentioned Chamberlain's appeal to the nation to make sacrifices for victory, concluding that: 'There is nothing which can contribute more to victory than that he should sacrifice the seals of office.'

Other major figures of the day such as Alfred Duff Cooper (who had resigned over the Munich agreement) and the former Labour minister Sir Stafford Cripps also spoke, and an intervention was also made by the young MP Quintin Hogg (later Lord Hailsham), but the House was waiting for Churchill to wind up the debate. It was not one of his vintage performances. He lost his temper, accusing the Labour MP Emanuel Shinwell of 'skulking in a corner' and angered the Labour Party with his jibes. His final plea to 'Let pre-war feuds die; let personal quarrels be forgotten, and let us keep our hatreds for the common enemy' went completely unheeded.

On the motion 'That this House do now adjourn', the Commons divided 281 in favour and 200 against, a government majority of eighty-one, far smaller than was normal in peacetime on a three-line whip. The rebels had included Lady Astor, Robert Boothby, Harold Macmillan, Quintin Hogg, John Profumo, General Spears, Lord Wolmer, Harold Nicolson, Leslie Hore-Belisha and of course Leo Amery and Admiral Keyes. Meanwhile there were rowdy scenes as two other rebels, Harold Macmillan and Earl Winterton, sang 'Rule Britannia!' until they were silenced by furious Tories. Labour MPs shouted 'You've missed the bus' at Chamberlain. In all, forty-one Government supporters had voted against Chamberlain and around fifty had abstained. The Government was certainly very badly damaged, and as Chamberlain stalked out of the Commons chamber after the result was announced his survival as prime minister was clearly in grave jeopardy. Churchill had done his bit for the Prime Minister, but fortunately for him it was not enough. He had, however, shown the necessary loyalty not to be suspected of treachery by the Conservatives who were still overwhelmingly sympathetic to Chamberlain.

Although numerically Chamberlain's National Government had won the Norway Debate the previous evening by eighty-one votes, because the majority was normally well over two hundred it was considered a moral defeat. The Government's business managers tried to ascertain exactly how serious this was on the morning of Thursday 9 May, as they attempted to limit the damage in the time-honoured way, by doing deals. First the whips tried to find out from the rebels who had voted against the Government or abstained the previous night what price needed to be paid for the recovery of their support. Then Chamberlain's parliamentary private secretary, Lord Dunglass (later the Prime Minister Sir Alec Douglas-Home), brought some leading backbenchers into Number Ten to listen to their grievances and let it be known that Chamberlain was willing to sacrifice the Chancellor of the Exchequer, Sir John Simon, and the Air Minister, Sir Samuel Hoare, in order to stay in office.

That morning Chamberlain also personally saw Leo Amery to offer him either the chancellorship or the foreign secretaryship, which Amery steadfastly refused. By 10.15 a.m. Chamberlain seems to have realised that he might have to resign, so he sent for his friend, Foreign Secretary and ideological soul mate Lord Halifax. At their meeting the two men agreed that the Labour and Liberal parties had to be brought into the Government. Since it was very unlikely that Labour would come in under Chamberlain, the Prime Minister asked Halifax whether he would form a government instead, one in which Chamberlain pledged to serve under him. According to his diary, Halifax 'put all the arguments that I could think of against myself', primarily that of the 'difficult position of a PM unable to make contact with the centre of gravity in the House of Commons'.

Perhaps significantly, Chamberlain does not seem to have argued that the rules could be changed to allow a peer to sit in the Commons under emergency situations, although it is now known that he had taken secret soundings with the Government's law officers to establish how this might be achieved.[3] Instead he made the dubious prediction that little opposition could be expected in the Commons anyhow because it would be a coalition government.

The whole drift of the conversation gave Halifax a stomach-ache. He had neither expected nor planned for the actual premiership to devolve upon himself. When he returned to the Foreign Office after the 10.15 a.m. meeting, he told his under-secretary, Rab Butler, that although 'he felt he could do the job', Churchill would effectively be running the war so he 'would speedily turn into a sort of honorary P.M.', and therefore possibly be less influential in restraining Churchill than he would be if he remained Foreign Secretary, heir apparent and the most powerful Cabinet minister.

As for Labour, then meeting at their annual party conference in Bournemouth, Butler had had two conversations the previous evening with Hugh Dalton and Herbert Morrison, who both wanted Halifax to know that their party would enter a Halifax-led government; Dalton added that 'Churchill must stick to the war'. Attlee had also told Churchill's friend Brendan Bracken that Labour would be prepared to serve under Halifax.

With the support of the King, who believed that Halifax's peerage could be put 'into abeyance' in such an emergency, the outgoing Prime Minister Chamberlain, the Labour leadership and the vast bulk of the Conservative Party, the premiership was Halifax's for the taking, had he demanded it. However, he knew that his lack of interest and expertise in military matters was an inadmissible lacuna in a wartime premier. In January 1942 Churchill joked about the situation, telling the House of Commons: 'When I was called upon to be prime minister, now nearly two years ago, there were not many applicants for the job. Since then perhaps the market has improved.'

Before the crucial meeting at Number Ten, Churchill had lunch with Anthony Eden and Sir Kingsley Wood, at which Wood – a formerly loyal Chamberlainite – advised Churchill to hold out for the premiership itself. Churchill played the whole crisis superbly, making himself the primary candidate without in any way being seen to undermine the sitting premier. It was exactly the kind of deft political leadership that he had often not shown in a past full of boisterous romanticism, but in this moment he displayed his nerve to devastating effect.

When Chamberlain, Churchill, Halifax and David Margesson, the Chief Whip, met in the Cabinet Room at 4.30 p.m. on Friday 9 May, Halifax was in a sincere mood of self-abnegation. Churchill left a famous account of the meeting: 'I have had many important interviews in my public life, and this was certainly the most important. Usually I talk a great deal, but on this occasion I was silent.' Churchill claimed that only after a 'very long pause', which seemed longer than the two minutes' Armistice Day silence, did Halifax, almost out of embarrassment, blurt out that his peerage disqualified him from the premiership and Churchill realised that 'it was clear that the duty would fall on me – had in fact fallen on me'.

Written eight years after the event, Churchill's account is open to question. He got the time and date of the interview wrong and even omitted Margesson from it altogether. The anecdote had been told so often by Churchill in the meantime that it had acquired the barnacles of exaggeration that adhere to every well-sailed story. From the contemporaneous accounts that survive and from Margesson's own memory, as well as from other circumstantial evidence, it is thought that there was no 'very long pause' at all, but in fact Halifax 'almost immediately urged Churchill's greater fitness for leadership in war'.

One compelling new piece of evidence has recently emerged to suggest that there was indeed a silence, after which Churchill asserted his own fitness for the job, or at least Halifax's unfitness, which amounted to the same thing. Far from the mantle having fallen upon him, Churchill grasped it. In 2001 the letters and diaries of Joseph P. Kennedy, the United States Ambassador to London, were published, edited by his granddaughter. They record a visit that Kennedy made on 19 October 1940 to Neville Chamberlain, who was by then dying of cancer at his home in the country. After a wide-ranging discussion about the war and about his terrible state of health, Chamberlain spoke about the interview after the Norway vote. Kennedy noted:

He then wanted to make Halifax PM and said he would serve under him. Edward as [is] his way, started saying 'Perhaps I can't handle it being in the H of Lords' and Finally Winston said, 'I don't think you could.' And he wouldn't come and that was settled.[4]

The capitalised word 'Finally' implies that a silence, or a long discussion, had in fact taken place, and then Churchill with brutal honesty agreed with Halifax 'and that was settled'.

Another interpretation is possible, which is worth mentioning only to dismiss. That is that the words 'he wouldn't come' refer to Churchill rather than Halifax, and meant that Churchill actually refused to serve in a Halifax government run from the House of Lords. Although this might fit the literary construction of Kennedy's sentence, such a construction would not fit the context of the political situation of the time, because Churchill would have been forced by patriotism to join a Halifax government in which the opposition parties were preparing to serve. There is no question of his holding out for the job through blackmail. Chamberlain clearly meant that Halifax 'wouldn't come' into the premiership. Equally, the historian David Carlton has put forward an ingenious theory that Chamberlain only saw Churchill as a stopgap prime minister to get Britain over the present crisis, after which he would replace him, and therefore secretly preferred Churchill to Halifax, whom it might prove impossible to dislodge later. This, too, is a theory too far, for all that it appeals to those who cannot overestimate the machiavellian nature of politicians.

Here was true leadership; Churchill believed he was the best man for the job and, by agreeing with Halifax, he made it clear that he wanted it. High posts like the British premiership rarely fall into people's laps unbidden; Churchill judged his moment and grasped it.

It still remained for Chamberlain to ask the Labour leaders whether they would join his Government or be willing to serve under someone else instead. When Attlee and his deputy leader

Arthur Greenwood arrived at Number Ten they said that they would consult their colleagues in Bournemouth and telephone their decision the next day, but they also warned Chamberlain privately that Labour would be very unlikely to be willing to serve under him. After his speech at the Norway Debate, Attlee could hardly have said anything less. Within a matter of hours, at dawn on 10 May, Hitler unleashed his Blitzkrieg on the West. That Hitler attacked on the same day as Chamberlain resigned was one of the great coincidences of history, but that is all it was. There is no evidence that he chose the time because Britain was in the middle of a political crisis.

The first Cabinet meeting after Hitler's dawn attack in the West took place at 8 a.m. on Friday, 10 May 1940. The news was not wholly unexpected; indeed, less than a week earlier Halifax had warned all British embassies that it 'seems likely we are shortly to meet the full force of a German onslaught on our-selves'. The Cabinet heard how Belgium and Holland, both hith-erto neutral, had been invaded in an attempt to outflank the Maginot Line, and thus deal a knockout blow to France. By the time of the next Cabinet meeting at 11.30 a.m. Chamberlain had concluded to his own satisfaction, but to few others', that the military situation was so serious that it justified postponing his resignation altogether. How could the Government change in the middle of such a crisis? he argued.

It was at this point that the Lord Privy Seal, Sir Kingsley Wood, hitherto a loyal Chamberlainite, bluntly informed the Prime Minister that, on the contrary, the new crisis meant that he had to step down immediately. The Air Minister, Sir Samuel Hoare, noted that 'No one said anything in the Cabinet except me. Edward [Halifax] quite heartless.' Many other ministers around the table, especially Winston Churchill but probably also including Halifax, felt that the dangerous new situation on the Continent actually made it more imperative rather than less that Chamberlain should go. What most did not know was that the day before, Wood had gone to Churchill to urge him to hold out for the premiership, or else he would soon be rewarded for this swift change of coat with the chancellorship of the exchequer.

When the Labour leadership telephoned from Bournemouth to say that the party would enter a coalition government, but not one formed by Chamberlain, it sealed the Prime Minister's fate. Crucially, however, they were in no position to decide who the new premier would be. It is quite wrong to think, as some politicians such as Roy Hattersley, Julian Critchley, Michael Foot and Barbara Castle persisted in doing for decades, that it was Labour that made Churchill prime minister. In fact, the party proclaimed itself just as willing to serve under Halifax at the time; the choice was therefore up to Chamberlain and the King. In such a small minority in the Commons, Labour was scarcely in a position to do anything else.

That afternoon, Chamberlain made one last effort to persuade Halifax to change his mind and take on the premiership, despite what seemed to have been agreed with Churchill the previous day. Lord Dunglass telephoned Henry 'Chips' Channon at the Foreign Office to have him ask the under-secretary there, Rab Butler, to try to persuade Halifax to accept the job. When Butler went to the Foreign Secretary's room he was told that Halifax had gone off to the dentist and could not be contacted. So Chamberlain went to Buckingham Palace where King George VI accepted his resignation, and, as he told his diary, 'told him how grossly unfairly I thought he had been treated and that I was terribly sorry that all this controversy had happened'. When they got round to the subject of his successor, the King 'of course suggested Halifax' as 'the obvious man', but Chamberlain told him that Halifax 'was not enthusiastic'. The King did not exercise his right to ask Halifax directly, although he might have been able to change his mind with a personal appeal from the sovereign to a devoted public servant.

Instead it was Churchill who kissed hands, at 6 p.m. on 10 May. The King had not much wanted Churchill, possibly partly because of the irresponsible role he had played in support of his brother Edward VIII at the time of the Abdication Crisis. None the less, when it became clear that his constitutional duty was to appoint him, the King alleviated any awkwardness by making a joke. As Churchill recalled: 'His Majesty received me most graciously and bade me sit down. He looked at me searchingly and quizzically for some moments, and then said, "I suppose you don't know why I have sent for you?" Adopting his mood, I replied: "Sir, I simply couldn't imagine why." He laughed and said: "I want to ask you to form a Government." I said I would certainly do so.'

Churchill knew that his first action must be to invite Labour and the Liberals into what he later termed his 'Grand Coalition', so he asked Attlee and Arthur Greenwood to join a drastically slimmed War Cabinet of five, along with Chamberlain and Halifax. Churchill knew he had to treat the Conservatives well too, for, as he wrote to Chamberlain that evening: 'To a large extent I am in your hands.'

At 9 p.m. Chamberlain explained his resignation in a broadcast to the nation, urging it to support his successor. Our present Queen, then aged fourteen, told her mother that it moved her to tears. Meanwhile Churchill worked into the night, and as he went to bed at three o'clock next morning, he was 'conscious of a profound sense of relief. At last I had the authority to give directions over the whole scene. I felt as if I were walking with destiny, and that all my past life had been but a preparation for this hour and this trial.'

Hitler's route to Compiègne

On 21 June 1940 Hitler visited the French monument in Compiègne outside Paris that commemorated Germany's defeat in the Great War. An American newspaper correspondent, William Shirer, recorded the Führer's body language on that triumphant day:

He steps off the monument and contrives to make even this gesture a masterpiece of contempt. ... He glances slowly round the clearing. ... Suddenly, as though his face were not giving complete expression to his feelings, he throws his whole body into harmony with his mood. He swiftly snaps his hands on his hips, arches his shoulders, plants his feet wide apart. It is a magnificent gesture of defiance, of burning contempt for the place and all that it has stood for in the twenty-two years since it witnessed the humbling of the German Empire.

A week later, on 28 June, Hitler did two things that were entirely out of character: he got up early and he went sightseeing. Like any dutiful German tourist, the Führer had prepared for the outing by reading up on the architectural highlights of Paris. As the convoy of black Mercedes-Benz limousines swept past La Madeleine towards the Arc de Triomphe, he delighted in showing off his detailed knowledge to his entourage.

At Les Invalides, Hitler gazed in silence at the tomb of Napoleon, that other European conqueror to whom the Führer frequently liked to compare himself. By now, Hitler believed that his leadership qualities made him, in the words of General Keitel, 'the greatest warlord of all times'. In just ten months the German Army had conquered half of Europe. Only the British and their imperial dominions and brave Greece remained defiant. Yet the method behind Hitler's initial successes as a war leader was, in time, to become his greatest weakness, and by capitalising on it Churchill was to set an example for anyone who aspires to leadership today.

When Hitler returned to Germany from his Blitzkrieg victory over France he was at the apex of his popularity. But Blitzkrieg, this new form of warfare, was not Hitler's invention. Nor was it Hitler who conceived the operational plan for the invasion of France. The credit for this must go to two generals, Erich von Manstein and Heinz Guderian. As early as the early 1930s, Guderian had been advocating rapid panzer operations designed to take the enemy by surprise. Based on Guderian's ideas, Manstein developed the so-called 'sickle-cut' plan to outmanoeuvre French fortifications and render irrelevant their superior numbers in men and matériel.

Manstein wanted to mount an armoured assault through the forests of the Ardennes mountains, an area generally considered to be impassable to tanks. Conventional wisdom said it would be crazy to try to attack through there, but that is exactly why the German strategy was so successful. The panzer divisions were to attack where the enemy would least expect it. This would enable them to drive a wedge between the Allied forces by swiftly advancing to the Channel coast – just like the cut of a sickle. (The metaphor originated with Churchill.)

Most generals in the High Command favoured a much more conventional operation, and envisaged the main line of attack coming from the north, either side of Liège. They considered Manstein's panzer manoeuvre through the Ardennes mountains to be simply too risky. Manstein was hurriedly transferred to an insignificant post. But then the Führer intervened. To him, the unimaginative plans of the Army High Command (OKH) seemed to be no more than 'the ideas of a military cadet'.[5] Manstein's sickle-cut, on the other hand, signified a great risk but it had the crucial element of surprise to commend it. So Hitler ordered the OKH to adopt Manstein's plan.

This was a case of inspired leadership. Hitler realised that the operational plans of the High Command actually involved a greater risk than the seemingly reckless sickle-cut manoeuvre, because a conventional attack from the north was exactly what the Allies were expecting. Successful leaders don't gamble; they take calculated risks because they realise that sometimes the most dangerous thing you can do is not to take a risk at all.

Had it not been for Guderian's boldness and initiative, however, the German invasion may well have bogged down in World War I-style trench warfare. When on the third day of the invasion Guderian's panzers had reached the River Meuse,

Hitler and the Army High Command ordered him to wait for the infantry divisions that were following as fast as they could. The result was the greatest traffic jam Europe has ever seen; columns of fifteen hundred tanks and one and a half million troops formed a tailback of 150 miles from the Meuse right back to the Rhine. Just as the blade of the sickle was beginning to cut deep, threatening to slice off the French and British forces in the north from their other armies in the south, the Führer was starting to have severe doubts. He was worried about the exposed flanks of the panzer spearheads under Guderian's command. Guderian knew that every day lost would give the Allies time to withdraw and regroup, so on 14 May he decided to ignore Hitler's orders and push forward, sweeping other divisions along with him.

The German Blitzkrieg of 1940 worked because the Allies feared a return to the costly stalemate of the First World War. But if one believes that the events of the past are going to replicate themselves precisely, one is almost guaranteed to fail. Hitler's entire career had been based on risk-taking, yet when it came to putting Manstein's daring plan into practice he showed a surprising lack of nerve, as he had in Norway.

On 17 May Franz Halder, the Chief of the Army General Staff, recorded in his diary: 'A really unpleasant day. The Führer is terribly nervous. He is frightened by his own success, does not want to risk anything, and therefore would rather stop us.'[6] Guderian was ordered to stop by the River Oise and wait for the infantry divisions to catch up. It was a major tactical mistake, showing that Hitler, although he was willing to take risks and employ Blitzkrieg tactics, astonishingly enough didn't really appreciate how they worked.

Guderian, on the other hand, fully appreciated that only speed and surprise protected him from a counter-attack. Vehemently protesting against the halt order, he relinquished his command. He only revoked his resignation after he had been given permission to undertake a so-called 'reconnaissance in force' – whatever that was thought to mean. Guderian decided to interpret it as a licence to act on his own initiative and to press on towards the Channel coast, which he hurriedly did.

Guderian's revolutionary form of mechanised warfare proved overwhelming and took the Allies completely by surprise. Ten days into the campaign, the first German units reached the mouth of the River Somme at the Channel coast. The sickle-cut was complete: the Allied armies in the north, including the British Expeditionary Force, were encircled. This was the worst day in British history for four hundred years. The British were about to lose their Expeditionary Force of a quarter of a million men. There hadn't been a disaster like it since the English lost Calais in the sixteenth century. Yet the success of the sickle-cut operation cannot be credited to Hitler's leadership, but to Manstein's planning and the boldness and initiative of Guderian. Had Guderian stuck to Hitler's directives, it would have been all 'Krieg' and no 'Blitz' – a lightning war without the lightning and, quite possibly, a campaign with a very different outcome.

Would Guderian have got away with such initiative in the British Army? For his exploits in the French campaign, Hitler rewarded him with a promotion to lieutenant-general. There is a persistent belief in Britain that the Germans were like automatons, their soldiers blindly obeying orders, but it's a myth. Guderian was able to use his initiative because he was acting in accordance with the German principle of *Auftragstaktik* (Mission Command).

Mission Command

First developed by the Prussian Army in the nineteenth century and now official NATO doctrine, Mission Command means that headquarters confines itself to setting the objectives while leaving it up to the commanders on the spot to decide how best to achieve them. Success or failure – rather than obedience – is

Hitler with
Blondi.

Hitler with his other
blondie. Eva always called
him 'mein Führer', right up
to their shotgun marriage.

The Führer pioneered the politicians' photo-opportunity with children.

A very rare shot of the short-sighted Hitler wearing glasses; he feared such photos would damage his superhuman image.

When the Italian dictator Benito Mussolini was photographed in his bathing trunks Hitler exploded with derision.

Churchill didn't much care what he looked like.

Hitler deliberately dressed down to emphasise his simplicity *vis-à-vis* his generals.

Goebbels used humour to get round the Führer, and to undermine his rivals.

The architect Albert Speer and Hitler admire their handiwork at the opening of the new Reich chancellery in 1938.

You had to walk through nine hundred feet of increasingly splendid halls before you reached the Führer's study.

Churchill would walk the streets of London even as wartime premier, as on
26th May 1940.

Hitler's secretaries smoked when his back was turned.

The Führer rated two Father Christmases at this party in 1937.

Hitler wanted to use the German diplomatic service to seduce Churchill's daughter Mary (left). It never happened.

Finance minister Hjalmar Schacht salutes the Führer's bust in 1935.

Kingsley Wood and Anthony Eden advise Churchill after a Cabinet meeting, only hours before he became prime minister on 10th May 1940.

Lord Salisbury looks down on Chamberlain's wartime cabinet in October 1939.

Back row, left to right: John Anderson, Maurice Hankey, Leslie Hore-Belisha, Winston Churchill, Kingsley Wood, Anthony Eden and Edward Bridges.
Front row: Lord Halifax, John Simon, Neville Chamberlain, Samuel Hoare and Lord Chatfield.

the ultimate criterion. Mission Command was the secret behind Hitler's startling victory over France. It is a crucial principle for effective leadership. The management gurus call it empowerment: leaders trust their subordinates and rely on their initiative and expertise. An important element was that everybody in the German Army was specifically trained to be able to take over the duties of the superiors in the event that they were called upon to take command.

Yet if the German Army's leadership was so efficient in 1939–41, how was it that these victories of the first years of the war were followed by ignominious defeats? The answer lies with the man who had appointed himself Supreme Commander of the Wehrmacht – Adolf Hitler. The fatal flaws of his leadership had already become evident in his Blitzkrieg against France. A key moment in the campaign took place in the Maison Blairon in the French town of Charleville-Mézières in the Ardennes close to the Luxembourg border, where Hitler came on the morning of 24 May 1940. This was the headquarters of General Gerd von Rundstedt, the Commander of Army Group A to the south-west of the encircled Allied forces. All German panzer divisions were under the command of Rundstedt, who was sixty-four years old and a general of the old school. He wanted his panzers to wait for the slower infantry.

The Commander-in-Chief of the Army, General Walther von Brauchitsch, and his Chief of Staff, General Franz Halder, strongly disagreed. They recognised that without continuing pressure the Allied forces would try to escape across the English Channel. On the night of 23 May, von Brauchitsch and Halder transferred command of the panzer divisions from Rundstedt to Army Group B in the north-east. Hitler learned of this change of command only on the following morning when he visited Rundstedt at his headquarters in Charleville-Mézières.

Von Brauchitsch and Halder had made the correct decision, but they had made it without their Führer. Hitler could not accept that the Army High Command had acted on their own initiative, as they were trained to do in accordance with the principles of Mission Command. Now, as victory was all but certain, the Führer was anxious to make clear that it was not his generals who were winning this campaign, but he himself. Since the Army were the only force in Germany powerful enough to depose him, all the kudos for the victory in the West had to be concentrated upon the Führer alone. He therefore immediately rescinded the transfer of command of the panzer divisions and authorised Rundstedt to issue a halt order to his Army Group.

It was this famous halt order that gave the Allies the necessary respite to evacuate 338,226 British, French and Belgian troops. No other decision of the Second World War caused such a storm of protest from German generals as the halt order at Dunkirk. Brauchitsch called several times on Hitler to have the order revoked – to no avail. The Führer gloated over the humiliation for the Army's Commander-in-Chief who, in his own words, felt 'forced to the wall'.

After it had become clear what a serious mistake he had made, Hitler claimed that he had intentionally spared the British to demonstrate that he wanted no war with them. Yet his true motives were very different. Hitler's decision to hold back the panzers had nothing to do with magnanimity towards Britain and indeed little to do with any strategic considerations at all. Its main purpose was to put the Army in its place, as modern historical scholarship has recently shown.[7]

Instead of the Army, Göring's Air Force was given the task of finishing off the encircled Allied troops. Hitler also wanted to give Himmler's SS enough time to move into position to join in the action at Dunkirk. By forcing the Army to share victory with Luftwaffe and SS, Hitler could be certain to receive the main credit for it.

The Luftwaffe failed ignominiously. When Dunkirk was finally captured, the vast proportion of Allied forces had been carried to safety across the English Channel to fight another day. Meanwhile the Führer had won a comparatively futile battle against the Army High Command. This was only the first of many grave errors Hitler made in the war. His striving to expand and protect his power base, even at the expense of military judgement, helped prepare the ground for his ultimate defeat. Hitler's army adjutant, Major Gerhard Engel, would later explain: 'Some of Hitler's decisions had nothing to do with military reasoning. They were only made to demonstrate to the head of the Army that Hitler was in command and nobody else.'[8]

Plain speaking from Churchill

It is hard to conceive how Hitler's new British adversary, Winston Churchill, could have refused to seek peace terms with the Nazis if the entire British Expeditionary Force had been captured at Dunkirk. As it was, Churchill turned the successful rescue of the Allied Army into a morale-boosting triumph in adversity. Being right about Hitler and the Nazis might have got Churchill to Downing Street in May 1940, but in order to stay there he needed to invent an entirely new kind of leadership – one that effectively abolished logic and appealed to the heart rather than to the mind. For the simple fact was that although Churchill had to tell the British people that the war was winnable, he himself did not have the first idea of how that could possibly be achieved. In a series of uplifting speeches he made a number of assertions about how the war might be won, each more improbable than the last.

He was imploring – as only remarkable leaders can, and only in extraordinary times – the public to feel rather than to calculate. If he had been proved wrong, he would have had to face the people's wrath for grievously misleading them. In the first speech he made as prime minister, in the House of Commons on 13 May 1940, Churchill was disarmingly honest when he admitted that he had 'nothing to offer but blood, toil, tears and sweat'. But he went on to offer much more than that when he said: 'You

ask, what is our aim? I can answer in one word: Victory – victory
at all costs, victory in spite of all terror, victory, however long
and hard the road may be; for without victory there is no
survival.'

By the time he spoke publicly again, six days later, the
Germans had broken through the French defences to the north
of the Maginot Line, and further suspension of belief was needed
on behalf of the British people before they could imagine how
they could possibly eventually prevail. Churchill did hold out
hope for the French Army, saying: 'We may look with confidence to the stabilisation of the Front in France, and to the
general engagement of the masses, which will enable the qualities of the French and British soldiers to be matched squarely
against those of their adversaries. For myself, I have invincible
confidence in the French Army and its leaders.'

It did not stay invincible, however, because only ten days
later the British Expeditionary Force was being evacuated from
the beaches of Dunkirk. But by showing indomitable courage
himself, Churchill effectively shamed the British – who had for
the past twenty years been zealous appeasers of Germany, and
who had embraced the Munich agreement as enthusiastically as
they had rejected him – into being heroic. His speeches assumed
that they were actually looking forward to the coming attacks
on the civilian population:

There will be many men, and many women, in this island who
when the ordeal comes upon them, will feel comfort, and even
a pride – that they are sharing the perils of our lads at the front
– soldiers, sailors and airmen, God bless them – and are
drawing away from them at least a part of the onslaught they
have to bear. Is this not the time for all to make the utmost
exertions in their power?

By treating people in this way even before mainland Britain
had fallen foul of attack, Churchill turned an understandably

nervous and fearful people into heroes. Even if not everyone shared his confidence in ultimate victory, they were not about to spread defeatism by voicing their fears. This was a supreme act of leadership on Churchill's part. As he told the House of Commons on 4 June 1940:

We are told that Herr Hitler has a plan for invading the British Isles. This has often been thought of before. When Napoleon lay at Boulogne for a year with his flat-bottomed boats and his Grand Army, he was told by someone 'There are bitter weeds in England.' There are certainly a great many more of them since the British Expeditionary Force returned...Even though large tracts of Europe and many old and famous States have fallen or may fall into the grip of the Gestapo and all the odious apparatus of Nazi rule, we shall not flag or fail. We shall go on to the end, we shall fight in France, we shall fight on the seas and oceans, we shall fight with growing confidence and growing strength in the air, we shall defend our Island, whatever the cost may be, we shall fight on the beaches, we shall fight on the landing grounds, we shall fight in the fields and in the streets, we shall fight in the hills; we shall never surrender.

'Long dark nights of trials and tribulations lie before us,' he warned in an especially bleak radio address. 'Not only great dangers, but many more misfortunes, many shortcomings, many mistakes, many disappointments will surely be our lot. Death and sorrow will be companions of our journey, constancy and valour our only shield. We must be united, we must be undaunted. We must be inflexible.' One man who immediately recognised the strategy behind Churchill's dismal honesty was Joseph Goebbels. 'His slogan of blood, sweat and tears has entrenched him in a position that makes him totally immune from attack,' wrote the Nazi propaganda chief in a magazine article entitled 'Churchill's Tricks'. 'He is like the doctor who prophesies that his patient will die and who, every time his patient's condition worsens, smugly explains that he prophesied it.' By preparing the public for bad news, Churchill denied the Nazis the full propaganda value of their victories. They could not wreck national morale if Britons had already heard the worst from the Prime Minister himself.

In his speech to the House of Commons explaining the evacuation from Dunkirk, Churchill knew that he had to hold out some hope – however slender – to encourage the British to fight on. The factor he chose to emphasise was the possibility, which he privately knew to be remote to the point of being negligible, that the United States might soon enter the struggle. In his peroration, he summoned up the prospect of carrying on the struggle 'until, in God's good time, the New World, with all its power and might, steps forth to the rescue and liberation of the old'. From his own conversations with President Roosevelt he knew that unprovoked direct American military intervention was still a very distant possibility, but to lead is to give hope, however false it might be.

The crucial point was that if the British people were being gulled, all but a tiny minority of them actually wanted to be. As professional confidence tricksters will affirm, in order for a 'sting' to be successful the 'mark' must at least subconsciously want to be taken for a ride. This is what happened to the collective subconscious of the British people in 1940–41; they believed Churchill because they willed themselves to, and because the only alternative – peace with Hitler – was simply too dreadful and dishonourable to contemplate. Yet if one had asked individual Britons rationally whether they truly believed it was possible to drag America into the war, or to blockade the whole European continent into surrender, or to defeat Germany by any of the other means that Churchill seemed to be holding out in that strange yet sublime thirteen-month period, they would have been hard put to explain the rationale behind his belief in ultimate victory.

Grasping plenary powers

Churchill had learned from the Dardanelles disaster of the Great War that it is a mistake, as he put it, 'to carry out a major and cardinal operation from a subordinate position'. He also wrote, 'My one fatal mistake was trying to achieve a great enterprise without having the plenary authority which could so easily have carried it to success.' With these memories, he decided to grasp exactly such authority when he came to power in 1940.

Wars are not won by evacuations, as Churchill said, and neither are they won by morale-boosting speeches alone. One of his first steps was to tackle the cumbersome and inflexible decision-making structure that he had inherited from Chamberlain. Churchill rightly complained that everything was 'settled for the greatest number by the common sense of most after the consultation of all'. Of the Committee of Imperial Defence, which was responsible for strategic plans but not for operations, he said that it represented the 'maximum of study and the minimum of action'.

Churchill's solution was to couple responsibility with the direct power of action. He didn't like purely advisory committees. War, he said, was 'more like one ruffian bashing the other on the snout with a club'.[9] He was equally straightforward when he complained to Harold Macmillan: 'Why, you may take the most gallant sailor, the most intrepid airman and the most audacious soldier, put them together – what do you get? The sum of their fears.' Macmillan recalled this being said 'with sibilant emphasis'.

Churchill had streamlined decision-making successfully as Minister of Munitions and at the Colonial Office during earlier periods in government. He recognised how it allowed the executives not to be smothered by detail and duplication. During the war his considerable organisational skills were brought into play as he sought to reduce overlaps in government and administration. He even had a gift for simplifying administrative language:

the Local Defence Volunteers became the Home Guard, Communal Feeding Centres became British Restaurants, and so on.

At ten people, the War Cabinet was too large, just as it had been at the start of the Great War. One error was that it included the three service ministers, encouraged Cabinet discussions to become too broad, often extending to the making of operational plans. Chamberlain's attempt to solve this had been to form a Military Co-ordination Committee chaired by Lord Chatfield. It was charged with the mission of co-ordinating the efforts of the military services with the policy set out by the War Cabinet. It suffered from being advisory without control of any department, and without the power to give orders. In April 1940 the office was abolished under pressure from Churchill, who was none the less soon complaining that he had 'no power to take or enforce decisions'. When he became Prime Minister he halved the War Cabinet to only five members. 'The days of mere co-ordination were out for good,' one senior figure later wrote. 'We were now going to get direction, leadership, action – with a snap in it!'[10]

Churchill did not stop there. He immediately set about obtaining even greater powers, believing that, as he put it, strategic failure in war was due to 'the total absence of one directing mind and commanding will power'. Running a war by committee was bad enough, but on top of that there was no clear distinction between political and military decision-making. Creating the new office of Minister of Defence, taking the post himself and making the trusted General Ismay his personal liaison with the Chiefs of Staff was a political and administrative master-stroke. The new structure gave Churchill greater authority than any previous prime minister. He had placed himself in the direct line of responsibility for the creation of war plans and their execution, but he had not created an actual or new Ministry of Defence with all its costs and bureaucratic apparatus. As he warned Ismay, 'We must be very careful not to define our powers too precisely.' By keeping them flexible and nebulous, they were in effect far greater than if they had been circumscribed by Whitehall, Westminster or – more powerful than either – by precedent.

Churchill also immediately sought to reduce the number of committees. In particular he amalgamated many of the British military and civil missions to the United States which were burgeoning but whose responsibilities often overlapped. Two weeks after becoming prime minister he sent a memo to his Cabinet Secretary: 'I am sure there are far too many committees of one kind or another which ministers have to attend, and which do not yield a significant result. These should be reduced by suppression or amalgamation.' He despaired at collective decision-making through committees, on which the entire basis of British administration had for so long been centred.

Yet the new powers were not undemocratic; Churchill had not taken on autocratic powers but continued to work through the Cabinet because he knew that ultimately his power would always rest with the House of Commons, which in December 1916 had brought down the sitting wartime premier Herbert Asquith and in May 1940 had repeated the process with Neville Chamberlain. (The historian in Churchill would also have been reminded of Lord Aberdeen's fate during the Crimean War: British premiers who begin wars often do not get to finish them.) 'I am a child of the House of Commons,' Churchill was to tell the United States Congress in December 1941. 'I was brought up in my father's house to believe in democracy. "Trust the people" was his message. . . . In my country, as in yours, public men are proud to be servants of the State and would be ashamed to be its masters.'

In practice, Churchill's streamlining of the system meant that he could push through controversial policies; one of these was the decision to use heavy bombers such as the Lancaster against German towns and cities. Under Chamberlain, bombing had been restricted to dropping leaflets and attacking naval targets. Air raids on land targets were off-limits, not only for fear of German retaliation but also for rather peculiar legal considerations. A Royal Air Force plan to attack military targets in the Black Forest had been rejected by the then Secretary of State for Air, Sir Kingsley Wood, with the words: 'Are you aware that it is private property? Why, you'll be asking me to bomb Essen next!'[11]

Churchill showed no such inhibitions and a few days after his assumption of the premiership he authorised attacks on military and industrial targets in Germany. When three months later, at the height of the Battle of Britain, the first German bombs fell on central London, Churchill bypassed both the Chiefs of Staff and the Secretary of State for Air and ordered Bomber Command directly to fly a reprisal raid on Berlin. Such swift decision-making would have been unthinkable under the structure of the previous government. And it was the right decision. For the next four years, strategic bombing would be the only means by which Britain could take the war to the German fatherland itself.

Other methods of taking control of the British war effort were Churchill's famous minutes, his 'prayers', and his 'Action This Day' tags. He had an astonishingly fertile mind: 'Winston had ten ideas every day,' his Chief of the Imperial General Staff Lord Alanbrooke used to say of him, 'only one of which was good, and he did not know which it was.' Roosevelt made a very similar remark, saying that the Prime Minister had a hundred ideas a day of which six were good (a much larger number if an even lower percentage).

Nothing was too minute a detail to escape Churchill's notice. He laid down the precise number of apes that should occupy the Rock of Gibraltar (twenty-four), tried to find out whether captured First World War trophy weapons could be reconditioned for use, worried about the animals in London Zoo during the bombing, and made sure that beer rations went to the fighting men at the front before those behind the lines. He even tried to discover whether wax might be used to protect the hearing of soldiers during bombardments.[12] Several of these requests, nicknamed 'prayers' because they often began 'Pray inquire...', were also tagged with a red marker demanding 'Action This Day'. On the very day that he became prime minister, 10 May 1940, for example, on top of all the other emergencies created by Hitler's assault in the West, Churchill came up with the idea that ex-Kaiser Wilhelm II be invited to defect to Britain from his exile in Holland. (It turned out to be one of Alanbrooke's nine or Roosevelt's ninety-four bad ideas and was not followed up.)

Sometimes Churchill's hands-on style simply went too far. His private secretary Jock Colville recalled how one night at Chequers:

> I was instructed, as usual, to ring up the duty captain at the Admiralty and find out if there was any news. There was none, and the duty captain promised to telephone immediately if anything of the slightest interest was reported. An hour later I was instructed to enquire again, and an injured duty captain reminded me of the promise he had given. When, at about 2am, I was bidden in spite of all remonstrations to try yet again, the angry officer, aroused from a few hours' sleep, let fly at me the full vocabulary of the quarter deck in times of crisis. Churchill, hearing a flow of speech, assumed that at least an enemy cruiser had been sunk. He seized the receiver from my hand and was subjected to a series of uncomplimentary expletives which clearly fascinated him. After listening for a minute or two he explained that he was only the prime minister and that he was wondering whether there was any naval news.[13]

Churchill wrote: 'Those who are charged with the direction of supreme affairs must sit on the mountain tops of control; they must never descend into the valleys of direct physical and personal action.' Yet, early in his premiership in 1940, he also admonished his staff that: 'An efficient and successful administration manifests itself equally in small as in great matters.' In his first few weeks as prime minister he even gave orders about the size of flag that flew outside the Admiralty. 'Churchill scrutinizes every document that has anything to do with the war and does not disdain to enquire into the most trivial point,' wrote one of his private secretaries. He gave orders about rabbits, how not to let the whisky industry suffer, and even altered the codenames of individual military operations.

Hitler also involved himself with the minutiae of fighting the war, at one stage personally banning horse-racing in Berlin, but there was one decisive difference between Hitler and Churchill: the Führer's orders were almost all issued by his private secretary, Martin Bormann, rather than being signed personally by him. Hitler himself put hardly anything in writing, which enabled him to deny his responsibility should things go wrong, or if they were too infamous to be directly connected with him. 'Never put an order in writing that can be given verbally' was his maxim. This enabled him (and his apologists, though with equal lack of credibility) to deny his responsibility for his crimes, up to and even including the Holocaust itself.

Churchill, on the other hand, had no difficulty about accepting responsibility. Indeed, on 21 April 1944 he told the House of Commons: 'I have no intention of passing my remaining years in explaining or withdrawing anything I have said in the past, still less apologising for it.' The following year he went further, saying: 'If I am accused of this mistake, I can only say with M. Clemenceau on a celebrated occasion: "Perhaps I have made a number of mistakes of which you have not heard."' Churchill had long been used to blame and indeed obloquy, and had developed a rhinocerine hide for criticism by the time the Second World War broke out. Anyone who had returned to active politics after the Gallipoli débâcle needed to be pachydermatous. As he wrote about something else in *My Early Life*, 'Everybody threw the blame on me. I have noticed that they nearly always do. I suppose it is because they think I shall be able to bear it best.'

Of course Churchill did not see why he should bear blame unnecessarily. In contrast to Hitler, he actually preferred things to be put in writing. As his wife Clementine advised General Sir Louis Spears: 'He often does not listen or does not hear if he is thinking of something else. But he will always consider a paper carefully in all its implications. He never forgets anything he sees in writing.' It had to be kept short, though, and entirely to the point. In July 1940 Churchill put out the following minute to the War Cabinet Secretariat and in large part he stuck to it throughout the war: 'Let it be very clearly understood that all directions emanating from me are made in writing, or should be immediately afterwards confirmed in writing, and that I do not accept responsibility for matters relating to the national defence on which I am called to have given decisions unless they are recorded in writing.'[14]

As the senior civil servant Lord Normanbrook recalled, this minute had a profound and immediate effect: 'Hitherto prime ministers wishing to seek information or to offer advice to a colleague had done so by letter – more often than not by correspondence conducted in their name by private secretaries. Now, ministers received direct and personal messages, usually compressed into a single quarto paper and phrased in language showing beyond doubt that they were the actual words of the prime minister himself.'[15] Minutes like this were usually written at the beginning and end of each day.

Churchill was one of the first modern political leaders to recognise the value of statistics and quantitative analysis. He appointed his friend Professor Lindemann to head his statistical office, which comprised about twenty people, including economists, at least one scientist, civil servants, and the usual retinue of clerk-typists to produce the reports. It soon proved invaluable to Churchill, who used data well. 'Do not think of making a case for a particular point of view,' he wrote. 'Let us just have the cold-blooded facts.'

Recognising himself to be an unusual creature, Churchill also wanted to ensure that abnormal people were allowed to thrive in the military and civil services. In a letter to Anthony Eden, the newly created Secretary of State for War, a few weeks after he became prime minister, Churchill wrote: 'We want live wires, and not conventional types.' Some six months later he wrote to Field Marshal Sir John Dill: 'We cannot afford to confine Army appointments to persons who have excited no hostile comment in their careers...This is a time to try men of force and vision and not be exclusively confined to those who are judged thoroughly safe by conventional standards.' As a result, thoroughly unconventional people like the half-mad Orde Wingate, the homosexual Alan Turing and the eccentric academics at Bletchley Park were permitted to make their significant contributions to the war effort. Churchill believed in using talent wherever he could find it, even if that meant looking beyond those who were conventionally qualified. In one letter to Field Marshal Sir John Dill about the brilliant but unconventional tank general, Percy Hobart, Churchill wrote: 'It is not only the good boys who help to win wars. It is the sneaks and stinkers as well.'

The primary example of Churchill inserting the roundest possible peg in the squarest Whitehall hole was the promotion of his friend Lord Beaverbrook to Minister of Aircraft Production in May 1940, knowing that the threat of invasion could only be beaten off through air supremacy. 'The Beaver' was a Canadian press baron who was thought to have made his money by unscrupulous means and who thus had a controversial reputation, but who had been Minister of Information in the Great War and whose ownership of the *Express* newspaper group made him a power in the country.

Churchill was an exponent of what management gurus today call 'MBWA' – management by walking about. He constantly visited factories, gun emplacements, searchlight units, and so on. Soon after becoming prime minister he visited Fighter Command to see for himself what they required. Air Chief

Marshal Sir Hugh Dowding told him he badly needed extra resources – pilots, night-defence capability, but most especially more planes. The major problem, Churchill quickly discovered, was the lack of available fighters. Churchill set about changing this by giving Beaverbrook his total support. He even overrode the objections of the King and others to appoint Beaverbrook a privy counsellor.

Fortunately, Beaverbrook soon proved highly effective. He used heavy-handed, often bullying techniques to get what he wanted and aircraft production soon significantly increased under his aggressive prodding. Resources were taken away from bombers, and he simplified the bureaucratic process to get at least a short-term boost in fighter production. His famous appeal for housewives' pots and pans for melting down did much to raise public awareness and morale, even if little of the metal produced found its way into actual aircraft.

At a meeting on 3 June, Sir Archibald Sinclair, the new Secretary of State for Air, reported that Britain was also dangerously short of pilots. During May fighter production had been critical, but now it was the number of pilots as well as of planes that had become the vital issue. Churchill told Sinclair that during a visit to Hendon he had noticed lots of pilots behind desks. 'Comb out the fluff and the flummery!' he ordered him in the authentic tones of a modern CEO. 'Keep me informed.'

By mid-August Sinclair had found more pilots to add to 'the Few'; he was helped by Churchill, overriding the complaints of the Royal Navy, to give Air Chief Marshal Dowding pilots borrowed from the Fleet Air Arm. The result of Churchill's leadership was that the overall number of fighter pilots rose despite the constant losses. The Germans, on the other hand, did not change a thing. They were very lethargic at the top level of the Luftwaffe; and in August Göring even went off hunting and playing with his train set.

On 15 September Churchill visited the headquarters of Fighter Command 11 Group on what turned out, coincidentally, to be the decisive day of the Battle of Britain. From there he watched the crucial air battle unfold and witnessed the glorious victory of the RAF. The success of that day meant that invasion was effectively no longer possible. On 17 September Hitler decided to postpone 'Operation Sealion' indefinitely, although it was not till 12 October that the invasion was formally called off, ostensibly until the following spring. In July 1941 it was postponed again by Hitler until the spring of 1942, 'by which time the Russian campaign will be completed'. Instead, on 13 February 1942 Admiral Raeder had his final interview on 'Sealion' and got Hitler to agree to a complete 'stand-down'. Yet Churchill recognised that the forging of a national commitment was stronger in the face of a perceived threat, so even after Ultra decrypts had informed him that the genuine danger had passed, he continued to warn of a possible invasion since he realised it was the perfect means to keep the nation focused and united.

If the Germans had invaded, and if the long history of British sovereign independence had come to an end in 1940, it would have happened in Neasden in north London. That was the location of the bunker to which Churchill and other senior government ministers were to move in the event of the Germans capturing central London, and where Churchill would have fought to the end. In his own words: 'If this long island story of ours is to end at last, let it end only when each one of us lies choking in his own blood upon the ground.' As he wrote of the death of the brave President Molara in *Savrola*: 'It often happens that, when men are convinced that they have to die, a desire to bear themselves well and to leave life's stage with dignity conquers all other sensations.'[16] So it might have been with Churchill. Although the Royal Family, Britain's gold reserves and the Royal Navy would have been evacuated to continue the struggle from Ottawa, Churchill was personally resolved to end it all in the nation's capital. (Of course, whether he would have been allowed to in the actual event is another matter, the exigencies of a real post-invasion scenario being impossible to predict, and a live prime minister in Canada being a lot more useful to the cause than a dead one in Neasden.) The Royal Family had a series of stately homes – including Madresfield Court in Worcestershire – to which they were going to be evacuated on their journey north towards embarkation from Scotland, and it is hard to believe that Churchill would not have also been prevailed upon to carry on the fight, especially if so ordered by the King. All such plans were of course kept strictly secret, because the primary purpose of the Government in the summer of 1940 was to counter any sense of defeatism, which had so sapped the will of the Continental Allies to continue the fight.

Defeating defeatism

In the midst of the Dunkirk evacuation in May 1940, Churchill circulated a memorandum to all Cabinet members and senior officials that read: 'In these dark days the prime minister would be grateful if all his colleagues in the Government, as well as high officials, would maintain a high morale in their circles; not minimizing the gravity of events, but showing confidence in our ability and inflexible resolve to continue the war until we have broken the will of the enemy to bring all of Europe under his domination.'

Stamping out defeatism, or worse still the supposed pro-Nazi Fifth Column that was thought to be operating inside Britain, was a central task for Churchill as he tried to lead the nation in 1940. In his post-Dunkirk speech he said that 'Parliament has given us the powers to put down Fifth Column activities with a strong hand, and we shall use these powers, subject to the supervision and the correction of the House, without the slightest hesitation until we are satisfied that this malignancy in our midst has been effectively stamped out.' One of the places this happened was at Ham Common in Richmond, where a secret MI5 base called Latchmere House was used to imprison the top forty suspected enemy spies in 1940–41, who were interrogated using methods expressly banned under the Geneva Convention. Although little is known about this shadowy place – because the secret service files that cover it are even now still kept under lock and key – we do know that it was there that MI5 first broke and then 'turned' those who it believed were working for the Germans, with an almost complete success rate.

The process of countering defeatism elsewhere in the country was carried out with sometimes absurd over-efficiency, with ordinary people being arrested for doing no more than complaining about prices in bread queues. It was even made an offence to discourage people's belief in achieving victory.[17] In 1940 the literary critic Cyril Connolly was arrested in an Oxford hotel by military police because he 'seemed very interested' in the conversation of British officers near by. His Viennese-issued passport and editorship of a literary magazine led to an inquisition by no fewer than eight policemen, and he was only released once he proved that he had attended both Eton and Balliol College, Oxford.[18] One Leicestershire man got a two-year gaol sentence for saying in a pub that he 'couldn't see how we could win the war'. Yet neither really could the Prime Minister, who was even reduced to arguing in 1940 that Germany's subject peoples would rise against her if there was a bad winter.

During the Fall of France in mid-June 1940, Churchill broadcast to the people, saying that: 'We are sure that in the end all will come right.' With Hitler master of the European continent from Warsaw to Brest and from Narvik down to Naples, with Germany's non-aggression pact with Russia still holding, with Italy in the war against Britain, and with the Nazis having swallowed up eleven independent nations in two years, Churchill was rather reduced to the position of Mr Micawber in Charles Dickens's *David Copperfield*, who hoped against hope that 'something will turn up'. On 18 June 1940, in what has become known as the 'Finest Hour' speech, Churchill tried to set out the grounds upon which, as he put it, 'there are good and reasonable hopes of final victory'. But beyond saying that the Dominion prime ministers had endorsed the decision to fight on, and that the French might continue to resist – which they very largely did not – he still did not have any kind of rational recipe for eventual victory, for all the wonderful tone of his language. He argued that in one-to-one fighting in the air individual British pilots were superior to their German counterparts, and that the United States would shortly send immense supplies and munitions; but these were at best reasons why Britain might be able to survive, not explanations as to how an army could be landed on the continent of Europe that would capture Berlin, overthrow Hitler and win the war.

Churchill even held out the possibility that Germany might suddenly and inexplicably collapse simply out of superior British morale, citing what he claimed had happened in 1918: 'During that war we repeatedly asked ourselves the question: How are we going to win? and no one was able ever to answer it with much precision, until at the end, quite suddenly, quite unexpectedly, our terrible foe collapsed before us, and we were so glutted with victory that in our folly we threw it away.' A sudden and unexpected collapse in German morale was simply not a credible war plan. What Churchill knew was that the British Empire could not defeat Germany on its own; it desperately needed allies.

Finding allies

Even before he became prime minister, Churchill had hoped to draw a reluctant America into the war. After a lunch with Churchill on 5 October 1939, Ambassador Joseph Kennedy confided to his diary: 'I just don't trust him. He almost impressed me that he was willing to blow up the American embassy and say it was the Germans, if it would get the United States in.' Churchill understood earlier than anyone else in the wartime Government, especially after the Fall of France, that American help would be vital, and he embarked on a concerted effort of coalition-building even before he became prime minister, and despite the anglophobic American Ambassador. His offers to the United States culminated in a speech at the Mansion House on 20 November 1941, in which he promised that: 'Should the United States become involved in war with Japan, the British declaration will follow within the hour.'

Hitler, by contrast, completely underestimated the importance of alliances. There was a pragmatic side to him, as the Nazi–Soviet Non-Aggression Pact of August 1939 proved, but it was only ever intended as a short-term measure. As he put it in *Mein Kampf*: 'Tactical considerations matter.' When, a decade later, he discussed Germany's need for *Lebensraum* he said: 'That does not mean that I will refuse to walk part of the road together with the Russians, if that will help us…But it will only be in order to return the more swiftly to our true aims.'[19] The idea of staying faithful to the terms of a treaty the moment it was no longer advantageous to him was completely foreign to Hitler's way of thinking. His ideological aim of winning German living space in the East weighed far heavier than the moral or legal considerations of lesser beings.

Just as the Nazis underestimated the importance of alliances, so they had nothing but contempt for international agreements. Treaties were to them, in Göring's typically scatological expression, 'so much lavatory paper'. More often than not, Hitler failed to consult his allies about his next steps. Hitler not only broke his treaty with the Soviet Union, thus opening a war on two fronts; he also failed to inform his other allies, the Italians and the Japanese, of his plans for 'Operation Barbarossa'. He treated Italy with particular disdain, as the junior partner whose concerns and wishes could be readily ignored. As he said of that country: 'Mussolini might be a Roman, but his people are Italians.' Small wonder then that Mussolini decided, in his own words, to 'pay Hitler back in his own coin' when he attacked Greece only three weeks after being warned not to by Hitler at their meeting at the Brenner Pass on 4 October 1940. This possibly had a fateful effect on 'Operation Barbarossa'. As Mussolini's Greek offensive misfired badly, Hitler was forced to occupy Yugoslavia in April 1941 in order to come to Italy's aid. It was another lightning campaign, over in six weeks, but it probably helped to delay the invasion of the Soviet Union. Just how vital those six springtime weeks were became clear when the German Army only just failed to reach Moscow before the onset of the Russian winter.

Hitler also failed to inform his other ally, Japan, in the spring of 1941 about the impending invasion of Russia. Indeed he deliberately misinformed them, saying that 'Russia will not be attacked as long as she maintains a friendly attitude in accordance with the treaty'.[20] Had Hitler consulted with the Japanese before the German invasion, they might have been persuaded to invade Russia simultaneously. In the Russian Civil War, Japanese forces had fought in Siberia, and an attack from the East to coincide with Hitler's attack in the West could have been devastating to Russian morale. As it was, the Japanese High Command decided in September 1941 to postpone any military action against the Soviet Union and then three months later assaulted Pearl Harbor without warning the Germans, causing the United States to enter the war. Hitler's failure in coalition-building thus indirectly brought into being Churchill's strategic dream of a 'Grand Alliance' of the British Empire, the United States and the Soviet Union. Roosevelt's magnificent statesmanship ensured that a counterintuitive 'Germany First' policy was adopted, and Hitler's fate was thereby all but sealed.

Of course, for all of his public life since 1917 Churchill had shared Hitler's contempt for the Communist dictatorship in the Soviet Union. Indeed, even at the time of the publication of *Savrola* two decades before the Revolution, the chief villain was Karl Kreutze, a socialist revolutionary. Churchill had led the call for armed intervention against the Bolsheviks after 1918, and some of the greatest philippics of his career had been directed against the Soviets, in which he called them 'deadly snakes', 'cold, calculating, ruthless, patient', 'nothing lower', and even 'the nameless beast'. Yet none of these past views were allowed to bias Churchill against the opportunity of joining forces with the Soviet Union after Hitler's Blitzkrieg invasion of the USSR.

On 22 June 1941 Churchill broke the news of 'Operation Barbarossa' to the British people with the words: 'At four o'clock this morning Hitler attacked and invaded Russia. All his usual formalities of perfidy were observed with scrupulous technique.' He went on to pronounce the policy that: 'Any man or State who fights on against Nazism will have our aid. Any man or State who marches with Hitler is our foe.' He was thus prepared to subordinate his ideological prejudices to the greater cause. To his private secretary Jock Colville he had even remarked the night before the attack: 'If Hitler invaded Hell [I] would at least make a favourable reference to the Devil.'[21] Churchill was able to compromise: first by making concessions to the Americans, then by making an alliance with his old ideological enemy, Joseph Stalin. This willingness to compromise for the greater good is a characteristic of inspired leadership.

Speaking of his wooing of the Americans, Churchill once told Colville: 'No lover ever studied every whim of his mistress as I did those of President Roosevelt.' In 1941, when a new edition of his 1937 book *Great Contemporaries* was printed, Churchill included a laudatory article he had written about FDR in 1934, saying of his presidency: 'It is certain that Franklin Roosevelt will rank among the greatest of men who have occupied that proud position. His generous sympathy for the underdog, his intense desire for a nearer approach to social justice, place him high among the great philanthropists. His composure combined with activity in time of crisis class him with famous men of action.'[22] Later that year he described Roosevelt to the Canadian Parliament at Ottawa as: 'That great man whom destiny has marked for this climax of human fortune.'

This desperate desire to flatter and charm the Americans, and especially their leader, was noted by Roosevelt's minister Harold Ickes, who remarked that Churchill would have fêted the President's friend and personal representative Harry Hopkins even if he had been carrying the bubonic plague.[23] Yet Churchill could also make the subtlest of threats. Consider the wording of the message he sent to Roosevelt via the American Embassy in London on 15 June 1940, begging for American intervention before France capitulated:

Although the present government and I personally would never fail to send the fleet across the Atlantic if resistance was beaten down here, a point may be reached in the struggle where the present ministers no longer have control of affairs and when very easy terms could be obtained for the British islands by becoming a vassal state of the Hitler empire. A pro-German government would certainly be called into being to make peace and might present to a shattered or a starving nation an almost irresistible case for an entire submission to the Nazi will. The fate of the British fleet...would be decisive on the future of the United States because if it were joined to the fleets of Japan, France and Italy and the great resources of German industry, overwhelming sea power would be in Hitler's hands. He might, of course, use it with a merciful moderation. On the other hand he might not. This revolution in sea power might happen very quickly and certainly long before the United States would be able to prepare against it. If we go down you may have a United States of Europe under the Nazi command far more numerous, far stronger, far better armed than the new [world's].[24]

For all that politicians claim not to deal in hypothetical questions, in fact any conscientious ones must deal with alternative future possibilities all the time, and Roosevelt was no exception. 'After reading this,' his close adviser Henry Morgenthau minuted the President, 'unless we do something to give the English additional destroyers, it seems to me it is absolutely hopeless to expect them to keep going.' The result was the deal by which the United States gave Britain fifty destroyers in return for 99-year leases on various military bases in the western hemisphere. Churchill's methods were therefore not always as soft and soapy towards the Americans as his detractors tend to depict.

As the war progressed, Churchill had to accept that overall military strategy was increasingly dominated by his partners, the Americans and the Russians, who were contributing far more in terms of men, money and amounts of war matériel than Britain. For a long time in 1942 and 1943 Churchill nurtured the adventurous idea of 'rolling up Europe from the South-East' through the river valleys of the Balkans. While the Chief of the Imperial General Staff, Field Marshal Lord Alanbrooke, regarded such a venture as little more than what he called a 'pipe-dream', Churchill thought it was a realistic – and indeed preferable – alternative to 'Operation Overlord', the planned cross-Channel liberation of France. The Americans shared Alanbrooke's assessment, and Churchill finally conceded to this view and abandoned the idea. There was constant give and take between Churchill and the Chiefs of Staff, of whom he said in January 1944, 'They may say that I lead them up the garden path, but at every turn of the path they have found delectable fruit and wholesome vegetables.'

As the war progressed, Churchill found that his role was increasingly that of counselling rather than leading, let alone of controlling, Washington and Moscow. It is a position to which Hitler could never have adapted; whereas Churchill was an occasional tyro, Hitler could only ever be a full-time tyrant. 'What a small nation we are,' Churchill observed of the Teheran Conference with Roosevelt and Stalin in November–December 1943. 'There I sat with the great Russian bear on one side ... and on the other side the great American buffalo, and between the two sat the poor little English donkey.' None the less, the donkey developed an effective way to maintain its influence on the conduct of the war. It was the same method that Churchill's staff officers used against him when they wished to delay one of his favoured schemes or to dissuade him from a plan they judged impracticable – they agreed in principle at the outset and then tried to drown the idea in a sea of reasoned objection.

After the war Dwight Eisenhower, the former Supreme Allied Commander, said of Churchill:

> I had a very hard time withstanding his arguments. More than once he forced me to re-examine my own premises, to convince myself again that I was right – or accept his solution. Yet if the decision went against him, he accepted it with good grace, and did everything in his power to support it with proper action. Leadership by persuasion and the wholehearted acceptance of a contrary decision are both fundamentals of democracy.

Churchill would use every possible dialectical and emotional weapon to ensure that decisions did not go against him. According to the Director of Naval Intelligence Admiral Godfrey, these included 'persuasion, real or simulated anger, mockery, vituperation, tantrums, ridicule, derision, abuse and tears'. It took a tough man, such as Field Marshal Lord Alanbrooke undoubtedly was, to put up with these methods and often to overcome them.

Triumph of the will

Churchill recognised that many of Hitler's victories had come from the superior power of the dictator's will, and resolved to show that his own willpower was just as strong. In his broadcast of 14 July 1940, he said:

I can easily understand how sympathetic onlookers across the Atlantic, or anxious friends in the yet unravished countries of Europe, who cannot measure our resources or our resolve, may have feared for our survival when they saw so many states and kingdoms torn to pieces in a few weeks or even days by the monstrous force of the Nazi war machine. But Hitler has not yet been withstood by a great nation with a will power the force of his own.

Churchill knew that part of the leader's task is to convince the people he leads that he has the necessary strength of will to fashion events, and not be merely swept along by them. His habit of sticking out his jutting jaw, almost in a caricature of a bulldog, emphasised this. He also somehow managed to turn his walking stick, which in any other pensioner might look like a sign of infirmity, into a potent symbol of defiance, as his statue by Ivor Roberts-Jones in London's Parliament Square eloquently demonstrates. He used his body language to convey the same message as his spoken language.

Although Churchill regularly and deliberately overestimated the chances of victory during 1940 and the first half of 1941, he never underestimated the dangers and difficulties. It made Churchill trusted as he took this stance to heights never seen before in politics. When the danger was real, as during the Battle of Britain in the late summer of 1940, the Prime Minister seemed almost to relish the long list of setbacks that had overcome Britain since he had taken office. It took an extraordinary leader in extraordinary circumstances to make an actual virtue out of such a series of catastrophes. In a speech he gave on 20 August 1940, he reported that:

Rather more than a quarter of a year has passed since the new Government came into power in this country. What a cataract of disaster has poured out upon us since then! The trustful Dutch overwhelmed; their beloved and respected sovereign driven into exile; the peaceful city of Rotterdam the scene of a massacre as hideous and brutal as anything in the Thirty Years' War; Belgium invaded and beaten down; our own fine Expeditionary Force, which King Leopold called to his rescue, cut off and almost captured, escaping as it seemed almost by a miracle and with the loss of all its equipment; our ally, France, out; Italy in against us; all France in the power of the enemy, all its arsenals and vast masses of military material converted or convertible to the enemy's use; a puppet Government set up at Vichy which may at any moment be forced to become our foe; the Western seaboard of Europe from the North Cape to the Spanish frontier in German hands; all the ports, all the airfields on this immense front employed against us as springboards of invasion. Moreover, the German air power, numerically so far outstripping ours, has been brought so close to our islands that what we used to dread greatly has come to pass and the hostile bombers not only reach our shores in a few minutes and from several directions, but can be escorted by their fighting aircraft.

It was an appalling litany, but Churchill somehow managed to convert the very ghastliness of the situation into a strange kind of virtue. The allegation that Germany had won her victories by surprise, lies and trickery regularly resurfaced during his speeches, but now, he seemed to be arguing, the hitherto-trusting British were up to their own dastardly methods, and sheer moral superiority would see them through to victory. Again, this might seem utterly illogical in the context of modern warfare, but Churchill understood that it was moral courage that Britons needed in 1940 as much as sheer physical courage, arms and ammunition, and all his leadership skills were set to the task of providing it. He might not have been the right man to take Britain into the peace in 1945 or to lead her again in the fifties, but his leadership techniques were instrumental in persuading the British to persevere in the crucial thirteen months between the Fall of France and Hitler's invasion of Russia. Much of this was done by sheer willpower, and there is a certain irony in Leni Riefenstahl's choice of title for her film about Hitler, *Triumph of the Will*, since in the end it was Churchill's will that triumphed.

The use of creative tension: Churchill and Alanbrooke

'On no account must the contents of this book be published,' wrote Field Marshal Lord Alanbrooke on the opening page of his wartime diary, and it is easy to understand why.[25] As the 'master of strategy', the man Churchill had implored to become Britain's senior soldier, Alanbrooke was the repository of all the most important wartime secrets. Even when they were published in 1957 as part of a biography of Alanbrooke, the diary entries were heavily censored both on grounds of national security and for fear of antagonising powerful figures such as the then American President Dwight Eisenhower and the past and serving prime ministers Winston Churchill, Anthony Eden and Harold Macmillan.

In 2001 they were published unexpurgated for the first time, and although it had long been no secret that Alanbrooke did not always see eye-to-eye with Churchill on strategic matters, it was only then apparent that for much of the war he could hardly bear working with the Prime Minister. (Churchill, on the other hand, seems to have harboured no reciprocal ill-will towards Alanbrooke.)

Alanbrooke's influence on global strategy can hardly be overestimated. It was he, more even than Churchill or the War Cabinet, who set out the stages by which Nazi Germany was going to be defeated. It was he who laid down the crucial sequence of North Africa, Italy and Normandy, as the prescribed path to Berlin. Once thought of as a typically strong, humourless, Ulster-born 'brass hat', it became clear that Alanbrooke was also a passionate man given to bouts of depression and elation, and also of fury against many of those with whom he had to work, especially Generals Marshall, Eisenhower and Patton, and much of the British political and military establishment.

Alanbrooke's painstaking approach often clashed with the more swashbuckling approach that came naturally to Churchill. It was the dichotomy between the chess player and the poker player. Yet Churchill never once overruled his Chiefs of Staff, however much he might have disagreed with them at times. The shadow of the Great War disaster at Gallipoli still hung over him, and he knew better than to trust his impulsive genius more than Alanbrooke's logical arguments. In his turn, Alanbrooke considered it his duty to prevent Churchill from getting Britain into another Gallipoli, a task in which he succeeded when quashing Churchill's plans for attacking in the Balkans in 1943 and Sumatra in 1944.

Although the minutes of the Chiefs of Staff Committee in the Public Records Office give the bare, factual outlines of what was discussed and agreed in the meetings, Alanbrooke's diaries flesh out the story and record the often volcanic rows that developed between the key players. Far from being the impassive, Olympian figures of wartime propaganda, Churchill and the British High Command were at times despairing of what to do next, and at bitter loggerheads over the way the war should be fought.

Where Churchill was romantic, boisterous and inspirational, the Chief of the Imperial General Staff was cautious, pessimistic, adamant and sober. Both men were combative, wilful, driven, and anxious to prevail. The personal tension between them eventually worked in Britain's favour, ensuring that grand strategy combined a mixture of Churchill's genius and Alanbrooke's professionalism. It was a pained, often exasperated working relationship that none the less helped to win the Second World War, even if it collapsed afterwards.

'Brookie wants to have it both ways,' commented

Clementine Churchill when his biography was published in 1957, after he had written a fulsome – if in the circumstances somewhat hypocritical – dedication in the copy that he sent Churchill. As Montgomery told the book's author, the historian Sir Arthur Bryant, Churchill was 'very angry indeed' at this, the first crack in the edifice of his wartime reputation. He would have been apoplectic if he had read what Alanbrooke and Bryant had already excised from the diaries.

Yet it must be recalled that Alanbrooke was often generous to Churchill in his journal and he regularly pointed out that it had been written at times of tremendous stress, often late at night, and as a way of letting off steam and thus preventing his irritation with his colleagues becoming apparent to their faces. The diaries therefore probably saved as many rows as they documented. In the major strategic arguments of the war, and especially in delaying the Second Front until June 1944 when the Allies were properly ready, Alanbrooke was proved right, and it was very fortunate that an admirable 'no man' was there instead of any weaker figure.

What saved Churchill from such potentially disastrous military blunders was that he respected people who stood up to him and did not mince their words. Indeed, it is to his great credit that he appointed Alanbrooke precisely because he knew he would stand up to him, something far removed from the standard practice in today's politics. As the American General George Patton once said: 'When everyone agrees, someone is not thinking.' Even the best leaders fail when they don't allow others to disagree with them; it was not a mistake that Churchill made.

Alanbrooke's diaries were a psychological safety-valve for a soldier who laboured under as great a weight of political and military pressure as any in history. As he snapped yet another pencil in half with the words 'Prime Minister, I flatly disagree', he was doing his duty better than any other Allied general on active service. Part of Churchill's greatness lay in the fact that he appointed Alanbrooke, and afterwards, however grudgingly, accepted his advice.

Part of his implicit self-belief stemmed from the fact that in one of his first major clashes with the Chiefs of Staff, Churchill's boldness had been proved correct. It was a very brave decision to reinforce the Middle East in July 1940, even while the Battle of Britain was being fought, involving sending nearly half of the available tanks around the Cape of Good Hope. Churchill's biographer Roy Jenkins believes that without this signal victory over the Chiefs, 'Egypt might not have been held in 1941/early 1942, and the Western Desert could not have been the scene of Britain's first decisive land victory at the end of the latter year.'[26] This led Churchill, not unnaturally, to take a more belligerent stance towards the Chiefs of Staff than he might otherwise have done.

As a result, Churchill was occasionally allowed to prevail over the Chiefs' more cautious and wiser counsel. As the military historian John Keegan has written:

Some of his initiatives resulted in actual disaster, such as his insistence, against American advice, in invading the Greek Dodecanese Islands in 1943. He also committed the cardinal military mistake of reinforcing failure, as by his decision to land the 18th Division in Singapore in 1942. It disembarked into Japanese captivity.[27]

Adopting his own staff's tactics of delay and veiled obstruction, Churchill succeeded in postponing 'Operation Overlord' until 1944, even though Stalin had been demanding a second front in the West ever since 1942, and Roosevelt aimed to launch the invasion in 1943. Fearing the disastrous consequences of a failed invasion, Churchill insisted that the Germans had to be weakened sufficiently before a cross-Channel operation should be attempted. He cunningly drew the Americans into diversionary campaigns in the Middle East and

Italy, and thus prevented the premature launch of 'Overlord'. In retrospect, Churchill was absolutely right. It is more than doubtful that an invasion in 1943 could have succeeded, and the delay of 'Overlord' was arguably – after stiffening Britain's resolve in 1940–41 – Churchill's most important single contribution to the Allied victory.

Hitler on Churchill

'It's a queer business, how England slipped into this war,' Hitler told his guests at the Berghof on the evening of 18 October 1941. 'The man who managed it was Churchill, that puppet of the Jewry that pulls the strings.'[28] Not surprisingly, Churchill cropped up in Hitler's table talk almost as much as Hitler did in Churchill's speeches in the House of Commons, with quite as much bile but not a particle of the wit. 'I never met an Englishman who didn't speak of Churchill with disapproval,' Hitler told his henchmen on the evening of 7 January 1942. 'Never one who didn't say he was off his head.' He went on to claim that Churchill was in the pay of America, and that he 'is a bounder of a journalist'. As a result, the Führer believed, 'The opposition to Churchill is in the process of gaining strength in England. His long absence [in the United States] has brought it on him.' He then predicted that Britain might quit the war before the end. Five days later, on the evening of 12 January 1942, he returned to the subject, saying: 'Churchill is a man with an out-of-date political idea – that of the European balance of power. It no longer belongs to the sphere of realities. And yet it's because of this superstition that Churchill stirred England up to the war. When Singapore falls, Churchill will fall too; I'm convinced of it. The policy represented by Churchill is to nobody's interest, in short, but that of the Jews.'

Before the month was out, Hitler was considering how 'England can be viable only if she links herself to the Continent.

Lieutenant-General Erich von Manstein, architect of the sickle-cut manoeuvre that led to the fall of France in 1940.

General Walther von Brauschitsch, Hitler and General Franz Halder operating Mission Command fitfully in that campaign.

Air Chief Marshal Sir Hugh Dowding of Fighter Command – victor of the Battle of Britain.

Bob Boothby was Churchill's close friend and confidant until he got involved in the sleaze story known as the Czech gold affair in 1941.

Field Marshal Sir Alan Brooke and General Sir Bernard Montgomery with Churchill in France in 1944.

Churchill was the only British prime minister who wore military uniforms, at the Teheran conference he looked more like Stalin than Roosevelt.

Hitler was merely
defenestrated in the
Bomb Plot of 20th
July 1944.

Bruno Gesche, the alcoholic commander of Hitler's SS Bodyguard,
twice let off pistols when drunk, but kept his job.

Some books have claimed that the Führer was gay.

„Was wir einmal haben, das halten wir fest."
Adolf Hitler
am 8. November 1942 in München

A photo forged and then distributed as a postcard by the British Political Warfare Executive. The caption quoted one of Hitler's speeches: 'What we have we hold.'

Hitler wearing the
Iron Cross 1st
class, swastika
armband and
peaked hat – his
only insignia of
rank.

Churchill with a few favoured props:
homburg hat, striped waistcoat,
polka-dotted bow-tie and flamboyantly arranged handkerchief. 'Never
forget your trademark' he once told a
fellow MP.

She must be able to defend her imperial interests within the framework of a continental organisation.' The ideal time for that to happen would be once the Eighth Army had recaptured Benghazi, which they had done on Christmas Eve and which Hitler thought would re-establish British military prestige and was therefore the obvious 'psychological moment to put an end to the war'. The major problem was still Churchill, who 'had Russia at the back of his mind. Hitler didn't see that, if Russia were to triumph over Germany, Europe would at once come under the hegemony of a Great Power.'[29]

This concentration on his opponent was amounting to something of an obsession because, only two days later, at noon on 2 February, Hitler was back on the subject, opining that 'Churchill is like an animal at bay. He must be seeing snares everywhere. Even if Parliament gives him increased powers, his reasons for being mistrustful still exist. He's in the same situation as Robespierre on the eve of his fall. Nothing but praise was addressed to the virtuous citizen, when suddenly the situation was reversed. Churchill has no more supporters.' Four days later the Führer predicted that: 'A day will come, during a [Commons] secret session, when Churchill will be accused of betraying the interests of the Empire...already several of his opponents are letting slip various disobliging remarks.' He then essayed a rather heavy gag: 'The English will have got nothing out of this affair but a bitter lesson and a black eye. If in future they make less whisky, that won't do any harm to anybody – beginning with themselves. Let's not forget, after all, that they owe all that's happening to them to one man, Churchill.'

Singapore fell on 15 February 1942, which brought Hitler to a new pitch of loathing, especially once it became clear that Churchill would not be ousted because of it. At dinner with Rommel three nights later, Hitler said that 'Churchill is the very type of corrupt journalist. There's not a worse prostitute in politics. He himself has written that it's unimaginable what can be done in war with the help of lies. He's an utterly amoral, repulsive creature. I'm convinced that he has a place of refuge ready beyond the Atlantic. He obviously won't seek sanctuary in Canada. In Canada he'd be beaten up. He'll go to his friends the Yankees.' The next evening, with Speer and Field Marshal Erhard Milch as his guests, Hitler discussed the terrible Russian winter that had descended on the German armies in the East: 'I've always detested snow; Bormann, you know, I've always hated it. Now I know why. It was a presentiment.'

Churchill felt that Hitler hardly needed a presentiment to know about the likelihood of it snowing heavily in Russia in winter. In a broadcast on 10 May 1942 he made the following sally:

> Then Hitler made his second great blunder. He forgot about the winter. There is a winter, you know, in Russia. For a good many months the temperature is apt to fall very low. There is snow, there is frost, and all that. Hitler forgot about the Russian winter. He must have been very loosely educated. We all heard about it at school; but he forgot it. I have never made such a bad mistake as that.

Four days after Hitler's attack on Russia, Churchill described him in a broadcast as 'A monster of wickedness, insatiable in his lust for blood and plunder'.

By the end of March 1942, with the British still not having overthrown Churchill, Hitler was starting to worry that Stafford Cripps might replace him. This led to an astonishing outburst from the Führer: 'I prefer the undisciplined swine who is drunk eight hours of every twenty-four, to the puritan. A man who spends extravagantly, an elderly man who drinks and smokes without moderation, is obviously less to be feared than the drawing-room Bolshevik who leads the life of an ascetic. From Churchill one may finally expect that in a moment of lucidity – it's not impossible – he'll realise that the Empire's going inescapably to its ruin, if the war lasts another two or three years.' What a tribute to Stafford Cripps that Adolf Hitler hated and feared him even more than Winston Churchill, and how self-deluding of Hitler to believe that Churchill would have ever been prepared to make peace with Germany after all that had taken place, even in order to save the Empire.

By 27 June 1942 Hitler had come up with a truly extraordinary plan to discover British intentions. In the course of a rant about the length of time Churchill and Roosevelt had been negotiating, from which he concluded that they had probably fallen out with one another, the Führer said: 'By far the most interesting problem of the moment is, what is Britain going to do now?' He believed that the job of finding the answer belonged to Germany's Foreign Office based on the Wilhelmstrasse, adding: 'The best way of accomplishing it would be by means of a little flirtation with Churchill's daughter. But our foreign office, and particularly its gentlemanly diplomats, consider such methods beneath their dignity, and they are not prepared to make this agreeable sacrifice, even though success might well save the lives of numberless German officers and men!'[30]

Quite how, in the middle of the Second World War, even the most 'gentlemanly' of German diplomats could have infiltrated the Auxiliary Territorial Service and achieved the seduction of the youngest of Churchill's three daughters – since Sarah and Diana were married, he presumably meant the nineteen-year-old Mary – was not explained. Hitler's propensity to micromanage campaigns clearly did not extend itself to those of the amorous type. The Führer was also exhibiting a bachelor's touching assumption that a father passes on the details of the higher conduct of the war to his daughter. (I am assured by Lady Soames that to her certain knowledge no such 'honey-trap' operation was mounted against her.)

By 1 July 1942 Hitler was still holding out hopes that Churchill would be overthrown in an internal coup, telling his guests that evening: 'For Churchill and his supporters the loss of Egypt must inevitably give rise to fears of a considerable strengthening of the popular opposition. One must not lose sight of the fact that there are already twenty-one members of parliament who openly oppose Churchill.' His accuracy was demonstrated when the very next day, in a motion of censure in the House of Commons, as Rommel pushed the Eighth Army back to El Alamein, Churchill's Government won by 475 votes to 25. 'I have never made any predictions,' the Prime Minister told the Commons, 'except things like saying Singapore would hold out. What a fool and knave I should have been to say it would fall!'

The next time that Hitler mentioned Churchill was a week later, on 9 July, when he made the fair point that the Prime Minister was wrong 'to portray his opponent in the manner in which Churchill has portrayed Rommel. The mere name suddenly begins to acquire a value equal to that of several divisions. Imagine what would happen if we went on lauding [the Red Army General] Timoshenko to the skies; in the end our soldiers would come to regard him as a superman.' In retrospect, it is hard to disagree with Hitler that the mythologising of Rommel as 'the Desert Fox' was a huge propaganda error by the Allies.

During Churchill's visit to Stalin in August 1942, Hitler again attempted to peer into the mind of his antagonist: 'I think Churchill was expecting some important development and went to Moscow hoping to return with the prestige of a great feat accomplished. They had had some great project in view, I am convinced: otherwise, why should they have sent the Mediterranean fleet to sea?' Of course it is part of the duty of a leader to try to understand what the opposition is thinking, but Hitler started out under such negative prejudices and absurd misapprehensions about Churchill – that he was drunken, near senile, and acting 'on the orders of his Jewish paymasters' – that he had no real chance of doing so. 'Churchill, the raddled old whore of journalism,' he ranted on 29 August 1942, 'is an unprincipled swine. A perusal of his memoirs proves it; in them he strips himself naked before the public. God help a nation that accepts the leadership of a Thing like that!'[31]

Churchill on Hitler

Churchill's strictures on Hitler were, as one might expect from such a master of parliamentary scorn, far less base, and they exhibited an understanding of Hitler's character that was entirely unreciprocated. He had made several positive references to Hitler in his journalism when the Nazis looked like a bulwark against German Communism, culminating in his remark in 1935 that: 'Those who have met Herr Hitler face to face in public business or on social terms have found a highly competent, cool, well-informed functionary with an agreeable manner, a disarming smile, and few have been unaffected by a subtle personal magnetism.' (Churchill had the moral courage to keep this sentence in the 1941 reprint of *Great Contemporaries*.) He also wrote of Hitler in that work: 'He it was who exorcised the spirit of despair from the German mind by substituting the not less baleful but far less morbid spirit of revenge.' Four decades earlier in *Savrola*, Churchill had written of the loathsome Iago-like private secretary Miguel who hailed from 'the infernal regions': 'He was small, dark, and very ugly, with a face wrinkled with age and an indoor life. Its pallor showed all the more by contrast with his hair and short moustache, both of which were of that purple blackness to which Nature is unable to attain.'[32]

It was in the early to mid-thirties that Churchill appreciated – long before anyone else of substance in British politics – that Hitler might develop into a greater threat even than the Communists. By June 1939 he was asking:

Is he going to try to blow up the world or not? The world is a very heavy thing to blow up! An extraordinary man at the pinnacle of power may create a great explosion, and yet the civilised world may remain unshaken. The enormous fragments and splinters of the explosion may clatter down upon his own head and destroy him ... but the world will go on.

Just before the outbreak of war, on 20 August 1939, Churchill was painting with his teacher Paul Maze, and as he worked at his easel he now and again made statements about the relative sizes and strengths of the German and French Armies. 'They are strong, I tell you, they are strong,' he said, before his jaw clenched, showing Maze the iron determination of his will. 'Ah, with it all, we shall have him.'[33]

Churchill had much practice of trying to put himself in the position of his enemy in order to divine his intentions, not least in the war games played out at the Admiralty. He had even been present as a guest of Kaiser Wilhelm II at the German Army's manoeuvres before the Great War. So, at a meeting at Chequers with General Sir Andrew Thorne on 30 June 1940 to discuss a possible German invasion of Britain, Churchill tried to put himself in the Führer's place, saying that he was 'inclined to think that Hitler's plans have had to be changed: H. cannot have foreseen the collapse of France and must have planned his strategy of invasion on the assumption that the French armies would be holding out on the Somme, or at least on the Seine, and that the B.E.F. would either be assisting them or else would have been wiped out.' Churchill therefore did not subscribe to the theory that Hitler was a master strategist who had drawn up plans for the invasion of Britain after knocking out France in a six-week campaign.

He was right: Hitler had given no serious thought to an invasion of the British Isles, and only ordered the OKW planning staff to draw up detailed proposals for 'Sealion' in September, by which time it was too late to put into operation. General Thorne came away from the Chequers meeting with an interestingly counterintuitive view, telling Colville: 'Winston was more vital to this country than Hitler to Germany, because the former was unique and irreplaceable and the latter had established a school of leaders.' To which Colville made 'the obvious comment' that: 'Hitler may be a self-educated corporal and Winston may be an established student of tactics; but ultimately Germany is organised as a war machine and England has only just realised the meaning of modern warfare.'[34]

Churchill enjoyed personifying the struggle at every opportunity, calling Hitler 'That Man' and at one point saying of one of the Führer's peace offers: 'I do not propose to say anything in reply to Herr Hitler's speech, not being on speaking terms with him.' A key element in his tactics was the utter demonisation of Adolf Hitler, who – unlike Rommel – was permitted no redeeming features. 'By all kinds of sly and savage means he is plotting and working to quench for ever the fountain of characteristic French culture and of French inspiration to the world,' Churchill said of Hitler in a broadcast to the people of France on 21 October 1940. 'Never will I believe that the soul of France is dead.'

Churchill enjoyed using powerful imagery in depicting Hitler, as in his speech in the House of Commons on 9 April 1941, after a coup had taken place in Yugoslavia toppling the pro-Axis government: 'A boa constrictor, who had already covered his prey with his foul saliva and then had it suddenly wrested from his coils, would be in an amicable mood compared to Hitler.' Churchill concentrated on the person of Hitler when he sought to visualise the enemy for himself and others; it was an image that never failed to draw forth Churchill's eloquent and bottomless ire.

At Chequers on 2 May 1941, when the war news was terrible and Colville recorded the Prime Minister as being 'in worse gloom than I have ever seen him', Churchill sketched out for Averell Harriman, General Hastings 'Pug' Ismay and his private secretary Colville a world 'in which Hitler dominated all Europe, Asia and Africa'. In this *ad hominem* mood about his enemy he went on to envision a Middle East in which Suez was lost and 'Hitler's robot new order' ruled. 'With Hitler in control of Iraq oil and Ukrainian wheat, not all the staunchness of [the British population] will shorten the ordeal.' Each time when he might have justifiably used the words 'Nazis', 'Reich' or

'Germans' in this gloomy rodomontade, Churchill concentrated on the person of Adolf Hitler. (Of course he might well have been playing up this nightmarish future, in order to impress upon Roosevelt's envoy Harriman the need for immediate and generous aid.)

The next day, in a message he broadcast to the Polish people, Churchill again spoke of Hitler and the way that 'Every week his firing-parties are busy in a dozen lands. Monday he shoots Dutchmen; Tuesday, Norwegians; Wednesday, French or Belgians stand against the wall; Thursday it is the Czechs who must suffer; and now there are the Serbs and the Greeks to fill his repulsive bill of executions. But always, all the days, there are the Poles.'

The night before Hitler invaded Russia, Churchill – who knew it was going to happen from intelligence decrypts and had warned the Russians, but been ignored – was teased by Jock Colville as they walked on the lawn at Chequers after dinner. Colville jibed that his proposed support for the USSR was a complete *volte face* for such an arch anti-Communist. Churchill replied that 'he had only one single purpose – the destruction of Hitler – and his life was much simplified thereby'. It certainly was; whereas Hitler was fighting for a New Europe free of Jews, with *Lebensraum* in the East and German domination of the Slav peoples in perpetuity, Churchill could – at least until just before the end of the war – concentrate on the single task of extinguishing him.

Of course this did carry with it the dangers of occasional gross oversimplifications or worse, as when he told the House of Commons on 2 August 1944: 'The Russian armies now stand before the gates of Warsaw. They bring the liberation of Poland in their hands. They offer freedom, sovereignty, and independence to the Poles.' The Red Army was indeed standing outside the gates of Warsaw, but was cynically waiting for the uprising inside the city to be crushed by the Wehrmacht before moving in; once they did, they offered Poland neither freedom nor sovereignty, much less independence. Churchill's single-mindedness about the destruction of Hitler allowed him to make compromises even over the issue for which Britain ostensibly went to war in the first place.

Just because Churchill despised Hitler personally and rhetorically, it did not mean that he underestimated him politically. Staying in a villa at the Mamounia Hotel in Marrakech on 5 January 1944, he took a vote at dinner over whether Hitler would still be in power in Germany on 3 September that year, the fifth anniversary of the outbreak of the war. Seven people around the table, including Churchill's doctor Lord Moran, and the Czech leader Eduard Beneš – voted no. Four voted yes, including Lord Beaverbrook, Colville and the Prime Minister himself.

When the news came through of Hitler's death, Churchill made precisely the comment that one would expect from a man who admired personal courage above all the other virtues. In the middle of dinner on Tuesday, 1 May 1945, Colville brought in a copy of the announcement that was being broadcast by German radio, stating that 'Hitler had been killed today at his post at the Reich Chancellery at Berlin...fighting with his last breath against Bolshevism'. Churchill's comment was: 'Well, I must say I think he was perfectly right to die like that,' to which Beaverbrook replied that it was just Nazi propaganda and he obviously had not.[35] Although Beaverbrook was correct, it showed Churchill's great generosity of spirit to accord his enemy the benefit of the doubt in such a way at such a time. (It turned out that the Nazis had withheld the announcement so that it might coincide with May Day, an important date in the German calendar.)

Seven years later in May 1952, and back at Chequers as prime minister, Churchill was quizzed by Montgomery as they walked along the monument hill above the house, making their way among the picnickers. How did the Prime Minister define a great man, asked the Field Marshal (who was probably fishing for a compliment): 'Was Hitler great?' 'No,' answered Churchill, 'he made too many mistakes.' They went on to discuss who could be classed as great, with Churchill fully accepting Jesus Christ's credentials because, among other reasons, 'the Sermon on the Mount was the last word in ethics'. In Churchill's view, therefore, it was Hitler's errors rather than his innate evil that disqualified him from the accolade of greatness. He had, after all, included Hitler among his *Great Contemporaries* in 1937, but that was before Hitler started making those mistakes for which Churchill came to despise him. Churchill too had made errors, but like a great leader – and unlike Hitler – he had learned from them.

Using secret intelligence

Churchill had certainly learned from the failure of the Norwegian campaign. One of the first things he did as prime minister was to ensure that he was kept personally informed of all the latest and most important intelligence. Not content with reading summaries and evaluations, he wished to examine personally the raw decrypts of the most important messages. Almost every day of the war, 'C', the head of the Secret Intelligence Service, sent over to Number Ten a buff-coloured box containing a selection of the most relevant items. This Ultra data derived from the success of the Poles in capturing an Enigma cipher machine and the staff of Bletchley Park in cracking the German military code.

A good illustration of Churchill's ability to keep his mind open and to try unconventional approaches can be found in his love of special operations. Nothing was too outlandish for the Prime Minister to consider in the war against Nazism. Churchill always had a special penchant for what he called 'funny' operations; he had a lifetime's fascination with spooks and codes, spying and secrecy. The appeal of unorthodox warfare chimed in well with his general wartime strategic concept for Britain: that a direct, full-scale, continental military engagement would cost more in terms of lives and resources than taking the more indirect route.

That had been the rationale behind the Gallipoli adventure in the First World War, and was to be the same behind the Italian and proposed Balkan campaigns in the so-called 'soft underbelly of Europe' in the Second. Between the wars, Churchill was a committed devotee to the theory that money spent on spying and collating information was rarely wasted. In 1909 he was instrumental in the creation of MI5 and on the eve of the Great War five years later he drew up the charter for the Admiralty's decrypting operation, codenamed Room 40.

From his time reporting to the Foreign Office when a subaltern in 1890s India, via his job of war correspondent in Cuba, to his active service behind the lines in the Boer War, Churchill nurtured his connections with British Intelligence. He made inspired use of the secret service in the Russian Civil War, in the U-boat war from 1914 to 1915 and even during the General Strike. After the Second World War he continued to be an enthusiastic player of the great intelligence game, before going on to appreciate its use in the Cold War.

Churchill's close links with British Intelligence resulted in his being able to set up a private spy network which served him very well during his wilderness years.[36] During the war, using an operative called Alan Hillgarth, he also ensured that several of Franco's senior generals were successfully bribed to ensure Spanish neutrality. Lord Halifax tended to find it uncongenial to, as he put it, 'slip them envelopes on the golf links', but Churchill saw himself as merely acting in the great British bribing tradition of eighteenth-century diplomacy.

Churchill ensured that the fact that the Allies had cracked the Enigma code was known to only thirty-one people, codenaming it 'Boniface' to decoy the enemy into thinking that it all came from a single (necessarily very high-level) agent. Such was its sensitivity that one of those not informed about Ultra was

Hugh Dalton – the director of the Special Operations Executive, whom Churchill had ordered to 'Set Europe ablaze!'.

'In wartime,' said Stalin first and Churchill soon afterwards, 'truth is so precious that she should always be attended by a bodyguard of lies.' The body set up to lie professionally for Britain was the Political Warfare Executive (PWE). In a house in Cambridgeshire the author has recently discovered an unpublished cache of PWE papers, documents and photographs that sheds fascinating new light on the way that the Allies planned to create chaos in Europe at the time of the D-Day landings in June 1944. This rich but hitherto untapped archive reveals the curious mixture of naïveté and ruthlessness that characterised PWE throughout its existence between 1938 and 1945.

The papers are those of David Garnett, which are held by his son Richard at Hilton Hall in Huntingdon.[37] In 1945 Garnett, the former Director of Training of PWE, was asked by the Foreign Secretary Ernest Bevin to write a secret history of the contribution the Executive had made to the war effort, for use in the Cold War in case of need. The result was so frank – indeed libellous – about so many prominent people in the Government and armed forces that it was distributed to only four people, at the War Office, Admiralty, Air Ministry and Foreign Office, and was then quickly buried in the archives of the Cabinet Office Historical Section. On its cover are the words: 'This Document is the Property of His Majesty's Government. SECRET. To be kept under lock and key. It is requested that special care may be taken to ensure the secrecy of this document.' It only finally saw publication in 2002, half a century after it was completed.[38]

Separate from Garnett's book are his private papers, which include his correspondence with scores of senior PWE officers. These cover a number of aspects of the work of the organisation that were not included in the secret history. Writing openly to their ex-colleague about their wartime experiences, many secrets were vouchsafed by these officers who otherwise would have gone to the grave with them. Just as with their secret sister-organisations MI5, MI6, Bletchley Park and SOE, such was the code of *omertá* surrounded PWE's wartime service that many of its officers felt that their duty to stay silent about its activities had not ended with the cessation of hostilities in 1945.

PWE was set up at the time of the Munich Crisis in 1938 to carry on the secret propaganda war against Germany along lines used in the First World War. Its purpose was to feed demoralising rumours to the Germans, by whatever means came to hand. In particular 'black' radio propaganda, which purported to come from within Germany but which was really being beamed from PWE's country headquarters at Woburn Abbey, was used to sow disinformation and misinformation in the homes of the Nazi enemy. Along with its American counterpart, the Office of War Information (OWI), PWE dropped no fewer than 265 million anti-Nazi leaflets on Germany, and broadcast hundreds of thousands of hours of propaganda of all kinds, including the frankly pornographic, which was designed to maximise listenership among ordinary German soldiers. It also spread bogus rumours such as the one that in 1940 the British had released in the English Channel two hundred man-eating sharks, imported from Australia, in order to eat Germans whose invasion boats had been sunk.

In a secret overview of the purpose of PWE, a senior officer, Lieut.-Col. R. L. Sedgwick, wrote: 'The fourth fighting arm, Political Warfare, attacks the mind. The chief forces which it employs are the dissatisfied elements in enemy countries or in enemy-occupied countries. Deceive your enemy, undermine his war effort, win the war of ideas.' This was to be done by 'bribery of newspapers, intrigue by women, personal flattery, sowing of internal dissensions, the setting of poor against rich and of rich against poor, young against old, soldier against general'. Rumours were to be sown in order 'to deceive and intimidate the enemy'.

Any organisation that called upon the diverse but undeniable talents of as varied a *galère* as Noël Coward, Raymond

Mortimer, Freya Stark, Denis Sefton Delmer, John Wheeler-Bennett, Robert Byron, Sir Robert 'Jock' Bruce Lockhart, E. H. Carr and Richard Crossman could never have been a dull place to work, especially as some of the operations that they devised were often so bizarre. What is one to make, for example, of the dropping of large numbers of dead carrier pigeons into Germany with messages attached to their legs, in the hope of deceiving the Gestapo into thinking that a huge German resistance movement was in close touch with British Intelligence? Tens of thousands of counterfeit German ration books were also forged to create confusion, as well as stamps bearing Himmler's face, in the hope that people would rise in revolt against the idea of his becoming the next Führer.

We know from the autobiography of the head of PWE's 'black' propaganda unit, the ingenious ex-journalist Denis Sefton Delmer, that a large number of PWE's files were destroyed after the war. Garnett's newly declassified *Secret History*, along with the archive from Hilton Hall, allows us, more than half a century after the end of the war, to cast more light than ever before upon the workings of this fascinating, dedicated, but until now very shadowy organisation.

A 'Minor Sabotage Booklet' was proposed, which would advise would-be resisters on the Continent how to help the Allies on D-Day (or 'Zero Hour' as it was rather transparently codenamed). Some of its suggestions were absurd and Heath Robinson-like, such as: 'Chemical devices. Strong laxatives, pernicious smells, harmless but bitter flavours for water, etc.' Other relatively harmless acts of resistance that were suggested were to call the fire brigade unnecessarily, 'to post all letters on one day and to post none at all on the next, to fill in all official forms wrongly, to queue up in railway stations asking how to get to some non-existent or hardly-known destination, to telephone the police station to complain that screams are coming from down the road'. It is hard to believe that these would have seriously inconvenienced the Wehrmacht on D-Day.

Other ideas would produce much more trouble for the Germans, such as the setting up of dummy roadblocks, the stencilling of false road signs, the mass puncturing of car and lorry tyres, and the cutting of field telephone wires. Finally there was advice on how to make incendiary bombs and tips on how to decapitate motorcyclists with wire strung between trees, which should always 'be placed at a slant so that when the rider is thrown off his machine it is into the ditch, where he will not be seen by the next motorcyclist'.

A postcard was mass-produced in December 1943 purporting to show Adolf Hitler masturbating, or at least holding his erect penis, with a broad grin on his face. Underneath the picture was a quotation from his Munich speech of November 1942, which translates as: 'What we have we hold.' A false news-sheet was also produced, allegedly by the OKW, denouncing this forgery, but reproducing it in full for the further delectation of anti-Nazi Germans.

A plan was made by the Director-General of PWE to flood Germany with 'ten times the amount of paper Reichsmark notes as there are in certain areas – particularly mining areas, the Sudetenland, Austria, etc, and starving Berlin. This will stop work in factories and mines, deplete stocks of goods in shops and produce chaos. Some parts of Germany will consume the goods of the rest.' It was feared, however, that the Germans might retaliate in kind, so the Director-General proposed as a pre-emptive measure to 'call in our own note circulation and replace it with a metallic currency'. The unimaginable costs and complications involved in putting such a plan into operation ensured that it never was.

Garnett's interview with the PWE operative M. Berman on 8 January 1945 finally clears up the mystery about the true extent of Noël Coward's contribution to the secret war effort. 'Mr Noël Coward was head of the French Department [of PWE] in Paris,' he stated. 'He was liaison officer for French propaganda. Lord Moore and Lord Strathallan assisted.' An undated, unsigned and uncopied 'Most Secret' document entitled 'Proposals for Joint P.W.E. and S.O.E. Action in Support of an Allied Invasion of Occupied Europe' provided for the selected assassination of quislings in the hours just prior to D-Day:

> In most countries there is likely to be a 'hard core' of traitors so compromised by their treachery that a fighting finish will be their only alternative to the lamp-post. This hard core is potentially dangerous at and about Zero Hour in relation to many of the activities being planned by or for patriots, and special measures against it are consequently worth contemplating. Planned liquidation in advance, even in a few cases, would obviously be of the highest importance.

Those quislings who could be 'kidnapped or taken into custody' and then 'blackmailed into turning King's evidence' would be expected to draw up 'lists of local traitors and their work; lists of prominent German (or other alien) civilians and their functions; names of persons or firms servicing the enemy; lists of stores and store-places; names of Gestapo agents and sub-agents; enemy plans in the event of retreat (i.e., scorched earth objectives); political movements secretly supported by the Germans', and so on. Among those who were deputed to undertake 'Operation King Rat' was the unlikely personage of the future royal dressmaker Hardy Amies.

In August 1941 Brigadier Ritchie Calder circulated a 'Most Secret' memorandum entitled 'Notes on Railway Sabotage', in which he went into loving detail about the best ways and places to destroy enemy trains: 'To secure maximum results a train should be derailed in a cutting (not on an embankment where the wreckage can be tumbled down the slope); in a tunnel (where there is no room for the breakdown cranes); on a bridge (so that the train falls over, damaging the parapet); or in a bottle-neck of a marshalling yard (so that all operations are jammed).' Removing between five and ten sleepers on the bend of a track was his recommended method of achieving this. There was further advice on how to damage points, signals, wagons, and axle boxes – 'remove the oil with a bicycle pump or pour in petrol, paraffin, water, sand, ashes or dirt'.

To celebrate the first anniversary of Battle of Britain Day, PWE considered calling a 'Tortoise Day' for 15 September 1941 during which Europeans would strike 'a blow for freedom by going slow'. 'Why sweat for the Germans?' they would be exhorted. 'Take your time. Where it normally takes one minute to walk from your cloakroom to your bench, make it take a minute and a half. If you go into a post office to buy a stamp, let it take longer. Engage the official in conversation. Let everything take longer than it usually does.' Again, it is doubtful that this would have made a significant contribution towards bringing the Third Reich to its knees.

The day before D-Day, the Oxford philosopher A. J. Ayer, then serving with the Inter-Services Research Bureau in Baker Street, approved a PWE leaflet entitled 'How to Live a Clandestine Life' that gave advice on how to survive on the run from the Gestapo. Among its tips were: 'Live in a friend's cellar, or out in the woods with a band of escapees. Assume a disguise, invent a story, choose a common – but not too common – name, remember a false date of birth and parents' names, leave before the curfews, never keep a scrap of paper, learn to use your memory, and avoid communicating with your family.'

Among the Hilton Hall papers is a copy of the 'Top Secret' letter that the Minister of Information, Brendan Bracken, wrote in January 1944 to General Brooks of PWE attacking the American Office of War Information, in which he described its directorate as 'incompetent, shifty and hare-brained'. In a coruscating paragraph that would undoubtedly have strained Anglo-American relations had it been made public, he went on:

They have no consistent policy. The content of their hectic output depends upon American political considerations. The

Polish vote, the Balt vote, the Jewish vote and above all the German vote will slant what politeness forces me to call their thinking. Their absurd actions followed by their gibbering explanations have earned them the contempt of most American newspapers. Why should we waste valuable time on this decaying and despised organisation? They will surely make you wallow with them in the squalid mess they created in America and wish to reproduce here.

Unsurprisingly, after this outburst, Brooks subsequently distanced PWE from OWI and cut it out of its next major operation, codenamed 'Operation Periwig'. This was a PWE plan to get the Germans to waste time and energy by providing 'proof' of a vast number of Allied spies within Nazi Germany itself. Parachutes and other gear were dropped, bogus messages were broadcast in Morse code either side of the BBC news, and one message was sent in a simple code that it was intended that the Germans should crack, saying: 'Will meet you Monday 9.30 in the 4th row of the stalls in the Ufa cinema.' Since there was a Ufa cinema in almost every German town, it was hoped this would take up huge amounts of Gestapo manpower.

Of 330 live pigeons dropped over Germany, five flew home to Britain with messages written by their German finders. One that returned in April 1945 bore a message saying: 'There are no German military personnel in our village, Hellensen. As far as I know Lüdenscheid will not be defended because there are many hospitals in the town. The [Nazi] Party swine have all cleared out, leaving in civilian clothes. I am also a pigeon-fancier and send my greetings. Good fight.' Unsurprisingly, it wasn't signed.

No one enjoyed and supported these unorthodox ways of making war more than Churchill, who had an incredibly fertile mind for invention. One of his pet projects was for the creation of, 'for use in northern waters, a device for transforming icebergs, embellished with frozen wood pulp, into unsinkable air bases'.[39] Codenamed 'Habbakuk', from the biblical prophet who promised 'a work which you will not believe', Churchill tested the idea in his bathtub and a model of a Habbakuk was also built on Lake Patricia in Canada. This soon proved how impractical the idea actually was: it would have taken eight thousand men eight months working in arctic temperatures to build an iceberg carrier of the size required.

Another idea that Churchill championed was for floating harbours, codenamed 'Mulberry', to be used in 'Operation Overlord', the planned seaborne invasion of Normandy. Once again, the Prime Minister's bathtub was employed as the test site. General Ismay later recalled the scene as Churchill sat in 'a dressing gown of many colours' surrounded by his advisers, with an admiral moving his hand in the bath to simulate the effect of waves and a brigadier stretching an inflatable sleeve across the bath to show how it broke up the waves. It was, as Ismay reflected, 'hard to believe that this was the British High Command studying the most stupendous and spectacular amphibious operation of the war'. Amazingly, the Mulberry harbours did work and would turn out to be an important contribution to 'Operation Overlord', as they allowed the Allies to select landing zones away from the Germans' major gun emplacements and fortifications.

Sacking people

As well as not dismissing ideas out of hand, however impractical they might at first seem, another key rule to be found in management guides is that a good leader selects the right people for the right job. Yet that is only half the truth; what is just as important is that leaders sack the right people too. If they failed to live up to his expectations, Churchill could be ruthless even to his close friends. Bob Boothby, for instance, had been one of Churchill's most loyal allies in the Commons during the anti-appeasement struggle, for which Churchill, when prime minister, initially rewarded him with the post of under-secretary at the Ministry of Food. Yet when Boothby soon afterwards became entangled in a sleaze story known as the 'Czech gold affair', Churchill dumped his old friend ignominiously. Privately suggesting that Boothby should 'join a bomb-disposal squad', Churchill declared in Parliament: 'There are paths of service open in war time which are not open in peace; and some of these paths may be paths of honour.' Boothby duly joined an RAF bomber squadron, although he never forgave his friend for his lack of support.

Another close friend, Alfred Duff Cooper, the only minister to have resigned over the Munich agreement, was made Minister of Information. Once it became clear that he wasn't particularly well suited to the job, Cooper fell out with the press which soon ran ever more aggressive attacks against him. Their criticism focused on what they dubbed 'Cooper's Snoopers' – government informants who they claimed were ordered to evaluate the state of public morale and report back to the Ministry. The *Sunday Pictorial* held a 'Duff Cooper ballot' featuring an extremely unflattering picture of him and including a coupon saying: 'He gets £5,000 a year for being Minister of Information. Do you think he should hold office?' Churchill didn't need any such ballot to show him that his friend had to be replaced and Cooper was sent away on a mission to the Far East. Although Churchill appointed him to important posts thereafter, he had in effect sacrificed a friend whom he had begun to see as a political liability. It was unfair on Duff Cooper, an extremely intelligent and talented man as well as a brave politician, but Churchill's primary concern had to be the interests of his Government and so Cooper had to go.

This kind of ruthlessness came even easier when administered against those who were not personal friends. The harsh treatment meted out to King Leopold III of the Belgians was such a case in point. Churchill needed a scapegoat for the 1940 defeat in the West, and the ideal person was the Belgian monarch who had capitulated to the Germans on 28 May, the day that the evacuations from Dunkirk began. Churchill blamed Leopold personally for the surrender, stating in the House of Commons on 4 June: 'Suddenly, without prior consultation, with the least possible notice, without the advice of his ministers and upon his own personal act, he sent a plenipotentiary to the German Command, surrendered his Army and exposed our flank and means of retreat.'

In fact, however, Churchill had been forewarned by his friend, Admiral Sir Roger Keyes, the liaison officer with the King of the Belgians, and according to Keyes he had not protested. As Keyes pointed out on several occasions:

The Belgian Army at the time of its surrender was no longer efficient but on the verge of complete collapse. King Leopold had given repeated warnings that his troops were at the end of their tether, and of his fear of imminent catastrophe. It was beyond his power to ask the advice of his ministers, for his ministers had fled the country on the 25th, after vain efforts to persuade him to abandon his army and accompany them. The eastern flank of the B.E.F. was already widely exposed before the surrender; and the British commander-in-chief [Lord Gort], realising on the 25th that the Belgians were on the verge of collapse, and that the only way of saving the B.E.F. was to evacuate it, leaving the Belgian King to his fate, had from that moment initiated his own arrangements for guarding his route to the sea, though without acquainting King Leopold of his intentions.

When reasons of state dictated, however, the scapegoating of the King became an absolute political necessity and Leopold spent the rest of his life under the shadow of Churchill's inaccurate denunciation in the Commons. Almost alone of the non-German European royalties, Leopold was not invited to Princess Elizabeth's wedding in 1947.

Another example of Churchill's ruthlessness at the time was

his order that the wounded should be the last people to be evacuated from the beaches of Dunkirk.[40] It made perfect military
sense, of course, since the able-bodied were needed to defend
Britain and it was initially thought that only 45,000 men could
be brought home, but it was an extremely harsh order to give
none the less. Or when he obtained the War Cabinet's permission in June 1940 to use mustard gas in Southern Ireland should
the Germans land there, with the reasoning that although the
storm troopers would have been issued with gas masks, the
thousands of horses they would bring with them would probably
not have been. Gas was also to have been used against the
Germans on the beaches of southern England in the event of an
invasion, with incalculable consequences for the civilian population of the south-coast towns, and for those who lived further
inland were the wind to blow in that direction. To lead is to
choose, and sometimes the decisions Churchill was forced to
take were ghastly ones. Yet he never hesitated.

Hitler, of course, was ultimately far more ruthless than
Churchill. A chilling example was the execution of those brave
army officers who had plotted against him in 1944. They were
hanged on hooks in Plötzensee prison in Berlin until they stran-
gled to death. Hitler ordered: 'I want them to be hanged, strung
up like meat-carcasses.' Some of them took as long as twenty
minutes to asphyxiate.

Yet, while this shows Hitler at his most vindictive, documents in the Bundesarchiv in Berlin – which incidentally used
to be the home of the SS Leibstandarte division that provided
the SS Führer Escort, Hitler's bodyguard – reveal that he could
be surprisingly forgiving to those who were loyal to him but
guilty of misdemeanours. Hitler liked the company of those
who had, in the words of Albert Speer, a 'flaw in the weave'.
Gauleiter Karl Hanke said of him: 'It is all to the good if associ-
ates have faults and know that the superior is aware of them.
That is why the Führer so seldom changes his assistants. For he
finds them easier to work with. Almost every one of them has

his defect; that helps keep them in line.' Immoral conduct, remote Jewish ancestry, or recent Party membership were all counted as flaws in the weave.

For the tasks that Hitler had in mind, particularly the undertaking of the Final Solution that was planned at the Wannsee Conference on 20 January 1942, it was important that his senior henchmen were absolutely not morally upright human beings. Albert Speer noted Hitler's genius at estimating the personality flaws in his lieutenants:

> He knew men's secret vices and desires, he knew what they thought to be their virtues, he knew the hidden ambitions and motives which lay behind their loves and their hates, he knew where they could be flattered, where they were gullible, where they were strong and where they were weak; he knew all this...by instinct and feeling, an intuition which in such matters never led him astray.

The fact that he despised his fellow man thus helped a great deal. In the crimes he was going to commit, Hitler knew that he needed morally compromised, largely under-educated, utterly loyal accomplices and when he found one he knew he could trust – such as Bruno Gesche, the head of his bodyguard – he hung on to him far beyond the time when he should have been sacked.

The Nazi Party and SS files on Gesche reveal that he had a chronic drink problem. In 1938 he had to promise Himmler that he would abstain from alcohol for three years. Yet in 1942 Gesche once more got so drunk that he threatened a fellow SS officer with his drawn pistol. Himmler imposed another three-year prohibition on Gesche and sent him to the Eastern Front. The Bundesarchiv documents show how Hitler would not let down his former bodyguard. After Gesche was wounded, this man – who was an alcoholic and a security risk – was nevertheless called back to be by Hitler's side. It was not long before

Gesche relapsed into old habits. On 20 December 1944, Himmler wrote to him:

1. You have again threatened a comrade with a pistol while intoxicated and fired shots senselessly.

[...]

4. I shall give you the opportunity to serve in the Dirlewanger Brigade and perhaps wipe out the shame you have brought on yourself and the entire SS, by proving yourself before the enemy.

5. I expect you to refrain from the consumption of alcohol for the rest of your life, without any exception. If your willpower has been so destroyed by alcohol that you are not capable of making such a decision, I expect you to submit your request to be released from the SS.

Gesche wasn't finally dismissed from the SS Führer Escort until just four months before the end of the war – this after many years of showing that he was a chronic drunkard. The indulgence shown him by Hitler was because he was what the Nazis called an 'old fighter from the years of struggle': he had joined the Nazi Party as early as 1922. Only one of Hitler's old comrades from that period could get away with so much.

The head of the Luftwaffe, Hermann Göring, was another, much more prominent example of Hitler's unwise loyalty to his cronies. A passionate hunter, Göring spent as much time at his country residence, Carinhall, as he did at the Air Ministry. As head of the German Air Force, Göring was all but a disaster. Time and again he promised more than he could deliver. At Dunkirk the vast majority of the encircled Allied troops were able to escape across the Channel, despite Göring having guaranteed that the Luftwaffe could finish them off by itself. He also promised that no single British bomber would ever reach Germany; if one did, Göring stated, his name would be Herr Meier (or Joe Bloggs, as we might say). As more and more

German cities were turned into rubble, Germans would increasingly (albeit in private) refer to Göring as 'Herr Meier'.

At Stalingrad, Göring's assurance that he could supply the encircled Sixth Army by airlift encouraged Hitler to issue a halt order when a breakout would still have been possible. As it was, only a small percentage of the promised supplies ever arrived. Any responsible leader would have relieved a serial failure like Göring of his command, but not Hitler. Like Gesche, Göring had been with the Nazi Party since 1922; he had been badly wounded in the groin in the Beer-hall Putsch. This, and his personal loyalty to Hitler, were more significant in the Führer's mind than Göring's string of blunders as the Luftwaffe's Commander-in-Chief. It was not until the last days of the war that Hitler turned against Göring, and only then because he incorrectly believed that Göring was preparing to take over from him. Hitler had him arrested and ousted him from the Party and all his offices. To Hitler, personal and ideological loyalty was more important than professional aptitude and performance.

Hitler was loyal to his staff so long as he could rely on their loyalty to him. What he failed to recognise is that loyalty alone was not enough. A leader like Churchill could subordinate almost everything – be it his ideological or even his personal feelings – to the one goal he had set himself and his country: victory.

Hitler's appointment of Joachim von Ribbentrop to such a key post in the Reich as Foreign Minister was another example of his desire to have a henchman who had 'a flaw in the weave' rather than the most professional person available. Unlike Göring and Gesche, Ribbentrop came late into politics, only joining the Nazi Party in 1932 with the distinctly unprepossessing membership number of 1,119,927. He had acquired the prefix 'von' by paying a distant aunt to adopt him while his parents were still alive. (He later reneged on the payments.)

Despite the time he had spent in the United States before the Great War, Ribbentrop gravely underestimated the power of

America at the time of Germany's declaration of war in December 1941. That miscalculation put the noose around his neck as surely as did the American GI who volunteered for the job at Nuremberg four years later. When the Allies questioned Ribbentrop's aunt-in-law about his whereabouts in May 1945, and asked which friends might be sheltering him, she truthfully told them that he didn't have any. His ignorance, incompetence and complete moral vacuity should have disqualified him for the post of Foreign Minister even in the Third Reich, but for Hitler they mattered less than his loyalty. Ribbentrop's hanging in the converted gymnasium at Nuremberg was badly botched; he took ten minutes to die.

As well as keeping the wrong people on because of their loyalty, one of the reasons for Hitler's failure as a leader was that he sacked some of his best commanders because of their perceived disloyalty. The Blitzkrieg pioneer Guderian was dismissed during the Russian campaign in 1941, only to be recalled in 1943. Erich von Manstein, the architect of the brilliant sickle-cut operation against France, was retired in 1944. One of Hitler's most senior commanders, Field Marshal Gerd von Rundstedt, was dismissed and re-employed no fewer than four times. Sooner or later, almost every senior general was replaced by Hitler, no matter how able and experienced he was, because Hitler didn't trust the German military. In the course of the war no fewer than thirty-five field marshals and generals were dismissed by Hitler, more often for lack of loyalty than for perceived or actual military incompetence.

Churchill too enjoyed the company of those who had 'flaws in the weave'. His greatest friend before his tragic death at the age of 58 in 1930, F. E. Smith, Lord Birkenhead, was a heavy drinker. Max Beaverbrook was widely thought of as crooked. Brendan Bracken also had a shadowy background and was suspected of deliberately failing to quash the unfounded rumour that he was Churchill's illegitimate son. Averell Harriman had an affair with the wife of Churchill's son Randolph, but was not penalised socially for it by the Churchill family. Yet there is a world of difference between Hitler's case – where the flaws were held as a form of blackmail – and Churchill's, where they were indulged in the knowledge that those people who are closest to moral perfection are often crashing bores. One could be guilty of almost anything and remain in Churchill's entourage, but not of either cowardice or wilful dullness.

Hitler would indulge stupidity to a surprising degree, certainly far more than Churchill. Although neither man attended university, Churchill generally got on well with academics, whereas Hitler despised them. Of the fifty Reichleiters and Gauleiters who formed the élite of the Nazi leadership, only ten had completed a university education. While some had attended university classes for a time, the majority had never got beyond secondary school.

Although most of his generals fervently supported the Nazis' expansionist policy, Hitler had little confidence in their ideological and personal loyalty, so he resorted to naked bribery. Of course, it is not uncommon in military history for generals to be specially rewarded – after a war. Churchill's ancestor the Duke of Marlborough had received the Blenheim estate, and Wellington had been given Stratfield Saye by a similarly grateful nation. The government payments of £5,000 per annum (the same as a Cabinet minister received) made to Admiral Nelson's descendants only ceased under the premiership of Clement Attlee.

Yet Hitler was conspicuously generous towards his commanders while the war was still being fought. A large number of generals and field marshals received cheques for 250,000 Reichsmarks – about half a million pounds in today's money – that were signed by the Führer personally. Others were given huge tracts of land and grand homes. The estate of Glebokie in western Poland was a gift to General Heinz Guderian from his Führer. While such an act appears to demonstrate his generosity, in fact it illustrates Hitler's cunning in ensuring loyalty through unashamed bribery.

Glebokie belonged to a Polish aristocrat, who during the Great War had served in the German Army as an adjutant to General Hindenburg. Despite this, the Nazis put him in prison and his family was sent to a forced labour camp. General Guderian didn't seem to care about the rightful owner of the estate that Hitler had given him. After the war he never tired of pointing out his distaste for the Nazis, but he conveniently forgot that he had had no scruples in making himself an accomplice to Hitler's brutal occupation policy. When the officers who plotted against Hitler approached Guderian to join them, he declined.

Instead, when their plot had failed, Guderian chose to serve on the infamous 'Court of Honour' against them, which condemned them to death for violating their oath to the Führer. The estate in Poland must have had a bearing on his decision to remain loyal. For all the post-war protestations of the German officer corps about fighting for the honour of their fatherland, very often it actually came down to cash. Hitler's gifts to his generals would nowadays be called 'golden handcuffs'. These were payments designed to keep people loyal, even though genuine loyalty cannot be bought or sold.

In the British Army, things were taken to the other extreme. After the war, Lord Alanbrooke found himself so impoverished that he was forced to put his house on the market and move into the adjoining gardener's cottage. A keen ornithologist, Alanbrooke even had to sell his bird-watching books. Yet he wasn't devastated by his decline in material fortunes since he didn't expect the country to give him a grand estate. He lived his life according to a code of duty that was entirely unrelated to financial reward.

Churchill had no reason to distrust his generals' commitment to the cause they were fighting for, but that does not mean that he always believed in their professional competence. In the first three years of the war, Churchill frequently tried to interfere with his commanders in the field. In August 1940, for instance, he personally drafted a directive to the Commander-in-Chief for the Middle East that went into minute tactical matters and even contained instructions for the deployment of troops down to battalion level. On several occasions in the Desert War, Churchill harried commanders into rushed and poorly prepared offensives, often with disastrous results – at least until strong-willed generals like Harold Alexander and Bernard Montgomery taught him to trust them.

Alexander was given command of the Middle East in the summer of 1942, with Montgomery as commander of the Eighth Army, which opposed the Afrika Korps of Erwin Rommel. So far, the British had only experienced humiliating defeats at the hands of 'the Desert Fox' and Churchill was eager to see some successes. Just as with his previous generals in the Desert War, such as Auchinleck and Wavell, he attempted to meddle with Montgomery's and Alexander's commands and urged them to 'take or destroy' Rommel's Afrika Korps 'at the earliest possible moment'. Yet Alexander replied coolly, effectively telling the Prime Minister to back off. As El Alamein showed, Montgomery would not disappoint him either.

The Battle of El Alamein was not only a turning point of the war, it was also a turning point in Churchill's war leadership. He finally learned to trust his commanders in the field and let them do their jobs without his constant interference. It certainly wasn't easy for him to stop meddling. He had been a soldier himself, having attended the Royal Military College at Sandhurst, and had seen plenty of action, most recently in the First World War. He would have loved to exercise command himself, at all times and in all places. Before the age of twenty-five he had written two books, *The Malakand Field Force* and *The River War*, in which he had sought to give the British High Command the benefit of his advice in India and the Sudan.

Churchill was not the great military commander that his ancestor Marlborough had been. His outstanding leadership qualities were sometimes marred by a startling lack of judgement. Very often it was his romantic vision of war as an adventure that nurtured his military thinking, rather than a realistic appreciation of operational practicalities. One of his favourite schemes, for instance, was an invasion of Nazi-occupied Europe from Norway, an idea he repeatedly returned to throughout the war. Each time, the Chiefs of Staff were forced to prepare detailed operational plans for this scheme, if only to prove that such an enterprise was doomed to failure.

It is fascinating to see how Churchill's and Hitler's leadership styles developed during the course of the war: while Churchill involved himself less and less with the day-to-day military conduct of the war, Hitler became more and more the micromanager. This was largely because the victories of the German Army in the first two years of the war had led Hitler to believe himself to be an infallible military genius. Meanwhile the British defeats reminded Churchill that he himself was not one.

Ever since the time when the German Army had been checked at the gates of Moscow, Hitler became increasingly involved with operational details and even tactical matters that would have been much better decided by the commanders in the field. It was the very negation of the principle of Mission Command that had made the early Blitzkrieg campaigns so successful.

Such was Hitler's exaggerated self-belief that when, one day, he was whistling a classical tune and a secretary suggested that he had made a mistake in the melody, Hitler retorted: 'I don't have it wrong. It is the composer who made a mistake in this passage.'[41] Yet as the war progressed, Hitler forgot that it had often been the initiative of individual commanders that had won him his early victories.

As the war in the East dragged on, Hitler more and more played the part of a divisional commander rather than a commander-in-chief. It allowed him to forget for a while the grim realities of the overall situation as he concentrated on interfering with his battlefield commanders in individual operations thousands of miles away. 'The other day I called off an attack that was to procure us a territorial gain of four kilometres,' he boasted at one staff meeting, 'because the operation didn't seem to me to be worth the price it would have cost.' If Hitler had had a Cerberus like Lord Alanbrooke, he would never have been allowed to get involved in such detailed decision-making, but the very nature of the Nazi State made that impossible. The situation got so bad that by 1945 General Günther Blumentritt complained how one plan from Hitler

> came to us … in the most minute detail. It set out the specific divisions that were to be used … The sector in which the attack was to take place was specifically identified and the very roads and villages through which the forces were to advance were all included. All this planning had been done in Berlin from large-scale maps and the advice of generals … was not asked for, nor was it encouraged.[42]

The contrast with the principles of Mission Command that had served Hitler so well in the West in 1940 could not have been more marked.

While Churchill had streamlined the decision-making process, Hitler operated a system of divide and rule that ensured that nobody but he could claim to have a comprehensive view of Germany's strategic situation. Yet the resulting fragmentation of command and blurring of responsibilities made effective military leadership all but impossible, as D-Day was to show. The 'Atlantic Wall', Hitler's fortification in Normandy, was designed to thwart an Allied attack across the Channel. It didn't succeed, of course, but the German failure was not primarily due to lack of armaments but rather to lack of leadership. Four years after the Blitzkrieg victory over France, the German command system was in a shambolic state.

The leadership technique that had helped Hitler to enhance his image of the charismatic, unchallengeable leader in times of peace proved to be his undoing in war, when he moved away from the rational – if albeit cynical and sinister – decision-making processes of his earlier years. This was particularly the case once the tide had turned in November 1942, the month both of Rommel's retreat after El Alamein and the encirclement of the German Army besieging Stalingrad. Hitler started to fit new information, especially discouraging news, into his already formulated patterns of hopes and beliefs. Evidence that his strategy was failing was minimised, and he could not accept that the war was being lost even when he received a report from Albert Speer that actually contained the words: 'The war is lost.'[43] On 20 July 1944 the German opposition to Hitler finally got round to making a serious assault on his life.

Resistance to Hitler

A new Second World War myth is about to enter the liberal canon. For as well as being responsible for concentration camps (started in the Boer War), the oppression of Weimar Germany (as the economist John Maynard Keynes effectively argued in his book *The Economic Consequences of the Peace*), and of course the so-called 'genocidal' bombing of Dresden and Hamburg, a theory is now emerging that the British were also guilty of failing to give active support to the German resistance so that they found it impossible to overthrow Hitler.

The publication in 1996 of *Plotting Hitler's Death* by the distinguished German historian Joachim Fest took the argument a stage further even than earlier works by Patricia Meehan, *The Unnecessary War* (1992), and Klemens von Klemperer, *German Resistance against Hitler: The Search for Allies Abroad* (1993). Herr Fest unequivocally blamed the British Government for their 'lack of flexibility, their hostility, their blindness, and a political obtuseness that to all intents and purposes represented an alliance with Hitler'. He argued that 'Nazi propagandists and

Allied spokesmen joined forces in a *de facto* coalition' in order to denigrate the German resistance. Several of the book's reviewers criticised Churchill and the British Foreign Secretary Anthony Eden for not doing more to support the plotters, and an editorial in *The Times* even argued that 'we too may wish to reconsider our wartime record' because of our 'misguided policy', which was only explicable because 'British leaders were fighting the wrong war'.

Yet far from being culpably blind or stupid, Churchill and Eden had sound, indeed politically unanswerable reasons for pursuing their 'perfect silence' policy towards the German resistance. As Fest, Meehan and Klemperer all acknowledge, there was no single resistance entity with which the British Government could reasonably deal to the exclusion of the others. There was little overlap between the Communist, Christian and military opponents of Hitler's regime. Even inside those circles that could genuinely pose a direct physical threat to Hitler's life there were wide differences over the intended outcome. Count Helmuth von Moltke's ideas for post-war democracy, for example, only involved elections for local councils and not for a national parliament. Claus von Stauffenberg and Karl Goerdeler wanted Germany to return to her 1939 borders, which of course included the re-militarised Rhineland as well as the Sudeten part of Czechoslovakia. Others, such as the politician Ulrich von Hassell, considered Germany's 1914 imperial frontiers desirable, yet they included parts of the very country, Poland, whose independence Britain and France had initially gone to war to defend in 1939. The possession of Alsace-Lorraine was another point of contention.

Furthermore, after June 1941, decisions over peace moves were no longer up to Britain alone. Once the war was being fought by the Soviet Union, and after December 1941 by the United States as well, it was unthinkable that Britain should enter into negotiations with any Germans behind the backs of her allies, especially after President Roosevelt's insistence in

January 1943 on Germany's unconditional surrender as a pre-condition for peace. As one of the officials in the German Department of the Foreign Office, Sir Frank Roberts, put it in his autobiography, *Dealing with Dictators*: 'If Stalin got the impression we were in contact with the German generals, whose main aim was to protect Germany against Russia, he might well have been tempted to see whether he could not again come to terms with Hitler.'

The British Government's stance was succinctly summed up by Sir D'Arcy Osborne, the British envoy to the Vatican, who, when told by Pope Pius XII that the German resistance groups 'confirmed their intention, or their desire, to affect a change of government', answered: 'Why don't they get on with it?' It is also questionable what genuine support the Allies could actually deliver. Logistical support in terms of providing bombs or rifles was hardly needed by the German military, and moral support was of little practical help. Any promises about the Allies' attitude towards a post-Hitler Germany would necessarily have been contingent upon its political make-up, which might even have included senior Nazis. Anyhow, to be seen as being supported or influenced in any way by the Allies would have spelt disaster to any German opposition group attempting to form a post-Hitler government with the support of ordinary patriotic Germans.

British decision-makers had seen quite enough of the Prussian officer class between 1914 and 1918 to have much faith in its commitment to anything approaching democracy. For them, Prussian militarism was almost as unattractive as full-blown Nazism; national-conservative Germans were nearly indistinguishable from national-socialist ones. One can understand why Eden should have said that the July bomb plotters 'had their own reasons for acting as they did and were certainly not moved primarily by a desire to help our cause', however harsh that might sound in retrospect.

Insofar as the German generals were a homogeneous entity, rather than a group of competing and often mutually antagonistic individuals, their complicity in fighting one of history's most vicious campaigns was total. In Poland in 1939 the Wehrmacht were accessories to the crimes of the SS, but by 1941 they were full accomplices. The defeats in Russia and the July Bomb Plot were hardly coincidental. The British Government can be forgiven for suspecting that if Russia had been defeated, or if the Allies had been repulsed in Normandy the previous month, no bomb would have been placed under the man who had been followed unquestioningly by the German people during the first bloodless, and then highly sanguine, victories of 1938 to 1942.

Although the plotters were undoubtedly in Churchill's words, 'the bravest of the best', it remains unclear whether supporters of the Resistance spoke for very many other Germans beside themselves, even on 20 July 1944. Had Hitler died in the Bomb Plot he would not have been succeeded by some neo-Christian Democrat government, but probably by Heinrich Himmler, who controlled the SS. With Bormann merely a bureaucrat and Goebbels's influence largely dependent on the dead Hitler, Himmler would have exploited his formidable power base and most likely become the new Führer. Nor would much have been different had the vice-Führer, Hermann Göring, succeeded to the Nazi throne. The historian Peter Hoffmann has written that: 'Göring would have sought to rally all the state's forces by an appeal to *völkisch* and national-socialist ideals, by vowing to fulfil the Führer's legacy and to redouble the efforts to fight the enemy to a standstill.' If either Göring or Himmler had taken over and not made the many strategic blunders perpetrated by Hitler in the final months of the war, Nazi Germany might even have lasted longer. Furthermore, the average German soldier would doubtless have continued to fight on doggedly to protect his fatherland (and his mother's honour) from the rampaging Red Army.

An assassinated Hitler would also have provided the ideal new *Dolchstosslegende* once Germany was defeated. It would undoubtedly have been argued that just as Hitler was about to launch his war-winning secret weapons to destroy the Allied Armies, which he had spent a year purposely luring towards Germany, he was murdered by a clique of aristocrats, liberals, Christians and cosmopolitans whose treachery was evident since they were working in league with British Intelligence. It would have been a potent recipe for revanchism that would have resonated in Germany almost to this day.

In his 1947 book *The Last Days of Hitler*, the distinguished historian Hugh Trevor-Roper called the German Resistance 'a creature as fabulous as the centaur and the hippogriff'. But quite apart from the question of whether it was really quite as large and influential as its post-war advocates claim – it might well have swelled somewhat after the war, rather like the French maquis – the fact remains that the British had good reason for suspecting its contacts among the Resistance of being double agents. In November 1939 two MI6 officers were kidnapped at Venlo on the Dutch–German border by Gestapo agents posing as Resistance figures. Fest does not mention the incident, but Meehan acknowledges that it had 'serious and long-lasting consequences' in making the Foreign Office understandably suspicious of future advances.

Seen in this light, the offhand attitude of Sir Alec Cadogan, the Permanent Under-Secretary at the British Foreign Office – 'As usual, the German Army trust us to save them from the Nazi regime' – becomes easily explicable. After the resister Karl Goerdeler asked for Danzig to remain German, colonial concessions and a £500m interest-free loan before attempting to depose Hitler in December 1939, Cadogan was equally scathing. 'We are to deliver the goods,' he wrote, 'and Germany gives the IOUs.' The Foreign Secretary agreed. On the subject of what Neville Chamberlain termed 'Hitler's Jacobites', Lord Halifax complained: 'The Germans always want us to make their revolutions for them.' Judging by Herr Fest's book, little has changed.

'Assassination,' said Benjamin Disraeli only a fortnight after

Abraham Lincoln's death in 1865, 'has never changed the history of the world.' Was he right? Considering the baleful effect that Hitler's leadership had on the German people between 1933 and 1945, would it have been justifiable to have assassinated him? Papers released at the Public Records Office at Kew in 2000 showed that 'Operation Foxley', the various British Intelligence plans to kill Hitler, were quite well advanced but were prevented from being carried out by a policy decision taken from on high.

The question of whether the assassination of Hitler would have dramatically changed the course of the war goes to the heart of the ancient debate about whether history is primarily driven by what T. S. Eliot called 'vast, impersonal forces' – so powerful that individuals, however seemingly influential, are in fact mere corks on history's waves – or whether great men, as Thomas Carlyle believed, determine by their own will what happens in human affairs. If Napoleon had been killed at the siege of Acre, or if Hitler had succumbed to 'Operation Foxley's' lethal cocktail of anthrax and bazookas, would the world be a different place?

Post-war American governments, or at least their Intelligence communities, seem to have cleaved to the 'great man' theory, authorising attempts on the life of Fidel Castro – once famously with exploding cigars – and bombing missions against Colonel Gaddafi in 1986 and Saddam Hussein in 1991. Although America has seen an inordinate amount of presidents (four) as well as other public figures such as Martin Luther King, Huey Long, Robert Kennedy and Malcolm X fall prey to assassins, it is still the most gung-ho of nations, willing to countenance an attack aimed specifically at an enemy leader, in a way that Wellington denounced as ungentlemanly when it was suggested that he fire a cannon directly at Napoleon during the opening stage of the Battle of Waterloo. By contrast with the Americans, Britain has been almost circumspect; indeed, it was said that the British politician Julian Amery's career never really prospered after he advocated that MI6 assassinate some of Britain's colonial trouble-makers.[44]

Assassination as a policy tends to fare very differently when carried out in representative democracies with established power hierarchies than in feudal, tribal or dictatorial countries. Whereas the assassination of a president – McKinley or John Kennedy – or a prime minister – Spencer Perceval – merely results in the smooth substitution of a lieutenant, who is usually at pains defiantly to continue the same policies, it is different when the dead individual personifies the nation. If a war can be foreshortened, and a significant change of government effected by an *ad hominem* attack, such as on Saddam Hussein, it is hard to balk at such action.

The assassinations of Jean Paul Marat, Tsar Alexander II, Archduke Franz Ferdinand, Admiral Darlan, Reinhard Heydrich, Hendrik Verwoerd, Benigno Aquino, Father Jerzy Popieluszko and General Zia ul-Haq all had far-reaching political consequences – albeit often the opposite of what the assassins intended – because they took place in undemocratic countries. Those of Empress Elisabeth of Austria, King Humbert I of Italy, Jean Jaurès, Mahatma Gandhi, President Diem of South Korea, Olof Palme, Indira Gandhi and Rajiv Gandhi, taking place in countries with representative institutions, did not, in Disraeli's typically flip generalisation, 'change the world'.

It is fairly safe to assume that Hitler's sudden death at the hands of the Special Operations Executive, by whichever of the splendidly James Bond operations was finally chosen for 'Operation Foxley', would have changed the course of the war, but for the better or worse? The war needed to be won by the Allies, but it also needed to be lost, comprehensively and personally, by Hitler himself. His suicide in the bunker after the total collapse of his dreams had to be the last chapter of the tale, the crucial prerequisite for the decent, democratic, peace-loving Germany we know today.

Before June 1944, Germany had wreaked far worse damage on

the rest of the world than it had on her. To have concluded an armistice on the demonstrable fallacy that the war was begun and carried on by one man's will, rather than through the whole-hearted support and enthusiasm of the German people, would not have produced the longest and most durable period of peace Europe has known for half a millennium.

A nation that had fought no fewer than five wars of invasion in the seventy-five years after 1864 needed to have the warlike instinct burned out of its soul. Only the horrors and humiliations of 1944 and 1945 could have achieved that. If they had been spared that ultimate calamity, somehow escaping Year Zero because of 'Operation Foxley', the Germans would not be the pacific democrats they undoubtedly are today. The ghastly, final scene of Götterdämmerung had to be played out, with Goebbels reading Thomas Carlyle's *Frederick the Great* in translation to Hitler in the Berlin bunker as the Red Army closed in. Ribbentrop, Kaltenbrunner, Streicher, Rosenberg and the rest could be hanged at Nuremberg, but Hitler himself needed to die by the one hand that would make his defeat truly complete – his own.

D-Day: Hitler's nemesis

Long before D-Day actually took place, Hitler was receiving contradictory reports on the time and location of the invasion from his three rival intelligence agencies. In line with Hitler's divide-and-rule principle, both the German Army and the Foreign Office had their own intelligence agencies, as well as Himmler's SS which ran the Sicherheitsdienst (SD). Each of these three agencies operated completely independently of each other, and often delivered contradictory analyses and reports. The British and Americans, by contrast, had a Joint Intelligence Committee that pooled and evaluated all incoming data, thereby rendering Churchill generally co-ordinated prognostications.

Even more serious for Germany was the fact that the commander responsible for the defence of France, Field Marshal von Rundstedt, had no direct control over many of the units operating in the area under his responsibility. Anti-aircraft units and parachute troops were under the control of Göring's Luftwaffe. The Waffen SS units reported only to Himmler. One Army Group was led by Rommel, but Rundstedt, although nominally his superior, was not permitted to give him direct orders. Two entire panzer divisions, held in reserve, were under the direct control of the High Command of the German Forces (the OKW), which in turn acted only on Hitler's orders. This greatly hampered Rundstedt's ability to manoeuvre fighting units effectively when the Allied landings began in the early hours of 6 June 1944.

Rundstedt immediately ordered the panzer reserves to speed towards the Channel coast to fling the Allies back into the sea before they managed to establish a firm toe-hold on the Continent, only to find himself reprimanded by the Army High Command (the OKH) for not having first obtained Hitler's authorisation. The panzer reserves were ordered to halt. But the Führer was not willing to give his authorisation and it was not until midday that Hitler finally reacted to the momentous news. It is not true that he was asleep, he was merely slow to make a decision. By the time he did so, the Allies had already seized the beachheads and Allied air superiority had made any large-scale movement of panzers during the day well-nigh impossible.

Churchill's promise to fight on the beaches had come true, but the fighting was not done at Brighton or Dover, but on the Normandy invasion beaches codenamed Juno, Omaha, Sword, Gold and Utah. Now it was only a matter of time before all of Europe would be liberated from the Nazi yoke. Yet the worse the military situation became for Germany, the more Hitler micromanaged, thereby making things even more dire than they were already. It was the very negation of the principle of Mission Command that had made Hitler's earlier Blitzkrieg successes possible.

After the Battle of the Odon had removed any chance that the Germans might have had to split Allied forces by striking at Bayeux, Rundstedt warned the OKW that the battle for Normandy was effectively lost. Field Marshal Keitel asked in despair: 'What shall we do?' Rundstedt's reply was harsh: 'Make peace, you fools.' He was relieved of his command and replaced by Field Marshal Günther von Kluge. A few days later, Rommel sent a letter to Hitler. 'Our troops are fighting heroically all along the line, but the unequal battle is nearing its end. In my view you should draw the necessary conclusions.' Kluge supported Rommel: 'Unfortunately, the field marshal is right.'

Yet Hitler would have none of this, especially when the failed assassination attempt of 20 July 1944 revealed a wide-ranging conspiracy against him within the High Command. His response was a ruthless purge of the military: 160 officers were executed, among them no fewer than two field marshals and seventeen generals. Rommel himself was offered no choice but to take poison.

The Bomb Plot weakened Hitler in other ways beyond the purely political. General Walter Warlimont of the OKH operation staff, who was injured in the blast, recorded how afterwards:

Hitler himself was now quite obviously a sick man. His actual injuries on 20th July had been minor but it seemed as if the shock had brought into the open all the evil of his nature, both physical and psychological. He came into the map room bent and shuffling. His glassy eyes gave a sign of recognition only to those who stood closest to him. His chair would be pushed forward for him and he would slump down into it, bent almost double with his head sunk between his shoulders. As he pointed to something on the map his hand would tremble. On the slightest occasion he would demand that 'the guilty' be hunted down.

One original aspect of the Führer remained, however, and that was the well-advertised effect of his glance. A military adjutant who saw him only days before Hitler killed himself recalled how, although the rest of him looked like 'a sick and senile old man...only in his eyes was there an indescribable flickering brightness...and the glance he gave me was strangely penetrating'.

Warlimont noted how the attempt on his life led Hitler, not surprisingly, to mistrust his generals even more after July 1944, which made them correspondingly less likely ever to contradict him: 'His responsible advisers gave the immediate observer the disturbing impression that they were now guided, not by sober military considerations, but by a discipleship complex if possible more unquestioning than before.' As a result, Hitler proceeded entirely to scrap the doctrine of Mission Command that had served him so well in Poland, Norway, the Netherlands and France (at least before he intervened with the disastrous 'halt order' for the panzers before Dunkirk). In consequence, Warlimont further recalled of this post-July period:

> Hitler succeeded...in setting the seal on his disastrous method of command by proclaiming as an order the principle that the sole responsibility of all commanders, even the most senior, was to carry out his orders unconditionally and to the letter. In face of the enemy a N.C.O. or private soldier had no right to question the soundness or likelihood of success of an attack ordered by his company commander; similarly the Supreme Commander of the Wehrmacht was not prepared to share responsibility for his decisions with commanders-in-chief of Army Groups or Armies. They were not allowed to ask to be relieved if they disagreed with his instructions.[45]

To make matters yet worse, Hitler's very survival of the Bomb Plot only served to reinforce his belief in his destiny. As Warlimont remembered:

He was presumptuous enough to consider that it was 'Providence' which had preserved him on 20 July and now expected that other 'miracles' would give the war a new turn, although in earlier days he had heaped scorn upon the heads of any enemy leaders who had used this sort of language.

Churchill meanwhile used Hitler's survival as an opportunity for one of his most crushing broadsides. He had in the past referred to Hitler as 'this bloodthirsty guttersnipe' and put Allied victories in Africa down in part to 'the military intuition of Corporal Hitler. We may notice the touch of the master hand. The same insensate obstinacy.' He had also refused to compare Hitler to Napoleon, since 'it seems an insult to the great emperor and warrior to compare him in any way with a squalid caucus boss and butcher'. Now, in September 1944, Churchill outdid even himself for scorn. Speaking in the House of Commons he said:

When Herr Hitler survived the Bomb Plot...he described his survival as providential. I think from a purely military point of view we can all agree with him. Certainly it would be most unfortunate if the Allies were to be deprived in the closing phases of the struggle of that form of warlike genius that Corporal Schicklgruber has so notably contributed to our victory.

As so often with Churchill's best jibes, it had the added but not wholly necessary advantage of being true. Three miracles had befallen Britain in the war, all of them the result of cardinal errors by Hitler: the 'halt order' of the panzers outside Dunkirk on 25 May 1940; the invasion of Russia on 22 June 1941; and the German declaration of war against the United States on 11 December 1941. None of these decisions had anything to do with Churchill, but they had collectively saved his cause. They had all come from one presiding mind. Leadership – in this case

Hitler's catastrophically bad leadership – had been crucial. Truly great leaders understand how vital it is to listen to people who disagree with them. While Churchill engaged in debate, Hitler simply stifled it. In the end therefore, although totalitarian states are good at starting wars, democracies are better at winning them.

Conclusion

'History may regard Winston Churchill as the architect of
the disastrous Gallipoli campaign or the maker of xenophobic speeches, but tonight we consider him, in philanthropic
old age, as Churchill the European.'

Radio Times, November 2001

'Winston Churchill High School in Harare, Zimbabwe, will
become Josiah Tongogara High, in memory of the commander of Mr Mugabe's 1970s guerrilla army....Warren Park
Primary School will become Chenjerai Hitler Hunzvi
Primary School, immortalising the regime's chief rabble-
rouser.'

Daily Telegraph, February 2002

'School Video On The War Gives Churchill Fourteen
Seconds.'

Newspaper headline, 2001

What will they say of Adolf Hitler and Winston Churchill long
after we are all dead? While there are still people alive who lost
family members to Hitler's War, while we still live in a world
the political contours of which are largely shaped by the post-
Hitler settlement, it is impossible to be truly objective about
them. What, though, will ordinary people make of Hitler and

Churchill in 2145 or 2245, when they are as chronologically distant to our descendants as historical figures like Napoleon and Wellington are to us today?

Most of us fondly assume that Hitler will always be seen as another Vlad the Impaler, Attila the Hun or Ivan the Terrible – a hate-filled bloodthirsty tyrant and no more than that. As Sir John Keegan has put it: 'He belongs in the company of Genghis Khan, Tamerlane, Stalin and Mao Tse-tung, inhuman megalomaniacs all. These men are, as the People of the Book have no difficulty in believing, in league with the Devil. May God rest their souls.'[1] Although in fifty years or so some revisionist biographies and television documentaries might occasionally attempt to rehabilitate the Führer, the judgement of posterity seems settled. But some distinguished thinkers, such as the American historian John Lukacs, are not so sure. Lukacs has identified a number of areas in which Hitler-revisionism has already made some (admittedly very limited) headway, and he fears that these will increase over time. Napoleon, after all, left over six million dead across Europe after two decades of wars of conquest, yet there is no shortage of intellectuals and writers who admire him today.

Lukacs believes that Hitler should be recognised as 'the greatest revolutionary of the twentieth century', superior even to Lenin in his ability to harness and then direct the politics of mass discontent, and that these ideas of nationalist triumphalism could still pose a threat in the future. His ultimate fear is that if Western civilisation melts away, and then threatens to disappear altogether, a danger lies before future generations. During a rising flood of barbarism, Hitler's reputation might rise in the eyes of ordinary people, who may come to regard him as a kind of Diocletian, a tough last architect of a desirable imperial order.[2] Fortunately, this outcome is hardly an immediate prospect, and if Western civilisation should ever dissolve to quite that extent, the state of Adolf Hitler's reputation will be among the last of our great-grandchildren's worries. Churchill himself said something to this effect in the House of Commons on 25 June 1941: 'If we win, nobody will care. If we lose, there will be nobody to care.'

In the Introduction to this book I tried to draw a distinction between the charismatic leader of Adolf Hitler's type and the inspirational one such as Winston Churchill. When we watch a magician performing his tricks at a children's party, half of us will stare at his hands trying to work out how he does them, while the other half of the audience will simply watch it for what it is, enjoying the sensation of being astounded. Natural sceptics will follow an inspirational leader, but be rightly suspicious of a charismatic one. In politics, therefore, scepticism is a healthy reaction that should be nurtured and encouraged.

The truth is that Hitler exerted far more power over people's imaginations and psyches than ever Churchill did. Hitler harnessed two of the most powerful, if vicious, of human emotions – envy and resentment – to his chariot wheels, and they took him an astoundingly long way. In the wake of the defeat of Germany and Austria in the Great War and their perceived ill-treatment in the subsequent Versailles peace treaty, it was pathetically easy to induce rampant self-pity in the German people. Indeed, Hitler was originally just one of a large number of competing far-right politicians trying to achieve this.

By contrast, neither envy nor resentment formed any part of Churchill's psychological make-up. The author John Julius Norwich recalls going to the cinema with his parents Duff and Lady Diana Cooper and with Winston Churchill: 'I remember a film about Irish peasants, during which he occasionally remarked: "Poor horse." And then at the end, he declared: "Envy – most barren of all vices."' The Germans' envy of the victorious powers of 1918, of their colonies and wealth certainly, but above all of their victory itself, made them easy victims for Adolf Hitler.

The Milgram and Asch experiments

'The art of leadership,' wrote Tony Blair in 1994, 'is in saying no, not yes. It is very easy to say yes.'[3] Two famous experiments undertaken in America some years ago – the Milgram and the Asch projects – illustrate quite how easy it is for people to say yes, and they have very disturbing implications for the way we view the tractability of human nature. In the experiment conducted in 1963 by Dr Stanley Milgram, volunteers were required to test a man who was strapped on to a chair with an electrode attached to his wrists. The volunteer was told that the experiment was being undertaken in order to test human tolerance to pain. The man had been required to memorise a text, and if he repeated it correctly, the volunteer would simply do nothing. If he stumbled or erred, however, the volunteer was instructed to flick a switch on a rheostat that administered an electric shock to the man in the chair. These shocks got progressively more powerful as the errors increased.

In truth, of course, there was no electric charge at all, and the man was acting as he yelled out in pain. Yet the volunteers did not know that, and no fewer than 65 per cent of them blindly obeyed their instructions, going on to administer shocks of up to 450 volts, which would constitute a lethal dosage. The man's screams of pain did not prevent them continuing with the experiment. As Brian Masters has put it in his autobiography, *Getting Personal*, the Milgram experiment 'demonstrated beyond question that timid, kindly decent souls could become monsters if offered the chance'.[4]

Then there are the equally worrying implications of the Asch experiment, in which three people were shown three lines on a screen and asked which was the longest. Again, unknown to one of the volunteers, the other two were in fact experimenters. The longest of the lines was always perfectly obvious; the true answer was not in doubt, even to someone with the worst eyesight and meanest intelligence. After a couple of rounds in which they all chose the correct lines, the two experimenters began to choose the same wrong line, one that was identifiably and clearly shorter than the longest. At first the volunteer would protest and point out the truth, but astonishingly quickly he would go along with the opinion of the other two. The Milgram and Asch experiments show how easily people can be led, both into acting cruelly and – just as worrying – into disbelieving the evidence of their own eyes.[5]

Leading people to commit horrific crimes, as Hitler did in the Second World War, and then to deny the evidence of everything about them, was therefore not so hard a task as it might at first appear. Academic work done by the historian Christopher Browning of Princeton University on the notorious Reserve Police Battalion 101, which was responsible for thousands of deaths in the Final Solution in Poland, shows how respectable working- and middle-class citizens of Hamburg became genocidal killers. It seems that peer pressure and a natural propensity for obedience and comradeship – rather than anti-Semitism or Nazi fervour – turned entirely ordinary people into mass murderers.[6]

The lessons are as applicable to today as to 1941–5, as we are reminded by a glance at what happened in the 1990s in places like Rwanda and the former Yugoslavia. How could a people as civilised as the Germans have perpetrated the most ghastly crime of human history? Browning's central conclusion – that far more than just anti-Semitism drove Germany's infamous Reserve Police Battalion 101 to commit atrocities in wartime Poland – was attacked by the historian Daniel Goldhagen in his controversial book of 1996, *Hitler's Willing Executioners*.

Goldhagen argued that the recruits of Battalion 101, who were not selected in any sense for their Nazi ardour but who indeed joined up largely to avoid active service abroad, killed Jewish women, the elderly, and children 'for pleasure' because they had 'fun' on their 'Jew-hunts', where their 'demonological anti-Semitism' was translated into 'a widespread eagerness to kill Jews'. Anti-Semitism, the author maintained, was so ingrained into German culture, society and history that Hitler and the Holocaust were simply the inevitable results. All it took was for Hitler to provide the necessary leadership for genocide to take place.[7] The early 1940s provided the perfect – in the stock phrase of detective fiction – motive, opportunity and method. Yet German Jews were far better integrated in Germany than in most other parts of Europe in the twenties and thirties and, as Keegan has pointed out, 'in 1918 the Kaiser's Reich controlled all the *shtetls* in Europe, but harmed their inhabitants not at all'. Was it therefore much more a case of, as Milton Himmelfarb has memorably put it: 'No Hitler, no Holocaust'? So was Hitler's leadership the central feature of the tragedy?

Battalion 101 represented a cross-section of German society and no one was coerced into killing Jews or taking part in any atrocity. Browning believes that there was nothing peculiarly German about the Holocaust, except perhaps in the perpetrators' heightened respect for authority and readiness to obey orders, and that apart from a relatively small number of fanatical Nazis, few Germans generally approved of what was happening 'out east'. Yet neither did they actively disapprove; the vast majority of Germans were simply indifferent and did not want to be told about the details. Yet when called upon specifically to help in the genocide, between 80 and 90 per cent of the members of Battalion 101 acquiesced without undue complaint. After some initial squeamishness they 'became increasingly efficient and calloused executioners'. Only twelve of the battalion's five hundred members actually refused to shoot 1,800 Jews in the woods outside the Polish village of Jozefow on 13 July 1942. During the remainder of that seventeen-hour day of slaughter – interspersed with cigarette breaks and a midday meal – another forty-five members or so absented themselves for various reasons. The remaining 85 per cent simply got on with the job of shooting Jewish women and children at point-blank range, even though they knew perfectly well that no retribution would have been exacted had they refused. 'At first we shot freehand,' one recalled. 'When one aimed too high the entire skull exploded. As a consequence, brains and bones flew everywhere. Thus, we were instructed to place the bayonet point on the neck.'

Using interrogation reports from the 1960s, it is possible to delve deep into the mindset of these killers. The reports make chilling but utterly compelling reading, as the authorities analyse the motives of men who for a large number of quite complex psychological reasons allowed themselves to become genocidal murderers. Most of these reasons – wartime brutalisation, 'segmentation', 'routinization', the desire for conformity and so on – do not end at the borders of Nazi Germany. We pride ourselves on the idea that the Holocaust could never have taken place in Britain, but in fact there were easily enough people in 1939–45 who would have staffed the gas chambers had they been erected in Argyll, Cardiff or the Home Counties.

Taking responsibility

Leaders take responsibility. When things went against Churchill he did not hesitate to take personal blame for them. In his speeches to secret sessions of Parliament he would readily admit to having made errors. Hitler, by contrast, constantly blamed others when the war began to go against him; first his generals and subsequently the whole German people, whom he wound up thinking unworthy of his genius. This dichotomy is well expressed by Churchill's willingness to visit bombed-out streets across Britain in order to raise morale, something Hitler virtually never did in Germany. Indeed, the Führer had curtains installed in his car. This distancing of himself from his people's suffering was undoubtedly an error for Hitler, who would probably have been received with adulation even up to 1944. His fear of being associated with images of failure and defeat meant that he passed up photo-opportunities that Churchill grasped enthusiastically. When, on 8 September 1940, Churchill started to cry at the sight of a flattened street in the East End of London, a local woman was heard to remark: 'Look, he really cares,' and the crowd cheered him spontaneously.[8] It helped, of course, that Churchill genuinely did care, and did not see people like Hitler did, merely as disposable units in his overall master-plan. Unfortunately for him, Hitler had no advisers who could change his mind. Successful leaders surround themselves with constructive dissenters; Churchill had Alanbrooke, Stalin had Marshal Antonov, Roosevelt had General George Marshall. Hitler, of course, received no such objective advice from 'no men'.

Hitler travelled very little during the war, just to his 'Wolf's Lair' headquarters in eastern Prussia, and four times to France – once to see Rundstedt, once to Paris to gloat at Compiègne, once to visit Marshal Pétain and Pierre Laval at Montoire and once to see General Franco at Hendaye. He was not much of a globe-trotter before the war either, having never visited Britain, America, Africa or the Far East. Some of his strategic blunders – especially his declaration of war against America in December 1941 – might have been avoided if he had been adventurous in early life and had an opportunity to discover for himself what the rest of the non-German world was really like. Churchill, by contrast, was by far the best-travelled Prime Minister in history: during the first four years of the war he covered no fewer than 110,000 miles, spending thirty-three days at sea and fourteen days in the air. It gave him a global strategic perspective entirely lacking in the mind of the Führer.

Knowing when to go

Part of the art of leadership is to know when to stop, but in common with all prime ministers of the twentieth century other than Lord Salisbury and Harold Wilson, Winston

Churchill stayed on in office too long. As with so many of his predecessors, he was too easily convinced by arguments about his own indispensability, despite the fact that they were being made by progressively fewer and fewer people. When, in the summer of 1954, an old journalist friend told Churchill that 'quite a few of your Conservative friends are saying that it would be a good thing for the party if you were to resign some time fairly soon', the Prime Minister glanced at him and then around the Commons bar where they were sitting, before replying: 'You know, as I look at this room and think back over my long association with this House, I think this is a pretty good pub. And as I look at the faces in the House, I wonder why I should leave this pub until someone says "Time, please!" in somewhat stronger accents than those of my friends to whom you have been speaking.'⁹

Churchill ought to have emulated Cincinnatus and Garibaldi and left active politics at the time of his triumph in 1945. He could have retired to Chartwell to build walls, write books, paint pictures, and enjoy global secular canonisation. For, by 1945, the greatest adventure story of the century was very obviously over, and the 'Indian Summer' premiership of 1951–5, with its labour appeasement, political sclerosis, foreign-policy reverses and general air of nostalgia and complacency was not at all what an exhausted and poverty-stricken Britain needed. Like Ronald Reagan at Reykjavik at the end of his career, but with far less success, Churchill longed for a summit with the Russians that would earn him the unaccustomed soubriquet 'Peacemaker'. Unlike Reagan he did not speak for a superpower, and it was not to be.

When Churchill and his Conservative Central Office adviser Reginald Maudling sat down to write the leader's speech for the 1947 party conference, it slowly dawned on Maudling that Churchill had not actually read the Industrial Charter, the cornerstone declaration of party policy on all matters concerning the economy. So Maudling handed him a paragraph that summarised its provisions, concerning centralisation, high employment levels, strong trade unions, no denationalisation, equal pay for women, increased spending on training, joint production councils and partnership schemes between industry, government and unions. Churchill said there was a great deal in it with which he did not agree. 'Well, sir,' answered the hapless speech-writer, foreseeing difficulties and beginning to get flustered, 'this is what the party conference adopted.' 'Oh well,' replied Churchill, 'leave it in then.'

The 1951–5 ministry was not Churchill's finest hour. When he returned to Downing Street he brought with him piles of the red 'Action This Day' tags that he had attached to important papers during the war. They were put in a drawer and left there, never to be used. Inattention to detail, lack of interest in domestic and economic issues, and sheer laziness over policy were the besetting problems of the 'Indian Summer' premiership. It is a sign of the sclerotic nature of that ministry that even though the Prime Minister suffered a stroke in the summer of 1953, the Cabinet never noticed that anything untoward had happened. On the few occasions when the Prime Minister intervened with his lieutenants' business it was to make matters worse.

Appeasement of growing trade union militancy only 'fed the crocodile' and introduced wage-induced inflation into the economy. The Chancellor of the Exchequer, R. A. Butler, was telephoned by Churchill just before Christmas 1954 to be told that he had solved the threatened rail strike. 'On whose terms?' inquired the worried Butler. 'Why, theirs of course, old cock!' replied a satisfied premier. If that was a leitmotif for a ministry which did not add to the lustre of Churchill's reputation, its most enduring image must be the huge hearing aid that had to be placed in the centre of the Cabinet table so that the octogenarian Prime Minister and several of his more elderly wartime colleagues could hear what was being said. Churchill was, after all, already an old-age pensioner even when he came to the premiership in 1940.

When Churchill finally retired in April 1955 he failed to leave enough time for his successor, Anthony Eden, to settle in to the job before the Suez Crisis was upon him. 'Many people say that I ought to have retired after the war, and have become some sort of elder statesman,' he told the young scientist R. V. Jones in 1946, 'but how could I? I have fought all my life and I cannot give up fighting now!'[10] What had changed was the quality of his enemies; from the excitement of fighting Hitler in 1945 he had to make do with far less riveting foes such as an under-skilled workforce, an over-regulated economy and increasingly militant trade unions. His place in history secured by VE-Day, Churchill could have bucked the twentieth century's baleful trend of prime ministers holding on too long for their own or their party's good. But as Churchill had written in *Savrola*: '"Vehement, high, and daring" was his cast of mind. The life he lived was the only one he could ever live; he must go on to the end.'[11]

Churchill as an historian

The first thing Churchill did when he finally retired was to publish his great work of Anglo-American history, which he had been working on in fits and starts for decades. Leaders who wish to make a lasting mark on history need to be great writers as well as great orators, and Churchill's Nobel Prize for Literature was well deserved. 'In broad principle I shall be willing to undertake to write *A History of the English-Speaking Peoples*, their origins, their quarrels, their misfortunes and their reconciliation for the sum of £20,000,' wrote Winston Churchill to Newman Flower, the managing director of Cassell & Co. on 30 October 1932. The project would take four or five years, he expected. Yet because of the great events that overtook not only Churchill but also the English-speaking peoples themselves, this four-volume work was not published for another quarter of a century.

It was during the first few months of that period of internal Tory opposition dubbed his 'wilderness years' that Churchill came up with the idea of writing a work whose 'object was to lay stress upon the common heritage of the peoples of Great Britain and the United States of America as a means of enhancing their friendship'. It was an act of tremendous foresight, for a decade later those two countries, along with their dominions and dependencies, were to be in the forefront of the struggle to save civilisation.

Although there were sound political reasons for writing the book, the principal and immediate reason for its inception was financial. A prodigious spender with no inherited wealth, Churchill throughout his life relied on his pen and his parliamentary stipends to pay for his grand style of life, and having recently resigned from the Conservative Shadow Cabinet over the issue of Indian self-government he knew he could not expect any ministerial posts in the near future. In the event, it took a full-scale European war to get him back into His Majesty's Government.

So his *History* was from the outset intended to be a bestseller, as he wrote to one of his assistants, the Oxford historian Keith Feiling, 'a vivid narrative picking up the dramatic and dominant episodes and by no means undertaking a complete account'. This was not going to be yet another dry-as-dust semi-academic history of the British and their worldwide cousinhood, but a fast-flowing work of literature starting with Julius Caesar's invasion of England in 55 BC and ending in 1902 with Britain's victory in the Boer War.

Although Churchill engaged a number of leading historians to help him prepare drafts, to explain periods of history to him with which he was unfamiliar and generally to ease the process of research and writing, this was very much his own work – as the annotations on the various proofs make abundantly clear. In 1937, informing his wife Clementine of their precarious financial situation, he wrote about how the *History* was 'entailing an immense amount of reading and solitary reflection if justice is to be done to so tremendous a topic'. The final £15,000 of his advance was not payable until the delivery of the manuscript, which he hoped he could achieve in December 1939.

Of course the rise of Nazism was to interrupt his writing with increasing force over the following two years, but it is astonishing how Churchill was able to compartmentalise his life, snatching time from his campaign against the appeasement of Hitler to get on with his writing. As the war clouds seemed to be gathering over Czechoslovakia in August 1938, Churchill wrote to Lord Halifax about how he was 'horribly entangled with the Ancient Britons, the Romans, the Angles, Saxons and Jutes, all of whom I thought I had escaped from for ever when I left school'. Indeed, if anything, the work on his *History* might have been a useful distraction, for as he wrote to a friend during the Munich Crisis: 'It has been a comfort to me in these anxious days to put a thousand years between my thoughts and the twentieth century.'

The expectation that the publication would make up about one-third of his income for 1939 meant that it provided his principal daily occupation that year outside politics. A team of historians – some paid, others not – continued to help him in various capacities, from writing treatises, to giving private lectures at Chartwell, to checking proofs for factual accuracy. By the time of the *History*'s eventual publication these included some of the most distinguished men of their profession. F. W. (now Sir William) Deakin was Churchill's principal assistant; also lending their help at different times and in different capacities were Maurice Ashley, A. L. Rowse, Asa (now Lord) Briggs, J. H. (later Sir Jack) Plumb, G. M. Young, Alan (now Lord) Bullock and several other highly respected scholars. These historians, recalled Ashley, generally kept enough restraint on an 'exuberant' Churchill to ensure that his statements could be sustained by the historical facts.

'In the main,' Churchill wrote to Ashley in April 1939, 'the theme is emerging of the growth of freedom and law, of the rights of the individual, of the subordination of the State to the fundamental and moral conceptions of an ever-comprehending community. Of these ideas the English-speaking peoples were the authors, then the trustees, and must now become the armed champions. Thus I condemn tyranny in whatever guise and from whatever quarter it presents itself. All this of course has a current application.' Yet however many hours the 'current application' of his principles might have taken out of his day in the last months of peace, Churchill always somehow managed to find time to work on his *History*, to the point that he was busy revising the final chapter of the fourth volume on the very evening that Germany invaded Poland in September 1939.

The delivery date for his completed manuscript obviously had to be postponed, but even the outbreak of war did not entirely close down work on the *History*. The Phoney War found Churchill, who was by then First Lord of the Admiralty, trying to complete the series. F. W. Deakin had joined the 63rd Oxfordshire Yeomanry Anti-Tank Regiment, but was also correcting proofs in his (rapidly dwindling) spare time, while Alan Bullock prepared a ten-thousand-word section on Canada. 'I do hope you will be able to get on with this during the week as the matter is so important and the stress here is very great,' Churchill wrote to Deakin from the Admiralty on 6 October 1939. By 1940 Churchill's project was nearing completion, but so too was Hitler's, and after Churchill became prime minister in May the *History* had to be put on ice for the duration of the war, although the film rights were sold to the great Hungarian-American film producer Alexander Korda for £50,000.

It was not until the last week of 1945 – by which time Churchill had saved civilisation but lost the British general election – that he was able to continue work on his *History*. By then, of course, the English-speaking peoples had added the greatest chapters of their history to the tale, but it was decided not to extend the work to an extra volume to incorporate that. Churchill took his proofs of the book on board the *Queen*

Elizabeth liner on his way to make his great 'Iron Curtain' speech in America, but no sooner did he return than another large-scale project was to intervene which would once again retard publication of his *History*.

Churchill considered it his duty to write six volumes of his war memoirs, and took advantage of his years in opposition to do this, helped by William Deakin. The work began in 1946 and the final volume, *Triumph and Tragedy*, also published by Cassell & Co., did not appear until 1954, by which time Churchill was once again prime minister, the Conservative Party having won the October 1951 general election. Yet again history had overtaken the *History*.

Ironically enough, it seems to have been Churchill's debilitating stroke in the summer of 1953 that led to the resuscitation of the project. His doctor Lord Moran had suggested that the Prime Minister should 'take up something that will calm your mind', at which Brendan Bracken, the former Conservative minister and Churchill's close friend, said: 'Well, why not finish *A History of the English-Speaking Peoples*?' As luck would have it, Bracken owned the journal *History Today*, which had been founded in 1951 and which was co-edited by his friend and former wartime assistant private secretary at the Ministry of Information, Alan Hodge. Hodge was something of a prodigy; he was only twenty-five when – after attending Liverpool Collegiate School and Oriel College, Oxford – he began writing avant-garde verse and collaborated with Robert Graves on *The Long Weekend* in 1940.

Co-editing the magazine with the author and poet Peter Quennell, in a highly productive partnership that lasted until Hodge's death in 1979, Hodge exercised, as *The Times* obituary of him states, 'a stewardship which was scholarly, imaginative and judicious'. He also published *The Past We Share* with Quennell in 1960, an illustrated history of Britain and America. Colleagues and friends of Hodge often lamented that his natural modesty contented itself with collaborative ventures rather than individual writings, through which he could have made a greater name for himself. A prime example of this was the way he headed the committee of historians who helped Churchill with the final research for *A History of the English-Speaking Peoples*.

A group of academics and historians was quickly brought together by Hodge to help Churchill, several of them the same men as had lent a hand before the war. 'I shall lay an egg a year,' Churchill announced to Moran, 'a volume every twelve months should not mean too much work.'

Aged seventy-nine, Churchill started to get the *History* ready for publication as he recuperated from his stroke. But on re-reading his early proofs he found that he wanted to recast the book substantially. The great events through which the world had passed in the intervening years since 1939 had put history into better perspective for him, and he wanted the work to reflect the wider lessons of history better than the first drafts had done. 'Hitherto after the opening chapters the story has been classified under titles of the reigns of kings,' Churchill wrote to Hodge. 'This was how we learned it at school. Of course it is not in accordance with the scale and temper of the work. We should consider only using monarchs for chapter heads when they represent some great phase or turning point in history.'

Magna Carta, the Hundred Years War, 'the Dawn of Parliament' and the Wars of the Roses were now to be given more emphasis than mere lists of monarchs, for, as Churchill put it: 'We are recording the march of events in what is meant to be a lively, continuous narrative. We are primarily concerned with the social and political changes as they occur, especially with those which have left their marks on today.' Churchill joked to his friend Lord Beaverbrook about this re-reading of his great work in the light of the Second World War: 'On the whole I think I would rather have lived through our lot of troubles than any of the others, though I must place on record my regret that the human race ever learned to fly.'

Just as Churchill had been working on the proofs the night that Hitler had invaded Poland in 1939, so he was revising them for the final time only two days after giving up his second premiership in 1955. This time no world event was going to be allowed to intervene. He had won the Nobel Prize for Literature in 1953 and had much to live up to, and, as he vouchsafed to friends, this was also to be his last literary endeavour. Talking to the historian A. L. Rowse from his bed at Chartwell in July 1955, Churchill admitted that he had been 're-reading the *History* he had written before the war, but he wasn't satisfied with it. However, there were people who would read it on account of his "notoriety".'

There were indeed; Cassell & Co.'s first print run of *A History of the English-Speaking Peoples* numbered no fewer than 130,000, with a further 30,000 being reprinted within a month. After that the reprints continued to come thick and fast, especially once the volumes – which were published between 1956 and 1958 – began to receive superlative reviews from historians such as C. V. Wedgwood, J. H. Plumb, Professor Michael Howard and Professor D. C. Somervell, scholars whose critical judgement was not blinded by Churchill's fame or grandeur. Even the notorious iconoclast A. J. P. Taylor wrote of the first volume, *The Birth of Britain*, that: 'It is one of the wisest, most exciting works of history ever written.'

Churchill fully deserved the massive critical acclaim that those volumes attracted when first published, and have continued to enjoy ever since. They should be read on their own terms, as a great work of literature, as much as – or perhaps even more than – a scrupulously accurate work of history. Pedants have been able to spot occasional sentences in which Churchill's natural exuberance and feel for the language or spirit of a story might have taken him over that thin dividing line between truth and myth – he cites (with caveats) Alfred the Great burning the cakes, for example – but the books are none the worse for that.

Churchill's place in history

'History,' declared Winston Churchill in his November 1940 panegyric to Neville Chamberlain, 'with its flickering lamp stumbles along the trails of the past, trying to reconstruct its themes, to revive its echoes, and kindle with pale gleams the passion of former days.' Churchill would probably have been very pleased by the historical cottage industry that has grown up around him and his reputation. Never far from controversy during his own lifetime, he would doubtless have taken enormous pleasure in defending himself from those who are today loosely called the 'revisionists'.

In one sense, of course, all history-writing is but a revision of the original version, and for some years after his death in 1965 writers about Churchill were merely seeking to restore the balance after the mass of hagiographies which had lauded him in the 1950s and early 1960s. Since then, however, and especially in the past decade, a new, highly critical tone has appeared. This is knocking, aggressively carping, and sometimes frankly contemptuous of Churchill and his achievements.

It has all had surprisingly little effect on the public perception of the wartime premier. The English-speaking peoples seem to have a settled view of Churchill's glory that no amount of historical debate will now alter. 'Churchill has a few detractors,' wrote the *Sunday Telegraph* on the fiftieth anniversary of VE-Day, 'but none has made much impression on the public view of him.' Today his popularity certainly shows no sign of abating. The numbers visiting his home, Chartwell, have been increasing steadily since it opened to the public in the year after his death; a United States warship was named after him in 2000, the first Englishman to be so honoured since the eighteenth century (although he was of course an honorary American citizen); more prosaically, a pair of his bedroom slippers recently fetched $10,000 at auction. He easily won the BBC's 'Great Britons' poll in November 2002, winning 447,423 votes, and was only just pipped at the post for Man of the Millennium by William Shakespeare in 1999, a defeat he would have taken much better than he did the result of the 1945 general election.

The virulence of the 1995 row over the purchase of Churchill's archives with money from the British National Lottery was a tribute to his continued pre-eminence in the national pantheon, as is the way in which both sides of the debate over the proper level of Britain's integration into the European Union attempt to appropriate his political legacy. When the would-be Führer of Austria, Herr Jörg Haider, criticised Churchill as a war criminal on a par with Hitler, it received far more attention than his other more immediate pronouncements about the widening of the European Union. When rioters daubed Communist and anarchist slogans on Churchill's Parliament Square statue on May Day 2000 there was a huge public outcry.

In the popular, non-academic sense at least, Churchill-revisionism is redundant. Like other national icons such as Lincoln, Washington and Napoleon – or his own antagonists Gandhi and de Gaulle – Churchill is so well-bunked that no amount of debunking books will have any appreciable effect on his standing. They continue to be written, of course, but they have the same impact on public perception as does a drawing pin stuck into the hide of a huge pachyderm. What in *Great Contemporaries* he called 'the grievous inquest of history' has sat in judgement on Churchill and has found that he has no case to answer. Only in certain historical and journalistic and outré academic circles is that verdict considered unsafe.

The first set of Churchill-knockers are the ideologists. From the author Clive Ponting on the Left across to David Irving on the far Right, these people have attempted to use various aspects of Churchill's career in order to make certain political points of their own. Depicting him as having a vicious or even evil personality, often by dragging quotations wildly out of context and ascribing motives so machiavellian that they might even have shocked Churchill himself, the ideologists rapidly lose the sympathy and patience of objective readers. If Churchill is so violently disliked by both extremes of the political spectrum, we rightly assume, he could not have been all that bad.

In 2001, admirers of Winston Churchill breathed a huge sigh of relief. For fourteen years, since the publication of David Irving's first volume on Churchill, they had been waiting to see what foul conspiracies the extreme right-wing historian might have managed to dig up in the hundreds of archives to which he had access yet in a 1063-page hymn of hate ironically entitled *Churchill's War: Triumph in Adversity* it was clear that he has not managed to land one single significant blow on the reputation of Britain's wartime leader.

All the old accusations were trotted out, of course: that Churchill was a rude, lying alcoholic who concealed Japan's intention to attack Pearl Harbor from the Americans, was behind the murder of Britain's ally the Polish leader General Sikorski, wanted to flatten Rome, and so on and so endlessly on. There were even a few new, equally groundless slurs; according to Irving's book, Churchill was also a flasher who enjoyed exposing himself to foreign statesmen, was responsible for tipping off the Nazis to the fact that Britain had broken their codes, and wanted MI6 to assassinate Britain's other ally, General de Gaulle.

There were a dozen such new accusations, most of which would be laughable if they were not so rabidly presented, complete with 160 pages of notes that were intended to look as if they backed them up. Yet when, for example, Irving claimed that the then Queen Elizabeth (the late Queen Mother) supported Hitler's peace offer in 1940, and that the proof was to be found in Box Number 23 of Lord Monckton's papers at the Bodleian Library in Oxford, I recalled from my own work on Monckton that that particular box had never been open to historians. Sure enough, the Bodleian Librarian officially confirmed to me that David Irving has not so much as seen the box, let alone opened it.

Many of Irving's assertions are completely contradictory. If Churchill 'invariably put the interests of the United States above those of his own country and its empire', why did he not warn the Americans about what was about to happen in Pearl Harbor? Or if Mr Irving's notorious views on Auschwitz are correct – that Jews were not being systematically killed there – why should Churchill be held to account for not ordering the RAF to bomb the place? Mr Irving consistently wanted it both ways in his book, but equally consistently wound up getting neither.

Despite the book's subtitle, Irving sees no redeeming features in the man who had the temerity to defeat Adolf Hitler. Churchill's funniest jokes are dismissed as 'jibes'. The imperative need to meet President Roosevelt in early 1942 to co-ordinate a post-Pearl Harbor global military strategy against Germany and Japan is explained in terms of the Prime Minister's 'desire to hobnob at the highest levels'. He is accused of winning the war 'in spite of himself'. Yet whenever the evidence for Irving's claims is minutely examined by someone who has visited the same archives and handled the same original documents, it utterly fails to justify Irving's ludicrous allegations.

The selective quotation is legion. When Irving claimed that Churchill wished to 'eliminate' de Gaulle, what Churchill in fact recommended to his Cabinet colleagues was that they should consider whether they should 'eliminate de Gaulle as a political force and face Parliament and France upon the issue'. Irving's entire Pearl Harbor theory also rested upon an obvious misreading of the diary of Sir Alec Cadogan.

If Mr Irving really has, as his publisher's blurb suggested, spent twenty-seven years researching and writing *Churchill's War*, then he has wasted half a lifetime. For in its long series of silly, snide, unproven innuendoes he has ultimately achieved a rather pathetic piece of work. Instead of trying to rebuild his historical reputation, which was destroyed by his defeat in the Irving *v* Lipstadt and Penguin Books libel trial in 2000, he has produced a book that will only convince the most extreme right-wing conspiracy theorists.

When Irving writes that Churchill was of 'partly Jewish blood, although safely diluted', he is simply being offensive. When he claims that Churchill 'was ambivalent about why he was really fighting this ruinous war', he is ignoring the evidence of dozens of the finest speeches ever delivered in the English tongue, which explained to Britain and the world between 1939 and 1945, in utterly uncompromising language, precisely why Nazism had to be extirpated for human civilisation to survive and prosper.

When Irving alleged that the Duke of Windsor was forced to leave Portugal in August 1940 at British 'pistol point', he was merely writing rubbish. Irving's profession of 'shock' that Churchill turned a blind eye to the affairs of his daughter-in-law Pamela Harriman is based on a failure to appreciate the mores of Churchill's class and time. Churchill's supposed desire 'to see Rome in flames' is utterly disproved by his message to Roosevelt that: 'We ought to instruct our pilots to observe all possible care in order to avoid hitting any of the Pope's buildings in the city of Rome.'

A second strand of Churchill revisionism comprises a critique which seems to be growing in American libertarian and isolationist circles. In Patrick Buchanan's 1999 book, *A Republic, Not an Empire*, Churchill is denied a place on the side of the angels, and in a single half-hour speech at a recent history conference, the New York State University historian, Ralph Raico, managed to level no fewer than thirty-two accusations against him. I have found that survivors of the London Blitz have their own comments to make on Mr Raico's statement that Hitler never had any intention of bombing their city and that Churchill was therefore wrong to advocate building a strong RAF in the thirties. According to Raico, Churchill was a crypto-socialist, an ethnic-cleanser, a war criminal and a 'stooge' of Stalin's. 'A man of blood and a politico without principle,' Raico described him in an article to support his thesis, 'whose apotheosis serves to corrupt every standard of honesty and morality in politics and history.' Rarely, I find, do the American libertarian revisionists take refuge in understatement.

Although he is British, the professional contrarian Christopher Hitchens was writing in an American publication, *Atlantic Monthly*, in April 2002 when he accused Churchill of being ruthless, boorish, manipulative, 'incapacitated by alcohol', myopic, and wrong about almost everything except the Nazis. He even accused Churchill of being 'vulgar and alarmist' for 'constantly drumming on the subject' of rearmament in the thirties, as though it was possible to be 'alarmist' about something like the rise of Adolf Hitler. In the course of his nineteen-page rant, entitled 'The Medals of his Defeats', Hitchens claimed that it was 'easy to imagine the R.A.F. helping the Wehrmacht in the Caucasus'. This is in fact an impossibility for anyone who is not an obsessive controversialist attempting simply to *épater les Churchillians*. Only a misunderstanding of the War Cabinet minutes could have produced Hitchens's statement that in 1940 'Churchill more than once favoured limited negotiations with Hitler', when Churchill was actually putting the case to the War Cabinet *against* any such negotiations. Hitchens puts Churchill's opposition to German hegemony down to 'pure ambition', thereby ignoring the great mass of his writing and speeches and political actions over forty years in support of the concept of a European balance of power. Even Adolf Hitler himself recognised Churchill's commitment to that balance of power theory, which he considered outdated, but which he did not deny (see p.136).

In his attack on Churchill for ordering the shelling of the French Fleet at Oran, Hitchens ignores the fact that Britain could not have known that Vichy would not have handed their fleet over to Hitler – if that was indeed the case. We must be thankful that Churchill and not the uncharacteristically gullible Hitchens was responsible for the security of Britain in 1940. When the writer then states of the Oran attack that Churchill's 'chroniclers prefer to skate over it or, where possible, elide it altogether', he is – unusually for so intelligent a polemicist – writing demonstrable rubbish. The episode has been discussed by Sir Martin Gilbert (in no fewer than twenty-seven pages), Roy Jenkins, John Keegan, John Lukacs, John Charmley, Joseph Lash, Philip Guedalla, Basil Liddell Hart, William Manchester, John Ramsden, Geoffrey Best, Norman Rose, A. L. Rowse, the present author, and, of course, by Churchill himself in the second volume of his memoirs.

Likewise, far from Churchill's retirement being 'a protracted, distended humiliation of celebrity-seeking and gross over-indulgence', in fact the four volumes of Churchill's *History of the English-Speaking Peoples* were acclaimed by academic historians and, as we have seen, are still in print over forty years later. After winning the Second World War, Winston Churchill had little reason or need to 'seek' celebrity. Yet it is only when Hitchens makes the claim that Churchill was responsible for deliberately putting the American liner *Lusitania* at risk in 1915 in order to bring the United States into the Great War that one starts to doubt whether Hitchens himself can really believe these ludicrous theses.

Churchill regularly used to joke that he knew that history would be kind to him because he himself would be writing it. Sadly, however, people who are uniquely disqualified by their lack of objectivity have been writing a great deal of history about him, and a good deal of cross-fertilisation goes on between them. Many of the quotations Mr Raico uses to illustrate his accusations are footnoted to have come from the work of Irving and Ponting; in turn Raico is quoted admiringly by Buchanan. Several of Hitchens's allegations seem to have originated from Irving. It is almost impossible to believe that these people have set out in genuine pursuit of historical truth, rather than to attack Churchill for the shock value (and sales) attendant on abusing such a totem figure of Anglo-American political culture.

Churchill is a powerful magnet for believers in conspiracy theories. The charge-sheet against him is as long as it is imaginative. Hardly a year goes by without a new book being published accusing him of luring Rudolf Hess to Scotland or having had prior knowledge of the bombing of Pearl Harbor or another such rank absurdity. He has been accused of engineering the Wall Street Crash of 1929 (in which he personally lost a fortune); a writer in the *Philadelphia Inquirer* has argued that if Churchill 'had been a little wiser in 1911, or 1919, neither World War II, nor the Korean, Vietnam nor Persian Gulf wars would have happened, nor the drug explosion, nor the vast [American] deficit'; some writers still maintain that he allowed the city of Coventry to be destroyed rather than risk revealing that Britain had cracked the Enigma code. The Internet has, needless to say, opened up an entirely new front on which Churchill revisionists can hallucinate, polluting cyberspace with ever more absurd fantasies. The excellent magazine *Finest Hour*, published by the International Churchill Society, has for years been collecting and systematically refuting these and dozens of other such allegations.[12]

A third and highly influential source of Churchill revisionism is provided by the press. Newspaper editors will readily affirm that Churchill stories make great copy, especially since the dead cannot sue for libel. We therefore see news stories in reputable newspapers which, had they been written in his lifetime, would have garnered Churchill hundreds of thousands of pounds in out-of-court settlements. According to some recent newspaper articles, Churchill was a drug addict who actively helped his daughter-in-law to cuckold his own son. He supposedly ordered Mussolini's assassination, and then tried to recover compromising documents relating to a secret Anglo-Italian peace deal he had allegedly tried to arrange. Churchill rarely smoked cigars, we have been told, but liked having lit ones around in order 'to accentuate his masculinity'.

According to various revisionists, he was also a plagiarist, an opportunist, a warmonger, a hypocrite, a fantasist, the true creator of Nazism – ingenious one, that – a terrible military strategist and a pathological liar. Someone has even written a book, which has inexplicably been catalogued according to its own estimation as non-fiction, stating categorically that Churchill helped Martin Bormann to escape from Berlin in 1945 and then found him a house near London in which to live out the rest of his days in comfort.[13] The advance offered to the author of this drivel was reputed to be in the region of a quarter of a million pounds, although it is said that it was not paid in full because the allegations did not stand up to scrutiny. As recently as September 2002 the Saudi Arabian Ambassador to London, Ghazi Algosaibi, wrote to *The Spectator* to claim that Churchill ordered troops to fire on suffragettes in 1917, an accusation that was comprehensively rebutted a fortnight later by the International Churchill Society.[14]

All that historians can do when faced with these patent absurdities is to stay calm, go back to the original documents and prime authorities – usually Sir Martin Gilbert's magisterial eight-volume biography with its fourteen companion volumes – examine the historical context and available evidence, and work out the truth as forensically as possible. Ninety-five times out of a hundred, Churchill comes off scot-free.

Of course Churchill is certainly not above all criticism. Quite obviously with a career so long and varied, involving twice crossing the floor of the House of Commons, and being called upon to make momentous decisions, his judgement on several issues can legitimately be questioned. Over issues such as the the Sidney Street siege of 1910, the Gallipoli débâcle, the partition of Ireland, rejoining the gold standard, the handling of the General Strike, Indian nationalism, the Abdication Crisis, Bomber Command's targeting policy, the 1943 'soft underbelly' strategy, the insistence on Germany's unconditional surrender, the refusal to help the July plotters, British official recognition of Soviet guilt over the massacre of Polish officers in the forest of Katyn, and the proposed bombing of Auschwitz, Churchill has been criticised by distinguished academics and responsible politicians and journalists, both during his lifetime and after it. Such criticism was and is fair enough, although this author personally believes that Churchill made the right choice in almost every single one of those cases, displaying a far better track record of good judgement than most of his contemporaries. What is now being seen, however, is not a reasonable and honest debate but a series of acerbic and hostile criticisms levelled at Churchill's very patriotism and honour.

By far the most cogent criticisms of Churchill's career, and the ones most capable of scratching the outer paintwork of the edifice of what is now an untarnishable reputation, are those that have been voiced by Dr John Charmley, Professor Maurice Cowling, and the late Alan Clark, who loosely make what might be called the British Tory nationalist critique. In January 1993, Dr Charmley published *Churchill: The End of Glory*, which he followed in 1995 with *Churchill's Grand Alliance: The Anglo-American Special Relationship 1940–1957*. Both were closely argued and well-written analyses of Churchill's personal responsibility for the collapse of British power in the twentieth century. Churchill is also blamed for preventing Charmley's hero, Neville Chamberlain, from successfully pursuing appeasement to its intended conclusion, namely a debilitating German–Soviet war in which both antagonists fought each other to a standstill and were left mutually weak and thus no threat to Britain or the West.

Churchill is further accused of effectively betraying the British Empire to the United States through naïveté and an over-exaggerated view of British post-war weakness, and also of letting socialism into Britain by the back door. This view is fundamentally flawed, in that it mixes up cause and effect and hardly allows for Churchill's limited alternatives by 1945. The Tory nationalist school none the less constitutes the most significant attempt to dislodge the great man from his Parliament Square pedestal.

It is worth while, therefore, to look closely at the contention that Britain ought to have made peace with Nazi Germany in 1940 or 1941. (Professor Cowling, by contrast, believes Britain should not have gone to war in the first place in 1939.) Far from saving the Empire, not fighting the war to the end would have been disastrous both for Britain and for the prospects of a civilised, peaceful, democratic Western Europe such as has existed since 1945. Any advantages that so craven a treaty might have produced would have been marginal, prohibitively expensive and probably also very short-lived.

Since before the time of the Spanish Armada of 1588 it has been British policy to oppose any hegemonistic Continental power which sought to control the Channel ports in France, Holland and Belgium from which an invasion of southern England might be launched. King Philip II of Spain, Louis XIV, Napoleon Bonaparte and Kaiser Wilhelm II all suffered significant reverses in successive wars over precisely this issue. To have left Hitler in undisputed control of these ports in 1940 would have entailed decades of danger, with astronomically high defence expenditure and the need for perpetual vigilance for the rest of the decade and probably beyond.

With Britain out of the war, Hitler would probably not have needed to swoop south into Yugoslavia and Greece in the spring of 1941. As was examined in the last section, he would thus have been able to launch his invasion of Russia six weeks earlier than he did, with divisions taken from France, the Low Countries and Africa as well as those he had originally earmarked in Germany and Poland. Even as it was, the Wehrmacht nearly reached Moscow's underground stations, captured Stalingrad and subjected Leningrad to a gruelling thousand-day siege. Had the Germans pushed the Soviets back beyond the Urals, Hitler would have been master of Europe from Brest to Sverdlovsk. Instead, Britain's alliance with Russia allowed the Allies – once Hitler's ill-advised declaration of war had brought the United States into the conflict against Germany – to supply the Red Army with five thousand tanks, seven thousand air-craft, fifty-one thousand jeeps and fifty-one million pairs of boots, assistance which contributed materially to its ultimate victory.

As the author Major-General John Strawson has asked of any peace negotiations that might have taken place in 1941:

> Would Great Britain have been left in possession of both her Royal Naval and merchant fleets, with absolute freedom of the seas for trading and other purposes? Would Italy have aban-doned her African colonies? Would Greece and Albania have been free? Would Rommel and the Afrika Korps have quit Libya? Would Britain have been at liberty to maintain her armed forces at their – by 1941 – not contemptible level, and to deploy them where she wanted other than in Hitler's domains? What would Britain have said to France, the Low Countries, Denmark, Norway, and to Poland? Would Hitler have agreed – the agreement to have been subject to rigid verification meas-ures – to cease research into and development of V-weapons, jet aircraft, new submarines – and nuclear weapons? Would he, after the subjection of all Eastern Europe including Russia, once more have declared that he had no further territorial claims? Would he have guaranteed the integrity of the British Empire? Or would the whole negotiated peace – on the bizarre assumption that it could ever have come off at all – simply have proved to be another Peace of Amiens, the truce between Great Britain and France of 1802–1803, during which Napoleon feverishly prepared for a resumption of hostilities?[15]

Merely posing this series of questions in itself highlights the improbabilities of a workable peace being successfully negotiat-ed, let alone the dangers inherent in leaving Hitler as master of Europe.

Just as disastrous for Britain's hopes of long-term independ-ence would be the scenario in which Stalin defeated Hitler, and the Red Army poured westward to Berlin and beyond, with no Anglo-American army in France and Germany to stop him pushing on further. Stalin's control of the Channel ports would have been no less dangerous to Britain's long-term independence in the late 1940s and 1950s than Hitler's.

Add to this the fact that Hitler was (albeit fitfully) undertaking his own nuclear research, while Stalin was learning about the Allied nuclear breakthroughs from his Western spies, and the necessity for full British participation in a drastically foreshortened war becomes obvious. For either dictator to have been left, perhaps for years, in control of Europe would have necessarily been disastrous for Britain's hopes of continued and genuine independence. Henry Kissinger once quipped of the decade-long Iran–Iraq War: 'A pity they both can't lose.' The risk of a Nazi–Soviet war resulting in something other than mutual defeat was too great a one for the British Government to take in 1940.

Furthermore, the great cause of trying to encourage the United States to adopt a 'Germany First' policy in the struggle to save civilisation would have been utterly wrecked if Britain had come to terms with Hitler after the British Expeditionary Force's evacuation from Dunkirk. It took the dogged resistance during the Blitz and the Battle of Britain to convince America of Britain's worthiness as an ally. Although Britain did indeed wind up in hock to America after the war, she would have been in no better financial state as a result of remaining in perhaps decades-long military readiness, waiting for the likely moment when Hitler suddenly revoked his peace treaty and attacked again. The Führer had, after all, reneged upon every other treaty he had ever signed.

Furthermore, the war had been going on at sea for nine months by the time of the Dunkirk evacuation; sailors had perished, ships carrying child evacuees to Canada had been torpedoed, and as a result British blood was up. To have made a palpably ignoble peace would have dealt a crushing blow to imperial pride and self-esteem, and would doubtless have caused severe internal ructions fatal to the sense of national unity fostered once the opposition parties entered Churchill's Government in May 1940. The demoralisation of the United Kingdom and her imperial allies was too high a price to pay to escape the perils of the Blitz; the only domestic political winners would have been the Communist Party and the British Union of Fascists.

As for the accusation that Churchill killed the thing he most loved: in fact, after the India Act of 1935 the British Empire was already well on the way towards self-governance. The Second World War accelerated that process, without doubt, but the great days of Empire were long over by the time that Churchill came to power in May 1940. On a more emotional level, what glory would there have been in the possession of an Empire mortgaged to Britain by the grace of Adolf Hitler?

To have made peace with Hitler in 1940 and thus to have forsworn the hope, however remote it might have seemed at the time, one day to liberate Europe from Nazism, would have been to condemn the Continent to what Churchill that year famously termed 'a new Dark Age, made more sinister, and perhaps more protracted, by the lights of perverted science'. Hardly a European Jew could have survived the extermination process which had been begun on an *ad hoc* basis in Poland in September 1939, but became fully industrialised by 1942, if Hitler had been allowed undisputed possession of Europe and no Allied invasion had taken place in 1944, 1945, or any time thereafter. The Great Powers are presently enjoying their longest period of peace since the rise of the nation state in the sixteenth century; would that really have been possible if Hitler had been allowed to keep the spoils of his victory in 1940?

Churchill knew that to have made peace with Germany would be to have forfeited his own and his country's honour. In his panegyric to Chamberlain, after speaking of history's 'flickering lamp' trying 'to kindle with pale gleams the passion of former days', Churchill asked:

What is the worth of all this? The only guide to a man is his conscience; the only shield to his memory is the rectitude and sincerity of his actions. It is very imprudent to walk through life without this shield, because we are so often mocked by the failure of our hopes and the upsetting of our calculations; but with this shield, however the fates may play, we always march in the ranks of honour.

Despite the unrelenting efforts of his revisionist detractors, Winston Churchill marches there still.

Notes

Introduction

1 Christopher Hitchens, *Atlantic Monthly*, April 2002, p. 121
2 *Daily Telegraph*, 29 August 2002
3 *Daily Telegraph*, 12 February 2002
4 Johnson, *Napoleon*, p. 193
5 Brian MacArthur (ed.), *The Penguin Book of Historic Speeches*, 1995, pp. 300–1
6 Churchill, *Savrola*, p. 156
7 Gilbert, *Winston S. Churchill*, vol. 8, p. 369
8 Rosebery, *Lord Randolph Churchill*, p. 81
9 A. N. Wilson, *Watch in the Night*, p. 32
10 *New York World*, 6 February 1928

Hitler and Churchill to 1939

1 Warlimont, *Inside Hitler's Headquarters*, p. x
2 Pearson, *Citadel of the Heart*, p. 243
3 Brendon, *Churchill*, p. 126
4 Irving, *Churchill: Triumph*, p. 62
5 Mosley, *Life of Contrasts*, p. 47
6 Brendon, op. cit., p. 110
7 *BBC History Magazine*, May 2001, p. 7
8 Patrick Kinna in Sir Martin Gilbert's 1992 TV biography of Churchill
9 Ibid.
10 Letter from Ian Weston-Smith, 1 May 2001
11 Churchill, *Savrola*, p. 50
12 Mary Soames, 'Winston Churchill: the Great Human Being', 9th Annual Crosby Kemper Lecture, 21 April 1991, p. 7
13 Churchill, *Savrola*, p. 226
14 Jablonsky, *Churchill and Hitler*, p. 260
15 Luke, *Hansel Pless*, p. 73
16 Hitler, *Mein Kampf*, pp. 740–2
17 Rhodes James (ed.), *Churchill Speaks*, p. 603

18 *Daily Express*, 5 October 1938
19 Grint, *Art of Leadership*, p. 267
20 Roseman, *Wannsee*, p. 113
21 Rauschning, *Gespräche mit Hitler*, p. 223
22 Grint, op. cit., p. 297
23 *Spectator*, 26 January 2002
24 *The Times*, 16 July 1998
25 Irving, *Churchill: War Path*, p. 20
26 Churchill, *Savrola*, p. 88
27 Brendon, op. cit., p. 143
28 Jablonsky, op. cit., p. 209
29 *Observer*, 5 August 1951
30 Speer, *Inside the Third Reich*, p. 151
31 Ibid, pp. 187–8
32 Churchill, *Savrola*, p. 79
33 Gilbert, *Winston S. Churchill*, vol. 4, pp. 446–7
34 Prof. R. V. Jones, 'Churchill as I Knew Him', 10th Annual Crosby Kemper Lecture, 29 March 1992, p. 10
35 Speer, op. cit., pp. 155–6
36 Kershaw, *Nemesis*, p. xvi
37 Burleigh, *Third Reich*, pp. 253–5
38 Overy, *Interrogations*, p. 38
39 Waite, *Psychopathic God*, p. 42
40 Churchill, *Savrola*, p. 99
41 Stone, *Hitler*, p. 86
42 Irving, *Winston S. Churchill: Triumph*, p. xviii
43 Proctor, Robert N., 'The Anti-Tobacco Campaign of the Nazis', www.freerepublic.com
44 *Time* magazine, 9 January 1995
45 Soames (ed.), *Speaking for Themselves*, p. 390
46 *Sunday Telegraph*, 12 July 1998
47 Jablonsky, op. cit., p. 270
48 Gilbert, *Winston S. Churchill*, vol. 6, p. 166
49 Ibid., pp. 59–60
50 Goleman, Boyatzis and McKee, *New Leaders*, p. ix
51 Colville, *Fringes of Power*, p. 319

Hitler and Churchill from 1940

1 Gilbert, *Winston S. Churchill*, vol. 6, p. 216
2 Keegan, *Second World War*, p. 38
3 Roberts, *Holy Fox*, p. 201
4 Smith (ed.), *Hostage to Fortune*, p. 476
5 Engel, *Heeresadjutant bei Hitler*, p. 75

6 Burdick and Jacobsen, *Halder War Diary*, p. 85

7 Frieser, *Blitzkrieg-Legende*, p. 392

8 Engel, op. cit.

9 Brendon, *Churchill*, op. cit., p. 140

10 Hayward, *Churchill on Leadership*, p. 73

11 Spears, *Assignment to Catastrophe*, p. 216

12 Wheeler-Bennett (ed.), *Action This Day*, p. 50

13 Ibid., pp. 52–3

14 Ibid., p. 20

15 Ibid., pp. 19–20

16 Churchill, *Savrola*, p. 307

17 Hinsley and Simkins, *British Intelligence*, vol. 4, p. 47

18 Thompson, *1940*, pp. 134–8

19 Kershaw, *Hitler Myth*, pp. 13–14

20 Jablonsky, op. cit., p. 159

21 Colville, *Fringes of Power*, p. 382

22 Churchill, *Contemporaries*, p. 343

23 Brendon, *Churchill*, p. 156

24 Kimball (ed.), *Churchill and Roosevelt*, pp. 49–50

25 Danchev and Todman (eds), *Alanbrooke War Diaries*, p. xi

26 Jenkins, *Churchill*, p. 629

27 *Daily Telegraph*, 29 August 2002

28 Trevor-Roper (ed.), *Last Days of Hitler*, p. 95

29 Ibid., p. 264

30 Ibid., p. 505

31 Ibid., p. 630

32 Churchill, *Savrola*, p. 22

33 Gilbert, *Winston S. Churchill*, vol. 4, p. 1103

34 Colville, op. cit., p. 180

35 Ibid., p. 404

36 Stafford, *Churchill and the Secret Service*

37 Richard Garnett's papers at Hilton Hall, Huntingdon

38 Garnett, *Secret History of PWE*

39 Gilbert, *Winston S. Churchill*, vol. 7, p. 455

40 Brendon, *Churchill*, p. 147

41 Jablonsky, op. cit., p. 22

42 Ibid., p. 256

43 Ibid., pp. 241–2

44 Author's 1993 conversation with the late Lord Home, p. 184

45 Warlimont, op. cit., p. 463

Conclusion

1 John Keegan, *Daily Telegraph*, 18 July 1998

2 John Lukacs, *Hitler of History*

3 *Mail on Sunday*, 2 October 1994

4 Masters, *Getting Personal*, pp. 57–8

5 Bryan Appleyard, 'Leaders of the Pack', *Sunday Times* magazine, 20 January 2002

6 Browning, *Ordinary Men*

7 Goldhagen, *Hitler's Willing Executioners*

8 Jenkins, op. cit., p. 635

9 Willans and Roetter, *Wit of Winston Churchill*, p. 106

10 Jones, op. cit., p. 11

11 Churchill, *Savrola*, p. 43

12 In order to subscribe to *Finest Hour*, contact *www.winstonchurchill.org* or write to PO Box 1257, Melksham, SN12 6GQ

13 Creighton, *Op. JB*

14 *Spectator*, 7 and 21 September 2002

15 Strawson, *Hitler and Churchill*, pp. 502–3

Bibliography

All books were published in London unless otherwise stated. The dates given are not for publication, but only for the edition used.

Adair, John, *The Effective Leadership Masterclass*, 1977
Addison, Paul, *Churchill on the Home Front*, 1992
Alldritt, Keith, *Churchill the Writer: His Life as a Man of Letters*, 1992
Ashley, Maurice, *Churchill as Historian*, 1968
Beevor, Antony, *Stalingrad*, 1998
  Berlin: The Downfall 1945, 2002
Below, Nicholas von, *At Hitler's Side: The Memoirs of Hitler's Luftwaffe Adjutant 1937–1945*, 2001
Berlin, Isaiah, *Mr Churchill in 1940*, 1949
Best, Geoffrey, *Churchill: A Study in Greatness*, 2001
Bethell, Nicholas, *The War Hitler Won*, 1972
Birkenhead, Earl of, *Churchill 1874–1922*, 1989
Blake, Robert, and Louis, William Roger, *Churchill*, 1993
Brendon, Piers, *The Dark Valley: A Panorama of the 1930s*, 2000
  Winston Churchill: A Brief Life, 2001
Browning, Christopher R., *Ordinary Men: Reserve Police Battalion 101 and the Final Solution in Poland*, 1992
Buchanan, Patrick J., *A Republic, Not an Empire: Reclaiming America's Destiny* (Washington DC), 1999
Bullock, Alan, *Hitler: A Study in Tyranny*, 1952
  Hitler and Stalin: Parallel Lives, 1991
Burdick, Charles, and Jacobsen, Hans-Adolf, *The Halder War Diary 1939–42*, 1988
Burleigh, Michael, *The Third Reich: A New History*, 2000
Callaghan, Raymond A., *Churchill: Retreat from Empire*, 1984
Carlton, David, *Churchill and the Soviet Union*, 2000
Carter, Violet Bonham, *Winston Churchill as I Knew Him*, 1965
Charmley, John, *Churchill: The End of Glory*, 1993
  Churchill's Grand Alliance: The Anglo-American Special Relationship 1940–57, 1995
Churchill, Winston S., *Savrola*, 1900

Secret Session Speeches, 1946

Great Contemporaries, 1962

Thoughts and Adventures, 1990

Clark, Alan, *Barbarossa: The Russian-German Conflict 1941–1945*, 1965

Cohen, Eliot A., *Supreme Command: Soldiers, Statesmen and Leadership in Wartime* (New York), 2002

Colville, John, *Fringes of Power*, 1985

Coote, Colin (ed.), *Maxims and Reflections of Winston Churchill*, 1947

The Other Club, 1971

Cosgrave, Patrick, *Churchill at War: Alone 1939–40*, 1974

Cowles, Winston, *Churchill: The Era and the Man*, 1953

Cowling, Maurice, *The Impact of Hitler: British Politics and British Policy 1933–1940*, 1977

Creighton, Christopher, *Op. JB*, 1996

Danchev, Alex, and Todman, Daniel (eds), *War Diaries 1939–1945: Field Marshal Lord Alanbrooke*, 2001

Day, David, *Menzies and Churchill at War*, 1986

Eade, Charles (ed.), *Churchill by his Contemporaries*, 1955

Ehlers, Dieter, *Technik und Moral einer Verschwörung. Der Aufstand am 20. Juli 1944* (Bonn), 1964

Engel, Gerhard, *Heeresadjutant bei Hitler 1938–1943* (Stuttgart), 1974

Evans, David, *Telling Lies about Hitler*, 2002

Fest, Joachim, *Plotting Hitler's Death: The German Resistance to Hitler 1933–1945*, 1966

Fraser, David, *Alanbrooke*, 1997

Frieser, Karl-Heinz, *Blitzkrieg-Legende der Westfeldzug 1940* (Munich), 1996

Garnett, David, *The Secret History of P.W.E.*, 2002

Gilbert, Martin, *Winston S. Churchill*, 8 vols, 1966–1988

Churchill's Political Philosophy, 1981

Churchill: The Wilderness Years, 1981

The Second World War, 1989

Churchill: A Life, 1991

In Search of Churchill, 1994

Giuliani, Rudolf, *Leadership*, 2002

Goldhagen, Daniel, *Hitler's Willing Executioners: Ordinary Germans and the Holocaust*, 1996

Goleman, Daniel, Boyatzis, Richard, and McKee, Annie, *The New Leaders: Transforming the Art of Leadership into the Science of Results*, 2002

Grint, Keith, *The Arts of Leadership*, 2001

Grunberger, Richard, *A Social History of the Third Reich*, 1971

Guedella, Philip, *Mr Churchill: A Portrait*, 1941

Hamann, Brigitte, *Hitler's Vienna: A Dictator's Apprenticeship*, 1999

Hardwick, Joan, *Clementine Churchill: The Private Life of a Public Figure*, 1997

Hart, B. H. Liddell, *History of the Second World War*, 1970

Hayward, Steven, *Churchill on Leadership*, 1997

Hinsley, F. H., and Simkins, C. A. G., *British Intelligence in the Second World War*, vol. 4, 1990

Hitler, Adolf, *Mein Kampf*, (Berlin: 162nd–163rd reprint, Eher Verlag), 1935

Hough, Richard, *Winston and Clementine: The Triumph of the Churchills*, 1988

Irving, David, *Hitler's War 1942–1945*, 1977
  The War Path: Hitler's Germany 1933–1939, 1978
  Churchill's War: The Struggle for Power, 1987
  Churchill's War: Triumph in Adversity, 2001

Jablonsky, David, *Churchill and Hitler: Essays on the Political-Military Direction of Total War*, 1994

Jenkins, Roy, *Churchill*, 2002

Johnson, Paul, *Napoleon*, 2002

Keegan, John, *The Second World War*, 1989
  Churchill's Generals, 1992

Kemper III, R. Crosby (ed.), *Winston Churchill: Resolution, Defiance, Magnanimity, Good Will*, 1996

Kershaw, Ian, *The 'Hitler Myth': Image and Reality in the Third Reich*, 1989
  Hitler 1889–1936: Hubris, 1998
  Hitler 1936–1945: Nemesis, 2000

Keynes, John Maynard, *The Economic Consequences of the Peace* (New York), 1971

Kimball, Warren F. (ed.), *Churchill & Roosevelt: The Complete Correspondence*, 3 vols, 1984

Kraus, René, *The Men Around Churchill*, 1971

Lamb, Richard, *The Ghosts of Peace 1935–1945*, 1987

Lash, Joseph P., *Roosevelt and Churchill 1939–1941*, 1977

Lawlor, Sheila, *Churchill and the Politics of War 1940–1941*, 1994

Lee, J. M., *The Churchill Coalition 1940–1945*, 1980

Lipstadt, Deborah, *Denying the Holocaust: The Growing Assault on Truth and Memory*, 1993

Lord, Walter, *The Miracle of Dunkirk*, 1982

Lowenheim, Francis L., Langley, Harold D., and Jonas, Manfred (eds), *Roosevelt and Churchill: Their Secret Wartime Correspondence*, 1975

Lukacs, John, *The Hitler of History*, 1997
  The Duel: Hitler vs Churchill 10 May–31 July 1940, 1990
  Churchill: Visionary, Statesman, Historian, 2002

Luke, Michael, *Hansel Pless: Prisoner of History*, 2002

MacArthur, Brian (ed.), *The Penguin Book of Historic Speeches*, 1995

Machtan, Lothar, *The Hidden Hitler*, 2001

Manchester, William, *The Caged Lion: Winston Spencer Churchill 1932–1940*, 1988

Martin, Sir John, *Downing Street: The War Years*, 1991

Masters, Brian, *Getting Personal*, 2002

Meehan, Patricia, *The Unnecessary War: Whitehall and the German Resistance to Hitler*, 1992

Megargee, Geoffrey P., *Inside Hitler's Command* (Kansas), 2000

Middlebrook, Martin, *The Battle for Hamburg*, 2000

Montague Browne, Anthony, *Long Sunset: Memoirs of Winston Churchill's Last Private Secretary*, 1995

Moran, Lord, *Winston Churchill: The Struggle for Survival 1940–1965*, 1966

Moriarty, David, *A Psychological Study of Adolf Hitler*, 1991

Mosley, Diana, *A Life of Contrasts*, 2002

Overy, Richard, *Interrogations: The Nazi Elite in Allied Hands 1945*, 2001

Parker, R. A. C., *Churchill and Appeasement: Could Churchill Have Prevented the Second World War?*, 2000

Parker, R. A. C. (ed.), *Winston Churchill: Studies in Statesmanship*, 1995

Pearson, John, *Citadel of the Heart: Winston and the Churchill Dynasty*, 1991

Pelling, Henry, *Winston Churchill*, 1974

Ponting, Clive, *Churchill*, 1994

Ramsden, John, *The Age of Churchill and Eden*, 1995
Man of the Century: Winston Churchill and his Legend since 1945, 2002

Rauschning, Hermann, *Gespräche mit Hitler* (New York), 1940

Redlich, Fritz, *Hitler: Diagnosis of a Destructive Prophet*, 2000

Rees, Laurence, *The Nazis: A Warning from History*, 1997
War of the Century: When Hitler Fought Stalin, 1999
Horror in the East, 2001

Rhodes James, Robert, *Churchill: A Study in Failure 1900–1939*, 1990

Rhodes James, Robert (ed.), *Churchill Speaks 1897–1963: Collected Speeches in Peace and War*, 1981

Roberts, Andrew, *'The Holy Fox': A Biography of Lord Halifax*, 1991
Eminent Churchillians, 1991

Roberts, Frank, *Dealing with Dictators: The Destruction and Revival of Europe 1930–70*, 1991

Rose, Norman, *Churchill: An Unruly Life*, 1994

Rosebery, Lord, *Lord Randolph Churchill*, 1906

Roseman, Mark, *The Villa, The Lake, The Meeting: Wannsee and the Final Solution*, 2002

Sandys, Celia, *Churchill Wanted Dead or Alive*, 1999

Smith, Amanda (ed.), *Hostage to Fortune: The Letters of Joseph P. Kennedy*, 2001

Soames, Mary (ed.), *Speaking for Themselves: The Personal Letters of Winston and Clementine Churchill*, 1998

Spears, E. L., *Assignment to Catastrophe, vol. I: July 1939–May 1940*, 1954

Speer, Albert, *Inside the Third Reich*, 1995

Spotts, Frederic, *Hitler and the Power of Aesthetics*, 2002

Stafford, David, *Churchill and the Secret Service*, 1997

Stewart, Graham, *Burying Caesar: Churchill, Chamberlain and the Battle for the Tory Party*, 1999

Stone, Norman, *Hitler*, 1980

Strawson, John, *Hitler and Churchill in Victory and Defeat*, 1997

Thompson, Laurence, *1940*, 1966

Thorne, Christopher, *Allies of a Kind: The United States, Britain, and the War Against Japan 1941–1945*, 1978

Trevor-Roper, Hugh, *The Last Days of Hitler*, 1947

Trevor-Roper, Hugh (ed.), *Hitler's Secret Conversations 1941–1944*, 1961

Waite, Robert, *The Psychopathic God: Adolf Hitler*, 1993

Warlimont, General Walter, *Inside Hitler's Headquarters 1939–1945*, 1964

Watt, Donald Cameron, *How War Came: The Immediate Origins of the Second World War 1938–1939*, 1989

Wheeler-Bennett, John (ed.), *Action This Day*, 1968

Willans, Geoffrey, and Roetter, Charles, *The Wit of Winston Churchill*, 1954

Willmott, H. P., *The Great Crusade: A New Complete History of the Second World War*, 1989

Wilson, A. N., *A Watch in the Night*, 1996

Wilson, Thomas, *Churchill and the Prof*, 1995

Woods, Frederick, *Artillery of Words: The Writings of Sir Winston Churchill*, 1992

Young, Kenneth, *Churchill and Beaverbrook*, 1966

Index

In this index WSC stands for Churchill; AH for Hitler

25; smoking restrictions, 62; rearmament, 73–4; food shortages, 74; attack and advance in West (1940), 87, 98, 100–5; and Mission Command, 104–5; British bombing campaign against, 114, 206; peace proposals, 143, 169–70, 208–11; Political Warfare Executive campaign against, 148–52, 154; resistance to Hitler in, 168–73; attains pacific democracy, 174; intelligence agencies, 175; indifference to cruel actions, 185–7; see also Hitler, Adolf; Nazi party

Gesche, Bruno, 159–61

Gibbon, Edward, 38

Gibraltar: number of apes on, 114

Gilbert, Sir Martin, 204, 206

Giuliani, Rudolf, xxiii

Gladstone, William Ewart, xxix, 38

Glebokie (estate) Poland, 163–4

Godfrey, Admiral John Henry, 129

Goebbels, Joseph: public speaking, 27–8; practical jokes, 44–7; public presentation of AH, 52; complains of Obersalzberg, 57; promotes Nazism, 59; loathing of homosexuals, 69; dislikes Ribbentrop, 75; reads to AH in Berlin bunker, 79, 175; and repression of Jews, 81; on WSC's 'blood, sweat and tears' speech, 109–10

Goerdeler, Karl, 169, 172

Goldhagen, Daniel: Hitler's Willing Executioners, 185–6

Goldwater, Barry, xxxiv

Göring, Field Marshal Hermann: on AH's appeal, 1; uniforms, 54–5; home, 56; four-year economic plan, 74, 81–2; and Jewish Question, 81–2; commands Luftwaffe, 106, 119, 160–1, 176; dismisses treaties of alliance, 124; AH's indulgence towards, 160–1

Gort, Field Marshal John Vereker, 6th Viscount, 157

Graves, Robert: The Long Weekend (with Alan Hodge), 195

Greece: Mussolini attacks, 124; AH invades, 208

Greenwood, Arthur, 97–8, 100

Grey, Sir Edward (Viscount Grey of Fallodon), 13

Grigg, Sir Percy James, 72

Grynszpan, Herschel, 80

Guderian, Lieut.-General Heinz, 101–4, 162

Guedalla, Philip, 204

Gulf War, xxxi

'Habbakuk' (proposed iceberg air base), 154–5

Hadamowski, Eugen, 45

Haider, Jörg, xxxvi, 199

Hailsham, Quintin McGarel Hogg, Baron, 42, 93

Halder, General Fritz, 103, 105

Halifax, Edward Frederick Lindley Wood, 1st Earl of: Clementine Churchill rebukes, 68; letter from WSC on Foreign Office business, 76–7; and Norway campaign, 86; and fall of Chamberlain, 88; proposed as successor to Chamberlain as premier, 94–9; warns of German attack in West, 98; in WSC's War Cabinet, 100; and bribing of Spanish generals, 147; on German opposition movement, 172; letter from WSC on writing history, 193

Hamann, Brigitte: Hitler's Vienna, 32

Hamburg: bombed, 168

Hamilton, General Sir Ian, 20

Hanfstaengl, Ernst ('Putzi'), 44–9, 71

Hanke, Gauleiter Karl, 46, 158–9

Hankey, Sir Maurice, 20

Harriman, Averell, 143, 162–3

Harriman, Pamela (earlier Churchill; Randolph's wife), 162, 202

Hart, Basil Liddell, 204

Hassell, Ulrich von, 169

Hattersley, Roy, Baron, 99

Hauptmann, Gerhart, 50

Hayek, Friedrich von, xxxv

Heath, Sir Edward, xxxviii

Heine, Heinrich: On the History of Religion and Philosophy in Germany, xxxv

Heseltine, Michael, Baron, xxxvii

Hess, Rudolf: AH dictates Mein Kampf to, 21; AH's relations with, 70; flight to Scotland, 205

Hewel, Walter, 75–6

Heydrich, Reinhard, 30

Hillgarth, Alan, 147

Hilton Hall, Huntingdon, 148–50, 153

Himmelfarb, Milton, 186

Himmler, Heinrich: AH rejects suggestion to use masseur, 53; dress, 54; restricts traffic at Berchtesgaden, 57; bans smoking to SS officers in uniform, 62; dislikes Goebbels, 75; commands SS, 106; and Gesche's drinking, 159–60; and SS intelligence, 175

Hindenburg, Field Marshal Paul von, 22

Hiroshima, xxi

History Today (magazine), 195

Hitchens, Christopher, 203–4

Final Solution, 30, 159, 185–7, 211; AH plans boycott of, 57; Nazi repression of, 80–1

Jodl, Field Marshal Alfred, 86

John the Baptist, St, xxxiv

Johnson, Paul, 64

Joint Intelligence Committee (US-British), 175

Jones, Jim: and Guyana suicides, xxv

Jones, R.V., 50, 191

Joseph, Sir Keith (later Baron), xxxv

Jozefow, Poland, 186–7

Kaltenbrunner, Ernst, 175

Kashmir dispute, xxviii

Katyn massacre, 207

Keating, Paul, 67

Keegan, Sir John, 135, 182, 186, 204

Keitel, Field Marshal Wilhelm, 86, 101, 177

Kennedy, John F., 174

Kennedy, Joseph P., 96–7, 123–4

Kennedy, Robert, 173

Kershaw, Sir Ian, 51, 57; The 'Hitler Myth', xxvii

Keyes, Admiral of the Fleet Sir Roger, 90, 157

Keynes, John Maynard, Baron: The Economic Consequences of the Peace, 168

Khalifa (of Sudan), xxv

Kim Il Sung, 64

King, Martin Luther, 173

King, William Lyon Mackenzie, 5

Kinnock, Neil, xxxiv

Kissinger, Henry, 210

Klemperer, Klemens von: German Resistance against Hitler, 168

Kluge, Field Marshal Günther von, 177

Korda, Sir Alexander, xx, 9, 194

Korean war (1950–3), xxi

Kristallnacht, 81–2

Labour Party: joins coalition government (1940), 100

Läffner, Siegfried, 32

Landsberg prison, Bavaria, 10, 21

Lash, Joseph, 204

Latchmere House, Richmond, 121–2

Lausanne Conference (1932), 24

Laval, Pierre, 188

Law, Richard (later Baron Coleraine), 79

Lawrence, Neville, xxxvi

Laziosi, St Peregrino, xxxii

leadership: nature of, xix–xxi, xxiii–xxiv, xxxiii–xxxiv; and saying no, 184; and responsibility, 187

Lenin, Vladimir Ilich, xxvi, 182

Leningrad, 208

Leopold III, King of the Belgians, 156–7

Lincoln, Abraham, 172–3

Lindemann, Frederick (Viscount Cherwell; 'the Prof'), 5, 48, 117

Lipstadt, Deborah, xxxv–xxxvi, 202

Lloyd George, David (later 1st Earl), 20, 26, 58, 92

London: bombed, 114, 202

Loraine, Sir Percy, 76

Lossberg, Lieut.-Colonel Bernhard von, 86

Louis XIV, King of France, 208

Ludendorff, Field Marshal Erich Friedrich Wilhelm, 22

Luftwaffe (German Air Force): fails at Dunkirk, 106, 160; organisation, 119

Lukacs, John, 182, 204

Lullenden, Sussex, 20

Lusitania (US liner), 204

McAlpine, Alistair, xxxiii–xxxiv

Macaulay, Thomas Babington, Baron, 38

Machtan, Lothar: The Hidden Hitler, 69–71

McKinley, William, 174

Macmillan, Harold (later 1st Earl of Stockton), 111, 132

Madresfield Court, Worcestershire, 121

Maginot Line, 87, 98, 108

Mahdi, the, xxv

Major, John, xxxiii–xxxiv

Malcolm X, 173

Manchester, William, 204

Manstein, General Erich von, 101–4, 162

Margesson, David (later 1st Viscount), 96

Marrakech, 145

Marshall, General George Catlett, Jr, 133, 188

Marx, Karl, 21

Masters, Brian: Getting Personal, 184

Maurice, Emil, 21

Maze, Paul, 142

Meades, Jonathan, 34

Meehan, Patricia: The Unnecessary War, 168, 172

Melbourne, William Lamb, 2nd Viscount, xxxiii, 64

Mellor, David, xxxiii

Mend, Hans, 70

MI5: interrogations at Latchmere House, 121–2; created, 147

Middle East: WSC reinforces, 135

Milgram, Stanley, 184–5

Minister of Defence: office created, 112

Mission Command, 105–6, 166–7, 176–8

Model, Colonel-General Walter, 74–5